THE GUIDE TO TAX BENEFITS FOR COLLECTORS, DEALERS & INVESTORS

THE GUIDE TO TAX BENEFITS FOR COLLECTORS, DEALERS, AND INVESTORS

SECOND EDITION

by Robert S. Persky

PUBLISHED BY:

THE CONSULTANT PRESS, LTD.

NEW YORK, NEW YORK

But in this world nothing can be said to be certain except death and taxes."

Benjamin Franklin in a letter to Jean Baptiste Le Roy, November 13, 1789

Over and over again courts have said that there is nothing sinister in so arranging one's affairs as to keep taxes as low as possible. Everybody does so, rich or poor; and all do right, for nobody owes any public duty to pay more than the law demands; taxes are enforced exactions, not voluntary contributions. To demand more in the name of morals is mere cant."

Judge Learned Hand, dissenting, Commissioner v. Newman, 159 F.2d 848, 2d Cir. 1947

ISBN 0-913069-32-9

Library of Congress Catalog Card No: 91-076614

Editor - Susan P. Levy

Printed in the U.S.A

THE CONSULTANT PRESS,LTD., 163 AMSTERDAM AVE., NEW YORK, NY 10023

TABLE OF CONTENTS

PREFACE

There are two inherent problems in writing a tax guide for the use of collectors, dealers, and investors.

The first problem is common to any literature on taxes written for the individual who is neither a lawyer nor an accountant. The author must convey the meaning of complex provisions of the Internal Revenue Code using language that neither confuses nor patronizes the reader. A danger exists that in the attempt to make the arcane comprehensible there may be oversimplification. Every effort has been made to avoid the sin of oversimplification. At the same time an effort was made to reduce the fog index. This is a guide not a treatise on tax law.

It must be remembered that the facts relating to each person differ. This guide is designed to aid in your tax planning by alerting you to problem areas. It is not a substitute for your own lawyer or accountant.

With the exception of the mention of sales and use taxes, this guide deals only with federal tax law. State and local income, gift, and inheritance taxes vary significantly from jurisdiction to jurisdiction. The preparation of complex tax returns, wills, trusts, and the documentation for gifts is in the province of your professional advisors.

The second problem is the difficulty of convincing many of those who inhabit the art, antiques and collectibles world that the words "taxes", "investments", and "deductions" are acceptable in polite company. The concept that aesthetics and investments are mutually exclusive dies hard.

Whatever your position, it cannot be denied that art, antiques, and collectibles are as much investments as a house or condominium. While the primary purpose of a home is to provide shelter, it cannot be denied that the family manse has, in most instances, substantially appreciated in value.

Similarly, although the primary purpose of acquiring art is to provide aesthetic enhancement, art appreciates in value. Works of art comprise a substantial portion of the tangible assets of many individuals.

Art As An Investment, a 1961 book by Richard H. Rush, stated the issue in the following manner:

> *To entitle a book* ***Art As An Investment*** *may seem to be a sacrilege. The general public has long considered art to belong to an elite group of intellectuals who seem to be the only ones who could really understand the greatness of the Old Masters, or decipher the otherwise intelligible abstractions that some extreme modern and contemporary artists produce. While fine works of art are certainly "above money", art, at the same time, is intimately connected and is an attribute of money. Recently a modern painting sold for $145,000 and a Rubens for $770,000.*

Prices reported in *ARTnewsletter* for contemporary art sold at Sotheby's during November of 1986, when we were preparing the first edition of this work, included "a towering $3,630,000 ....unprecedented for a work of contemporary art ....for Jasper John's 1959 *Out the Window*."

That work was completed two years before Rush's book and most certainly was first sold for below $100,000. It is doubtful that even Rush anticipated the investment potential of the art that was being produced during the time frame in which he wrote his book.

On December 10,1986 a Rembrandt portrait sold for $10,381,000 at Sotheby's, London.

During the four years that elapsed between the first and second editions of this book Van Gogh's *Portrait of Dr. Gachet* sold for $82,500,000 and *False Start* by Jasper Johns sold for $17,100,000. During the same time frame the prices of antiques and other collectibles also rose dramatically.

Regardless of the intellectual positions taken on the issue of whether art, antiques, and collectibles are investments, the facts support the proposition that they have the attributes of investments.

Whether you choose to think of your collection as an investment or to confine yourself to aesthetics is a personal decision. The Internal Revenue Code, however, denies benefits to those whose vision is restricted to aesthetics.

The information in this guide may open the eyes of many readers to the fact that, unless paying taxes is an experience you enjoy, tax planning should be a factor in acquiring and administering a collection.

Nothing in this volume is meant to suggest that your aesthetic judgment should be influenced by tax planning. One can be both a person who makes informed decisions relating to tax planning as well as a connoisseur.

> *The avoidance of taxes is the only intellectual pursuit that carries any reward.*
>
> *John Maynard Keynes*

CHAPTER ONE

AN OVERVIEW

The purpose of this guide is to demonstrate how the Internal Revenue Code grants benefits and denies benefits to collectors, dealers and investors. You should decide which status serves you best at the earliest opportunity.

A similarity exists between obtaining the maximum tax benefits under the Internal Revenue Code ("I.R.C.") and commencing play in a game of chess. The opening moves may determine the outcome!

The acceptance of a painting as a gift from the artist may dramatically affect the tax consequences of donating that painting to a museum fifteen years later. Claiming dealer status to avoid sales tax on a print may have dramatic tax consequences should you donate or sell that print long after its acquisition.

A second similarity to chess exists in that the state of mind of both the chess player and the person involved with art, antiques, and collectibles is a critical factor. In championship play, knowledge of the moves may be insufficient if your opponent is in better state of mind.

Whether you consider yourself a collector, dealer or investor and the substantive steps you undertake to be consistent with that state of mind is critical in obtaining or being denied tax benefits. It must be remembered that your actions must be consistent with your state of mind.

The Tax Reform Act of 1986 (T.R.A.'86) focused increased attention on tax planning. Many of the rules and all income tax rates have been changed. Nevertheless many of the basic rules remain unchanged. In the past many of these basic rules have been ignored, often with expensive consequences for those with collections.

A key determination in the granting and denial of benefits under the I.R.C. in the areas of expense deductions, offsetting losses on sales against gains, and charitable contributions is made on the basis of whether you are a collector, dealer or investor.

Prior to T.R.A.'86 whether gains realized on the sale of all or part of your collection were taxed at the ordinary income rates or the lower long term capital gains rates was a key question. T.R.A.'86 temporarily eliminated the rate differential but it did not excise all the old concepts of capital assets and gains from the I.R.C.

Subsequently there was a reinstatement of the differential in tax rates, although the differential is not currently as great as prior to T.R.A. '86. The distinction between ordinary income and capital gain, and between capital assets and ordinary assets remains significant in relationship to other I.R.C. sections. That distinction will, more likely than not, remain significant even in the rate differential is again eliminated.

Beginning in 1991, capital gains are subject to a maximum rate of 28 percent, while ordinary income may be taxed at 31 percent. Whether you are considered to be a collector, dealer, or investor, has again become the key fact in determining whether you can take advantage of the lower capital gain rates.

Among the questions that are be covered in this guide are:

- What changes did T.R.A.'86 make in the I.R.C. that directly affect the person who acquires art, antiques, or other collectibles?
- Is there a substantial tax benefit significance to the determination of whether you are collecting as opposed to investing or acting as a dealer?
- What strategies may be used to strengthen the status you determine to be in your best interests?
- When to beware of artists bearing gifts?
- When does the I.R.S. require dealers to keep two sets of books?
- Why may a knowledgeable expert may not be a qualified appraiser?
- How does one practice the art of donating art?

Individuals who refuse to concern themselves about taxes are inviting the I.R.S. to become a partner in their collections.

A Brief Look At T.R.A.'86

The T.R.A.'86 made one significant change targeted at those with appreciated property, including works of art, antiques and other collectibles, who contemplate charitable donations. That change came in the application, for the first time, of the

Alternative Minimum Tax (the "A.M.T.") to donations of appreciated property (see Chapter Seven).

Other changes that affect primarily collectors and investors include:

(i) the imposition of a floor on the deductibility of certain itemized expenses by individuals;

(ii) the elimination of the deductibility of sales taxes by individuals;

(iii) a change in the statutory presumption regarding whether an activity is a hobby or a business;

(iv) a change in the rules for casualty loss deductions for non-business property;

(v) the elimination, except for dealers, of the deductibility of the expenses for attendance at seminars and symposiums,

(vi) the elimination of the deductibility of consumer loan and credit card interest by individuals;

(vii) limits on the deductibility of investment interest by individuals; and

(viii) the elimination of the deductibility of charitable contributions for individual non-itemizers.

Reference will be made to each of these changes in the following chapters of this guide.

CHAPTER TWO

TAX BENEFITS

The question of whether you are a collector, dealer or investor is not merely relevant for cocktail party conversation, symposium discussions and articles in the media. The question is not merely one of aesthetic taste or emotional temperament...it is a question which involves your dollars, often thousands of them.

All the dollar questions fall within four areas that are relevant to all who own works of art, antiques, and collectibles. The four areas may be broadly described or formulated into four questions which are posed in the order in which they normally arise:

(1) Is your acquisition subject to a state or local sales tax?

(2) Are the expenses incurred in your activities relating to the acquisition deductible?

(3) Is the acquisition in your possession as a capital asset or as inventory?

(4) What is the tax consequence of your making a gift, charitable donation, or bequest of the acquisition?

The answers to these four questions are determined by first answering the question, "Are you a collector, dealer or investor?"

Before answering this key question it is important to understand (i) the economic significance to the answer and (ii) the differences from the point of view of federal tax law.

The differences are not merely of academic interest. The status into which you fall determines the tax benefits available to you.

In our discussion of benefits we shall, in most instances, use the term "art" to include antiques and other collectibles.

It may seem strange to talk of tax "benefits", but as presently structured, the law permits certain owners of art to deduct the expenses of maintaining their collections while denying in whole or part those deductions to others.

Among the expense items are:

1. insurance premiums
2. alarm and other security systems
3. storage materials and space
4. temperature and humidity controls
5. home office expense
6. mounting, matting and framing
7. cleaning and restoration
8. lighting
9. books
10. magazines and newsletters
11. membership dues
12. seminar and symposium tuition
13. travel

14. acquisition costs

15. selling costs

16. interest

17. rent

18. phone, postage and stationery

The ability to obtain a full deduction for the expenses of maintaining your collection is a benefit. It is equivalent to having more income!

Certain donors are permitted to obtain larger charitable deductions than others even when the cost basis and the present fair market value for each donor is identical. The person who obtains the larger deduction has a benefit unavailable to the person who is limited to a smaller deduction.

The fact is that there are benefits to be obtained provided your status is appropriate to the benefit. An informed approach is necessary to obtain those benefits.

From the point of view of the I.R.C. all owners of art can be classified within one or more of three categories. We shall refer to each category as a status.

Collector Status

The collector from the point of view of the I.R.C. is merely engaged in a hobby. In tax code terminology a hobby is an activity not engaged in for profit. If enjoyment of your art collection is your only or primary purpose in owning art you are a collector.

I.R.S. staff members generally commence their determination of whether you are entitled to a deduction for the expenses of maintaining your collection on the assumption that you are engaged in a hobby. You generally have the burden of proving that you are a dealer or investor. In Chapter Three we will discuss how you can be prepared to establish you are not merely a collector.

Dealer Status

A dealer is, in tax code terminology, a person who carries on a trade or business. It was recently determined that the term "trade or business" appears in over 490 subsections of the I.R.C. and over 660 regulations.

"Trade or business" is, however, nowhere defined in the I.R.C., and it has been left to the courts to set down general guidelines and to apply them on a case by case basis.

The importance of the meaning of "trade or business" lies in the fact that it is one of the three legs of support for taking deductions under I.R.C. §162(a).

Before a deduction can be taken, the expense must be:

1. ordinary and necessary
2. paid or incurred during the tax year
3. incurred carrying on a trade or business.

The definition of "trade or business" has proved more elusive than one would initially think. The evolution of the definition has been complicated, in part, by the fact that both taxpayers and the I.R.S. are likely to argue for or against trade or business status depending on the particular I.R.C. section at issue and the consequence of being in trade or business.

We will return to dealer status, but not wanting to leave you totally in the dark concerning the definition of "trade or business" the following is a list of evidentiary facts considered when there is a contested determination:

1. a good faith intention of making a profit or producing income,
2. extensive activity over a substantial period of time,
3. whether the activity has actually begun, and
4. whether the taxpayer holds himself out to others as being engaged in the selling of goods and services.

Investor Status

An investor is commonly defined as one who puts money into business, real estate, securities, or other assets for the purpose of obtaining an income or profit.

As an abstract proposition it is obvious that works of art, antiques, and collectibles may be the subject matter of investment. However, the establishment of investment intent, for tax purposes, is more difficult than with stocks and bonds.

Prior to 1970 there was little or no case law regarding art and investors. In that year a tax case involving the noted collectors Charles B. and Jayne Wrightsman sent shock waves through the ranks of collectors who had been deducting the ordinary and necessary expenses of collecting and maintaining their works of art.

At issue was the deductibility, over a two year period, of $34,000 by the Wrightsmans. The deductions were taken in 1960 and 1961 and would, in 1987 dollars, be substantially larger.

The *Wrightsman* case, 428 F2d. 1316 (Ct. Cl. 1970), is analyzed in Chapter Three of this guide, but it necessary that it be summarized at this point.

At issue was the interpretation of I.R.C. §212 which then and now reads, in relevant part:

> In the case of an individual, there shall be allowed as a deduction all the ordinary and necessary expenses paid or incurred during the taxable year
> (1) for the production or collection of income;
> (2) for the management, conservation, or maintenance of property held for the production of income;

A provision of the Treasury Regulations issued under §212 denied deductibility for expenses in connection with activities "carried on primarily as a sport, hobby, or recreation".

The regulation to this date reads:

> ...expenses of carrying on transactions which do not constitute a trade or business of the taxpayer...which are carried on primarily as a sport, hobby, or recreation are not allowable as non trade or nonbusiness expenses. The question whether or not a transaction is carried on primarily for the production of income or for the management, conservation, or maintenance of property held for the production or collection of income, rather than primarily as a sport, hobby, or recreation, is not to be determined solely from the intention of the taxpayer but rather from all the circumstances of the case.
>
> Reg. §1-212-1(c)

As will be discovered, the key word turned out to be "primarily".

The taxpayers lost on a set of facts and findings that were almost totally in support of their position except for the interpretation of the word "primarily".

They lost even though the court found that they considered their art collection to be an investment!

What you can do to avoid the result in *Wrightsman* is covered in our discussion of establishing investor status.

Capital Gains Has Risen Like A Phoenix

Prior to T.R.A.'86 a primary concern was whether the profit on a sale of a work of art was taxed at ordinary income or long-term capital gains rates. T.R.A. '86 eliminated the rate differential between long-term capital gains and ordinary income.

A differential has been reinstated. Although the differential is not as great as prior to T.R.A. '86 there is constant lobbying to revise the rate so as to increase the spread between the rate on capital gains and ordinary income.

It is important to remember that T.R.A.'86 did not change the character of gain as ordinary or capital, or as short-term or long-term capital gain. The statutory structure for capital gains was retained in the Code to facilitate reinstatement of a capital gains rate differential. In fact a differential was reinstated. As we go to press the top rate on capital gains is 28%. There is a distinct possibility that any future increase in the differential may be limited to securities and other traditional investments, as opposed to art, antiques, and collectibles.

Summary

The question of whether you are a collector, dealer or investor is of primary importance in determining tax benefits.

In planning your strategy, substantive actions will, in most instances, be determinative of whether you will prevail in your claim as to a particular status.

As will be discussed later it is possible to have a dual status. In some instances it will be of great benefit to you to be able to substantiate dual status.

Do not wait until you are questioned as to the factual basis for your claiming a benefit. The time to determine and establish your status as a collector, dealer or investor is now.

CHAPTER THREE

ESTABLISHING STATUS

The term status, as used in this guide, relates to a legal position, not social or professional standing in the art, antiques, or collectible world. A person owning art created by others can simultaneously fall into one or more of three categories. You may have the status of a collector, a dealer, and/or an investor. It is legally possible and permissible to own works of art as an investor and others as a dealer.

Your status is determined by the facts, the facts of form, substance and state of mind.

Your status has a direct relationship to the tax consequences of each transaction involving the acquisition or disposition of art. There is a tax consequence resulting from the receipt of a work of art as a gift from the artist as opposed to the purchase of the same work of art from the artist. There is a tax consequence to the disposition of that work of art by gift to a museum. The status from which you initiate that gift may result in a significant dollar difference in tax consequences.

Your status determines whether you obtain the benefit of deducting none, some or all of the expenses of owning a collection.

In this chapter we explore and explain the differences in status. Establishing status requires a conscious effort to comply with the complex provisions of the I.R.C., the Regulations, and court cases. Remember that to avoid repetition we are using the term "art" to include antiques and other collectibles. The only instances in which all three terms are not interchangeable in this guide are in the discussion relating to gifts from artists. Obviously, by definition, it is unlikely that you possess an antique that was a gift to you from the creator of the antique.

The Collector

A collector is a person whose primary purpose in owning works of art is personal pleasure or satisfaction. *Wrightsman v. U.S.* 428 F2d. 1316, 1322 (Ct. Cl. 1970).

By definition a collector does not acquire works of art for resale and therefore pays state and local sales and use taxes. Prior to 1987 the deductibility of sales and use taxes diminished the dollar cost of these acquisition taxes. T.R.A.'86 eliminated the deductibility of sales and use taxes by a collector.

From the point of view of the I.R.S. a collector is merely engaged in a hobby. As will become clear when we examine the *Wrightsman* case, the mere fact that art may be a good investment matters not to the tax collector if your *primary* purpose is personal pleasure or satisfaction.

The expenses of maintaining your collection are deductible only (i) up to hobby income, I.R.C. §183 or (ii) if they would be allowed whether or not the activity was carried on for profit. Prior to T.R.A.'86 interest charges on debt incurred in connection with the acquisition of art was the most important item in category (ii).

The permitted deductions fall within a total category of expenses that are now deductible only to the extent that they exceed 2% of your adjusted gross income, I.R.C. §67(a).

When the collector sells a work of art at a profit, the gain must be reported and the tax paid. Losses by a collector from the sale of art, however, are not deductible but may be used only to offset gains from the sale of works of art, I.R.C. §183.

The collector who borrows money to pay for a work of art can no longer deduct the loan interest since consumer interest is no longer a deductible expense.

Under T.R.A.'86 the collector who suffers a casualty loss, e.g. the destruction of art by fire or flood must file a timely claim for insurance proceeds or be denied the deduction for a casualty loss, I.R.C. §165(h)(4)(E).

The only benefit from having the status of a collector is that the works of art in your collection are considered capital assets, as opposed to inventory. When they are donated to an art museum, the result is a deduction valued at fair market value as opposed to cost. See Chapter Six for a discussion of the use related requirement and other rules and regulations relating to charitable gifts.

The I.R.S. is not above attempting to claim that a collector is a dealer under certain circumstances. One attempt that was not successful arose in connection with what became known in the 1970's as "art donation tax shelters".

The typical transaction resulted in a taxpayer's acquiring multiple copies of one or more newly created prints. The acquisition cost was allegedly substantially below fair market value. After a holding period sufficiently long to comply with then existing

I.R.C. provisions relating to long term capital gain, the prints were donated to museums.

The taxpayer would then take a deduction for the gift. The value claimed would be fair market value, invariably a figure which dramatically exceeded cost. The I.R.S. attacked the transactions as being sham on a number of grounds.

One prong of the attack was to challenge the fair market value. Establishing that the fair market value was below that claimed by the taxpayers required the use of appraisers and the taking of testimony. The I.R.S. looked for an easier way of establishing a lower value. They hit upon the idea of claiming that since the taxpayers were acquiring relatively large quantities of prints, often multiple copies of the same print, and then making a series of gifts, that they were in fact dealers.

A dealer of course was limited to a deduction for his cost. The I.R.S. staff apparently felt that a single decision establishing that a taxpayer engaging in that type of transaction was a dealer would eliminate the need to prove a lower fair market value in a multitude of cases. If the deduction were limited to cost there would be no tax saving, and the art tax shelter would fall out of favor.

That position was not pressed with any great degree of success. It was based on a concept of "dealer" that the I.R.S. would not willingly accept if the taxpayer were the one claiming dealer status. Changes in the law and other problems with the transactions effectively ended the art donation shelters of newly created art.

The point of relating the art donation tax shelter episode is that the I.R.S. can be as inventive as taxpayers and their advisors in attempting to establish status.

Two Traps To Avoid

Should you make a donation of a painting which has substantially appreciated in value during your ownership, you may well find your return and underlying records under scrutiny.

There are two fact traps which may deny you a fair market value deduction even if there is no question concerning fair market value. Since the traps await you at the time you acquire art, they are discussed here as opposed to at a later point.

The first is an innocent mistake made by collectors, dealers and investors. The mistake is to accept a gift of art from the artist who created the work.

We will explain the problem in detail in Chapter Six, but the bottom line is that your deduction will be limited to the artist's cost of materials.

Always pay for the work by check or obtain a dated receipt for cash payments. Payment to the artist will suffice to save the fair market value deduction for you at the time of a charitable donation.

Although usually not a major problem you should be aware that a sale by an artist to you below the normal selling price is a gift from the artist to the extent of the difference between your cost and the normal price.

A second trap results from a less innocent but common ploy by collectors and investors. The ploy involves claiming dealer status when acquiring works of art in states where a sales or use tax exists. By claiming dealer status and that the work is purchased for resale, the collector initially saves sales tax. This ploy became more tempting when T.R.A. '86 eliminated the deductibility of state sales taxes.

Having saved the sales tax the purchaser may find that a subsequent charitable donation is deductible only to the extent of cost, not fair market value. If there has been substantial appreciation in value, the initial saving of sales tax will result in a greater loss of tax savings at the time of donation. The less than innocent ploy may come back to haunt the collector or investor!

The claiming of dealer status to avoid payment of sales tax also deprives a collector of the favorable capital gains tax rate. Further discussion of sales and use taxes may be found in Chapter Five.

Collector status is the most common status and is least likely to be challenged by either state or federal tax authorities. The other side of the coin is that the collector receives the least tax benefits.

The Dealer

Dealer status requires substantiation of a claim that you are conducting a trade or business and attempting to make a profit. There are few challenges to the status of full-time dealers with galleries or private dealers who have no other source of income. Problems may arise in situations where dealer status is claimed by taxpayers who have other sources of business or professional income and are part-time dealers.

Conducting a trade or business requires:

(i) a good faith intention of making a profit, or producing income,

(ii) extensive activity over a substantial period of time,

(iii) that the activity has actually begun, and

(iv) a holding out by the taxpayer to others that he or she is engaged in the selling of goods and services.

The majority of the cases arise in the context of the taxpayer's claiming to be in a trade or business and the I.R.S.'s claiming that the activity is a hobby.

What is usually at issue is the question of whether the expenses incurred by the taxpayer in connection with the activity are deductible.

T.R.A.'86 amended §183 of the I.R.C. which deals with the hobby presumption. The presumption section now reads in so far as it is applicable to art:

> *(d) If the gross income derived from an activity for 3 or more of the taxable years in the period of 5 consecutive taxable years which ends with the taxable year exceeds the deductions attributable to such activity (determined without regard to whether or not such activity in engaged in for profit) then, unless the Secretary establishes to the contrary, such activity shall be presumed for the purposes of this chapter, for such taxable year to be an activity engaged in for profit.*

Although T.R.A.'86 tightened the rule by changing the number of required profitable years from 2 to 3 out of five, it did preserve an important presumption for the taxpayer.

I.R.C. §183(e) permits you to elect to defer the determination as to whether the presumption applies until the fourth taxable year of activity. The judicious timing of profitable transactions may enable you to avail yourself of the presumption.

Since §183 merely establishes a presumption which can be overcome by I.R.S., it is important that a taxpayer desiring to claim dealer status establish by form and substance that there is a business.

Moreover the mere fact that the presumption is unavailable because of insufficient gross income does not necessarily mean that it is impossible to establish that the taxpayer is a dealer.

The indicia which would seem to add substance to the claim are a regular course of transactions and the holding of the taxpayer out to others as being a dealer.

It is difficult, to say the least, to prevail a claim to being a dealer if all your transactions are purchases. Implicit in being a dealer is a course of conduct as a seller. Hopefully the sales are at a gross profit even if overhead expenses result in a loss.

Acts which assist in establishment of the claim to be in a trade or business are the establishment of a separate bank account for the dealer activities, the formation of a corporation, partnership or the filing of a certificate of doing business under a trade name. The use of a business card, business stationery, participation in trade groups, and advertising are additional indicia of a trade or business.

Obtaining a resale certificate and the collection of sales taxes from clients is strong evidence of being a dealer while omitting to collect and remit sales tax would seem equally strong in rebutting a claim of not being in business.

Before proceeding to examine some of the case law we must return to the four criteria for establishing that an activity is a trade or business. The first is the good faith intention of a profit or producing income. The best evidence of such an intent is success in producing a profit or income. All business enterprises are not profitable and unfortunately the I.R.S. is prone to deny deductions to unprofitable business enterprises using the bootstrap argument that the failure to make a profit is evidence of the lack of a good faith intention to make a profit or produce income.

The I.R.S. position most often arises when the business venture is a part-time or second occupation and where the subject matter is also the possible subject matter of a hobby. Collecting is a hobby for many taxpayers. Care must be taken to establish in both form and substance that your dealer activities are a business and not merely hobby activities conducted under the mantle of what appears to be a business.

The test of extensive activity over a substantial period of time is in many instances subjective.

The easiest fact situation is where the taxpayer rents a retail space and commences a business with regular hours on a full-time basis over the tax year.

The most difficult set of facts arises when the taxpayer has a primary business or profession. The art dealer activities are part-time, appear sporadic, and involve operating from the taxpayer's home.

The phrase "full-time" does not appear in the I.R.C., the Regulations or case law as a requirement for conducting a trade or business, but it seems to be a factor.

Many private art dealers do work full time. Buying and selling art, however, is not like buying and selling groceries. Both acquisitions and sales may take weeks, months and in some instances years. The number of individual sales in the most successful gallery never approximates the number of sales in a retail store selling, for example, expensive clothing. Part-time efforts, assuming all other indicia are present, are not inconsistent with being in a trade or business.

There is admittedly a distinction between no sales and few sales. A taxpayer may be able to successfully urge that one sale in each calendar quarter is sufficient activity if each sale involves a substantial sum and it can be demonstrated that a good faith, but not necessarily full-time, effort was made to conduct a business.

Recently the I.R.S. amended Reg. 1.6050I-1 which relates to the reporting of cash transactions of $10,000 or more by those engaged in a trade or business. The transactions, reported on Form 8300, are now defined so as to treat as "cash" cashier's checks, bank drafts and money orders. If you claim dealer status you are required to file Form 8300. The filing, when appropriate, will help substantiate your claim of dealer status. Failing to file derogates from your claim of being a dealer and subjects you the criminal and civil penalties for failing to file.

It must be remembered that the taxpayer claiming to be a dealer in the face of I.R.S. objections is always doing so when there has been a deduction for losses in excess of income.

When the taxpayer shows a profit in the activity, the issue of whether the taxpayer is a dealer or a person engaged in a hobby never arises. The I.R.S. accepts the tax without question.

When the issue arises in the context of a charitable deduction, the taxpayer who found himself claiming unsuccessfully to be a dealer may now be told by the I.R.S. that the activities in question clearly establish that he is a dealer. A dealer of course receives less of a tax benefit when donating a work of art from inventory. The maximum deduction is cost and not fair market value!

There is a method for the *bona fide* dealer to avoid that problem, and it will be covered in Chapter Six.

It cannot be said there are no problems as to when an activity has begun, but it is the easiest of the criteria to quantify. Opening a separate bank account, filing a trade name, forming a Sub-S corporation, obtaining stationery and a business card all fix commencement dates. Sending out a notice or taking an advertisement in a publication all document the commencement of a business.

Mailed notices and advertisements serve to comply with the "holding out to others as being engaged in the business" requirement.

Actually making purchases and sales is of course the best objective evidence. The purchase side is easier to commence than the sale side.

Sales at auction do count and, in fact, are much used by dealers to move inventory.

What is clear is that merely claiming dealer status without taking substantive steps to act as a dealer is not good tax planning.

What Do The Court Cases Tell Us?

The majority of all disputes concerning tax liability are settled by negotiation. The majority of taxpayers have neither the time nor the resources to fight with the I.R.S. over every disallowance of a deduction. The I.R.S. does not have the staff to fight every claimed deduction. The result is that disputes reaching the courts involve (i) difficult cases, (ii) reasonably large sums, (iii) matters of great principle to the taxpayer, and (iv) situations where the I.R.S. feels that the facts are sufficiently in its favor to establish a position taken by the I.R.S. as being correct not only in the particular case but in subsequent cases and negotiations.

In *Higgins v. Commissioner* 312 U.S. 212 (1941) the issue before the Supreme Court was whether the activities of the taxpayer constituted a trade or business. There was no question that the claimed deductions were ordinary and necessary.

The taxpayer, Mr. Higgins, owned real estate, stock and bonds. He devoted a major part of his time to his real estate and stock market activities. He rented offices and employed a staff. He deducted the expenses and salaries as ordinary and necessary business expenses incurred in a trade or business.

The I.R.S. conceded that the expenses related to the real estate holdings were associated with a trade or business and thus deductible. They contested the portion of the expenses related to the securities.

The Supreme Court ruled against the taxpayer finding that he was an investor but not engaged in a trade or business.

Had Higgins been a stock trader as opposed to an investor he would have been engaged in a trade or business and prevailed.

The Supreme Court recognized the possible distinction between traders and investors in *Snyder v. Commissioner*, 295 U.S. 134 (1935). In *Levin v. United States*,

597 F2d 760 (Ct. Cl. 1979) the Court of Claims held that a full time securities trader was in a trade or business. For the year in question, Levin conducted 332 transactions involving 112,400 shares worth $3,462,125.

The activity requirement makes sense when attempting to frame a distinction between one who invests and one who is in a trade or business. In *Levin* the court said that a trader is an "active investor" who "manipulates" his holdings in an attempt to produce the best possible yield.

A person who acquires ten paintings from the Hudson River School and stores them in a temperature and humidity controlled warehouse with the hope that they will appreciate in price is an investor.

A person who acquires ten paintings from the Hudson River School (1) with the intention of selling them as soon as possible, (ii) at a profit, and (iii) takes steps to do so is a dealer.

The "takes steps to do so" is important because there is an activity commenced test, I.R.C. §195(c)(2)(A). What constitutes commencement is not always clear. Renting gallery space, printing a business card, obtaining a resale number, and placing an advertisement would all seem to be indicia of commencing an activity.

In the instance of art, "commencement" may not necessarily be indicated by the first acquisition of artwork in the absence of other indicia. This is particularly true because the art might be acquired by a hobbyist or an investor.

A person who acquired forty overcoats of different sizes probably would have little difficulty in arguing that the acquisition was the commencement of the trade or business. Overcoats are not normally the type of tangibles that people collect or acquire for investment!

Some courts have also imposed a test of goods and services. It would seem that works of art would have no problem in being classified as goods.

In *Higgins v. Commissioner* 312 U.S. 212 (1941), the stock investment case we have previously mentioned, the Court stated that the determination of whether the activities of a taxpayer constitute "carrying on a trade or business" requires an examination of the facts of each case.

Stanley v. Commissioner T.C.M. 1980-217 involved the question of whether Mary L. Stanley's activities with respect to antique glass novelties were engaged in for profit. The issue was the deductibility of expenses including what we today call "home office expenses". The facts were, for the most part, undisputed. During the tax years in question, 1975 and 1976, Mary served as president of a family owned corporation. Prior to that time she was treasurer of the corporation. During the tax years in question the family income came from her salary and that of her husband.

Her acquisition of antique glass novelties began in 1969. The number of items rose from 500 in 1969 to 2,281 in 1978. It was agreed that her permanent collection was not held for resale. She had a separate inventory which she did hold for resale. They ranged in number from 0 in 1970 to 83 in 1973 and back to 25 in 1978. She purchased for inventory and sold and traded from inventory. In large part the "inventory" was made up of duplicates that she acquired as part of larger collections purchased. Mary wrote a book about her collection which was published. She also wrote articles for *Antique Trader* and *Tri-State Trader*.

She kept detailed records of here collection but she did not have a separate bank account, business phone listing, or income and expense records. The collection was kept in the Stanley's home which was in a residential zone. No variance or permit for business use had been sought.

The Court noting that *the mere fact that a collector is aware that the value of his collection may increase does not mean that he is primarily motivated by the expectation of profit rather than the personal satisfaction derived from pursuing a hobby and a hobby is not thereby converted into an activity engaged in for profit.* The Court also noted that here sales were always of duplicates and that she never sold from the "permanent collection". It was conceded that she had no present intention of selling the collection in the immediate future. Relying on *Wrightsman* the Court held that Mary had not demonstrated by the weight of the evidence that her activities were engaged in for profit.

Mary Stanley was guilty of the tax sins of displaying her collection in her home, failing to keep separate business records, failing to create the indica of an active business, and failing to sell from the permanent collection. While the Court seemed to primarily base its decision on a failure of investor status, it impliedly found a failure to establish dealer status. The residential zoning was not relevant on the investing issue but certainly was relevant on the issue of dealer status.

I.R.S. *Publication 535* bearing the title *Business Expenses* lists nine factors to be considered whether an activity is carried on for profit, perhaps the most fundamental distinction between hobbies, investing and trade or business:

1. Whether you carry on the activity in a businesslike manner.
2. Whether the time and effort you put into the activity indicate you intend to make it profitable.
3. Whether you are depending on income from the activity for your livelihood.
4. Whether your losses from the activity are due to circumstances beyond your control (or are normal in the start-phase of your type of business).
5. Whether you change your methods of operation in an attempt to improve the profitability of the activity.
6. Whether you, or your advisors, have the knowledge to carry on the activity as a successful business.
7. Whether you have been successful in making a profit in similar activities in the past.
8. Whether the activity makes a profit in some years, and how much profit it makes.
9. Whether you can expect to make a future profit from the appreciation of the assets used in the activity.

All 9 factors are relevant although Item 3, the "depending on income from the activity for your livelihood" factor should be considered only if the answer is "yes".

A "no" answer could be honestly given by many wealthy individuals who commence new businesses with every intention of making a profit, but who nevertheless do not depend on the activity for their livelihood.

I.R.S. publications are helpful, even though they usually present a narrow view of tax benefits. They do not have the force of law and are binding on neither the I.R.S. nor the courts. Nevertheless when arguing a contested point with a staff member or before a court the taxpayer is usually at some advantage in demonstrating compliance with advice contained in one of the publications.

The bottom line in establishing status as a dealer is that your activities must be consistent with being in business and attempting to make a profit.

The operative word, in our opinion, is activity. Assuming a profit motive as being primary, the major distinction between an art dealer and an art investor will always be the nature and frequency of the activity.

Note that I.R.C. §469 limits the use of losses arising from passive investments in a gallery or private dealer. Generally, loses generated by "passive activities" can offset only "passive income". They can, however, be carried over to future years and applied against passive income. §469 diminishes the attractiveness of being a "silent partner" in a gallery that is not expected to show a profit.

The Investor

An investor obtains the same benefits as a collector plus the benefit of deductions for many of the expenses incurred in connection with maintaining a collection.

Prior to the landmark case of *Wrightsman v. United States*, 428 F2d. 1316 (Ct. Cl. 1970) there was little or no case law involving art as an investment.

The *Wrightsman* case presents a difficult scenario for the investor in art. The Court of Claims was probably in error on its interpretation of the tax law, but the case has remained as an authority since 1970.

The case arose when certain expenses incurred by Charles B. Wrightsman and Jayne Wrightsman were disallowed on an audit of their 1960 and 1961 returns. In addition a claim of $1000 as part of a capital loss sustained on their 1961 sale of certain works of art was disallowed.

The Wrightsmans paid the additional tax and brought an action in the Court of Claims to recover the payments. An order of reference was made by the court referring the matter to a Commissioner to make findings of fact and render an opinion. The Commissioner found that the Wrightsmans had held their works of art as investment properties. He found that the use and enjoyment of the works of art by the Wrightsmans did not preclude the treatment of the works of art as investment properties. The Commissioner went on to hold that:

> *The facts and circumstances in evidence in this case clearly establish that in the taxable years involved, and for several years prior thereto, plaintiffs held their works of art as investment properties. Their personal declarations of investment purpose and intention, consistently made during that substantial period of time, are supported by circumstances and conduct evincing such intention....Their extensive and thorough study and exploration of the field of 18th century French art and related fields, their devotion of much personal attention and time to the acquisition and holding of their works of art, their maintenance of businesslike methods of accounting for their acquisitions...all confirm investment intent. Report of Commissioner To The Court*

The Commissioner also stated, "It would seem obvious as an abstract proposition, that works of art could be the subject matter of investment."

The Commissioner found that Mr. Wrightsman's art acquisitions were motivated by (1) a substantial change in his financial position in 1951, resulting in the availability thereafter of a large cash flow for investment purposes; (2) his personal fear of investment in stock of any corporation, in which he lacked intimate knowledge of its operations and had no management control; and (3) his firm belief in certain theories concerning long-range economic trends.

Among the facts established were that by the end of 1960 the Wrightsmans had purchased $5.2 million of art and by the end of 1961 the total had reached $5.5 million. As of March 31,1967 their total purchases exceeded $8.9 million. At that time their collection was insured for over $16.8 million.

The Wrightsmans were found to have engaged in an active and extensive course of self education by visiting major museums and art dealer establishments, studying works of art, reviewing auction catalogs and price lists, and participating in discussions with recognized art experts, such as collectors, museum curators, and dealers. They did extensive reading in the area of their major interest, 18th century French Art. They acquired a substantial art library and Jayne Wrightsman engaged in extensive research. Charles Wrightsman concentrated on the restoration and conservation of art objects and the conditions of the art market.

By 1956 Charles Wrightsman was sufficiently prominent to be elected to the Board of Trustees of the Metropolitan Museum of Art and became a member of its

Purchasing Committee, and a Trustee-Visitor of its Department of Conservation. As a member of the Purchasing Committee he participated in the museum's acquisition by purchase and gift of art objects involving millions of dollars annually.

In 1963 Charles and Jayne Wrightsman became members of the Council of Advisors of the Institute of Fine Arts of New York University.

The Commissioner accepted the evidence introduced which demonstrated that as each work of art was acquired it was invoiced, assigned an inventory number, and noted as an approved purchase by one of the Wrightsmans. Each invoice was sent to their business office, checked for accuracy, and a check request prepared. Each work of art was reflected in the investment control account of the general ledger. A detailed investment card record was maintained for each acquisition.

The Wrightsmans were diligent in cataloging their purchases, and at the time of the trial the catalogs consisted of 26 three-ring binder volumes, requiring a shelf space of five feet.

Except for occasional displays of items at other locations, the works of art were kept at a New York apartment, a Palm Beach home, and in the Metropolitan Museum on loan for display.

As of March 31,1967 about 77.8% of the art (on an insurance evaluation basis) was in the New York apartment, about 17.7% in the Palm Beach home, and about 4.5% in the Metropolitan Museum. The works of art were on display, or in use as in the case of such items as French period furniture, in the New York apartment and the Palm Beach home. A small amount of furniture was stored in one room at Palm Beach.

The premises were air conditioned and humidity controlled in accordance with standards consistent with the preservation of works of art. The Commissioner found that humidity and temperature controlled storage facilities for works of art were, at that time, not readily available.

Before the Court of Claims the I.R.S. argued that because of the nature of the property, the failure to segregate the art [so as to preclude personal pleasure] was a bar to the deduction of the expenses and, in the alternative, that the Wrightsmans did not demonstrate any action on their part inconsistent with the holding of their collection for pleasure.

The Court of Claims rejected both positions of the I.R.S. but ruled against the Wrightsmans basing the decision on the language of a Treasury Regulation 1.212-1(c) which to this day reads in relevant part:

> Expenses of carrying on transactions which * * * are not carried on for the production or collection of income or for the management, conservation, or maintenance of property held for the production of income, but which are carried on **primarily** as a sport, hobby, or recreation are not allowable as non-- trade or nonbusiness expenses. The question whether or not a transaction is carried on primarily for the production of income or for the management, conservation, or maintenance of property held for the production or collection of income, rather than **primarily** as a sport, hobby, or recreation, is **not to be determined solely from the intention of the taxpayer but rather from all the circumstances of the case.** [Emphasis supplied.]

While accepting that the record established that the Wrightsmans had established an investment purpose, the Court went on to say that the evidence did not "establish investment as the most prominent purpose for...acquiring and holding works of art. The complete record does establish, to the contrary, personal pleasure or satisfaction as ...[the Wrightsmans'] primary purpose."

The Court implied that had the Wrightsmans taken less of an interest in art, learned less about art, and participated less in art activities, the result might have been different. The Court referred to a case decided in favor of a taxpayer involving a stamp collector who... "exhibited scant interest in or knowledge of stamps; and ... participated little in those activities generally associated with stamp hobbyists..." and purchased stamps only through a professional philatelist. *G. F. Tyler*, 6 TCM 275 (1947). In *Tyler* investment intent was found to be primary.

The problem with the Court's reasoning, as we perceive it, is that all of the facts which appeared to be used against the Wrightsmans are not only consistent with intelligent investing but also consistent with being a dealer.

What apparently was unspoken was the image of an investor, in the minds of the judges, as a passive person. Nothing in the law or regulations, at that time, dictated a result based on the concept of an investor being passive. The idea of a coupon clipping aristocrat clearly prevailed.

What the result would have been had the Wrightsmans done what the I.R.S. urged, but was rejected by the Court, i.e. stored their collection out of view, can only be left to speculation. Would segregation have been sufficient to reduce enjoyment and pleasure to a secondary role?

T.R.A.'86 embodies a passivity concept but in a different context. That concept was previously discussed.

It is simplistic to conclude that the lesson to be learned from *Wrightsman* is that the enjoyment of and appreciation of art is inconsistent with being an investor for tax purposes.

While the Wrightsmans had a large collection and evidently managed to display almost all of it in their two homes, much, in our opinion, to their tax detriment, what is the investor to do with five works of art? Must such an investor store the work in a warehouse or vault?

The Court of Claims recognized that there is a "pleasure-giving quality commonly recognized as inherent in art object". How does one sublimate the pleasure to the point where it is superseded by investment intent?

If *Wrightsman* is applied to what everyone would concede is a pure business situation, it could be argued that if a takeover magnate enjoys the "game" or "victory" more than the money then he is pursuing a hobby!

The decision was, in our opinion, in error but must be lived with until another taxpayer prevails on similar facts.

A factor which did not appear to be crucial but which may have lurked in the minds of the Court is that with few exceptions the Wrightsmans were always on the buy side. The word "investor", in the minds of the Court, may have involved the concept of realizing gains. The Wrightsmans apparently kept every work of art that met with their long term critical approval.

In terms of a suggested course of action for an investor, we believe that prudence dictates that (i) a major portion of your collection be stored other than at your home, (ii) that there be sales which result in the realization of profits, and (iii) that your social life not be totally fused with your interest in art.

One strategy may be to acquire works that you admire but which you would be willing to sell once they have appreciated. The sale of those works would work to substantiate your investment intent. At the same time you would be able to continue to indefinitely hold those works which you see as long term investments.

The suggested strategy is simple to practice for investors in of prints, photographs, and other multiples. Having made an acquisition decision you purchase two identical prints with the intention of selling one.

The concept of selling works of art that have appreciated in value, and not having all your works of art hanging on the wall, may not appeal to all collectors, but if you desire to claim investor status they may be the factors that tip the scale in your favor. The image of the stock market investor keeping his securities in a bank vault and buying low and selling high does persist in the minds of jurists.

The profit motive presumption raised by §183 I.R.C. (the hobby loss provision) may be invaluable if you have profits from your activities in three of the past five years.

You cannot, of course, have profits in absence of sales.

Even though T.R.A.'86 eliminated some of the benefits of investor status, e.g. the deductibility of expenses in connection with seminars and symposiums, I.R.C.

§274(h)(7); the limitation of allowable deductions to an amount in excess of 2% of adjusted gross income, there remain substantial income tax benefits for investors as opposed to collectors. The most significant of those benefits, for the majority of those with collections, is the deductibility of insurance premiums.

QUICK REFERENCE CHART FOR DEDUCTIONS

EXPENSE	*COLLECTOR*	*DEALER*	*INVESTOR*
Insurance	No-1	Yes	Yes-2
Alarm & Security Devices	No-1	Yes	Yes-2
Storage Materials	No-1	Yes	Yes-2
Temperature & Humidity Controls	No-1	Yes	Yes-2
Mounting, Framing, Cases	No-1	Yes	Yes-3
Cleaning & Restoration	No-1	Yes	Yes-3
Lighting	No-1	Yes	No
Reference Books	No-1	Yes	Yes-2
Magazines & Newsletters	No-1	Yes	Yes-2
Dues	No-1	Yes	Yes-2
Seminars & Symposiums	No	Yes-5	No
Related Travel	No	Yes-5	No
Acquisition & Selling Cost	Yes-3	Yes-3	Yes-3
Interest	No	Yes	Yes-4
Rent	No	Yes	Yes-2
Phone, Postage, Supplies	No-1	Yes	Yes-2
Home Office Deduction	No	Yes	Yes-2

Notes:
1. If there is hobby income these expenses are deductible up to amount of income.
2. Deductible only to the extent they exceed 2% of adjusted gross income.
3. These expenses, including sales tax, are added to cost basis.
4. For investors the interest expense deduction is limited to extent of investment income.
5. There are limitations on the deductibility of expenses in connection with conventions and seminars outside of the North American area.

CHAPTER FOUR

SALES: THE EFFECT OF STATUS ON TAX BENEFITS

Collectors, dealers, investors and artists receive or are denied the benefit of the lower long-term capital gains rate on the sale of art held for the required long-term capital gains holding period as follows:

Status	*Received*	*Denied*
Collector	x	
Dealer		x
Investor	x	
Artist		x

T.R.A. '86 temporarily eliminated the difference between tax treatment by eliminating the benefit accorded on the sale of long-term capital gains property but a differential in rates has been reinstated.

Capital Gains

A primary, but not overly significant, concern is whether the profit on a sale of a work of art is taxed at ordinary income rates or at the long-term capital gains rates.

The capital gains issue, in so far as the tax rate differential, is not settled and may become more significant.

Pre-T.R.A.'86 noncorporate taxpayers could deduct 60% of their net capital gain (excess of net long-term capital gain over net short-term capital loss) from gross income. The remaining 40% of net capital gain was included in gross income and taxed at the regular rates applicable to noncorporate taxpayers. In the highest tax bracket of 50% the deduction resulted in a maximum effective tax rate on long-term capital gains of 20% (50% maximum rate x 40% of net capital gain included in gross income = 20%).

It is important to remember that T.R.A.'86 did not change the character of gain as ordinary or capital, or as short-term or long-term capital gain. It is unlikely that the importance of the character of property will ever be totally eliminated from the I.R.C.

The pre-1986 statutory structure for capital gains was retained in the Code to facilitate reinstatement of a capital gains rate differential and in fact a there was a reinstatement of the differential, although the spread is now only a 3 percentage point difference (28% v 31%).

Your Planning

The collector and investor are accorded capital gains treatment on the sale of works of art held for the requisite holding period.

Dealers who hold all works of art as inventory are denied the benefit of capital gains treatment.

It is possible for dealers to have an investment account of art and to receive capital gains treatment. That idea was addressed by Gilbert Edelson, Esq. at an *ARTnews Art Marketing Conference* held in the spring of 1982.

A dealer setting up an investment account should remember to act as an investor in all respects. If art work for the investment account is acquired at auction, the sales tax should be paid. A separate account or set of books should be maintained for the works of art held for investment. A separate insurance policy and even separate storage facilities would be advisable.

As will be discussed in Chapter Six, a dealer, in the absence of an investment account, will lose the benefit of the appreciation in the value of artworks which are the subject of a charitable donation.

In this instance it may be said that the I.R.S. requires you to keep two sets of books!

CHAPTER FIVE

SALES AND USE TAXES

Prior to T.R.A.'86 state and local sales and use taxes were deductible on federal income tax returns by collectors and investors. Dealers, acquiring artwork for resale, did not have to pay such taxes but were required by state and other local laws to collect the tax from their clients. Not all states have sales taxes, but New York, the site of most major United States art auctions, has a sales tax.

Effective for tax years beginning on or after January 1,1987, the deduction previously permitted by I.R.C. §164 for state and local taxes was repealed.

For business and investment property the state and local sales taxes are now added to basis, or if the tax is on the disposition, it is subtracted from the amount realized, I.R.C. §164(a).

For collectors, the effect is to increase the cost of the acquisition by an amount equal to the amount of the sales tax multiplied by their maximum tax bracket.

For dealers, local law still applies in terms of an exemption from the tax when purchasing for resale. The importance of your payment of the sales tax or claim of an exemption should not be underestimated.

Why Is The Sales Tax Important?

The rationale behind our devoting a separate chapter of this guide to sales taxes is that your payment or claim of an exemption from the sales tax may be an important evidentiary element in establishing your intent as to status.

During those time frames when the tax rate on long-term capital gains is in effect, it is strong evidence *against* investment intent if you claim dealer status as a purchaser by using the resale exemption from the sales tax.

Even when there is no favorable rate on long-term capital gains, you must consider basis when making charitable gifts (see Chapter Six). A dealer is permitted a deduction only for basis, i.e. cost. An investor or collector is permitted to deduct fair market value, except in the certain situations described in Chapter Six.

When your painting or antique has appreciated substantially in value, your unwarranted claim of dealer status on acquisition may be an expensive ploy.

We are not suggesting that *bona fide* dealers pay sales taxes on acquisition for inventory. If, however, you are a dealer with an investment portfolio of artwork, you should pay the sales tax on the acquisitions for your separate investment portfolio.

You should even go so far as to have two accounts at auction houses, a dealer account and a personal account.

Changing Your Intent

Should you elect to transfer a work of art from dealer inventory to investment status, it is suggested that you establish a record of that transaction by purchasing the work from inventory.

If you keep separate bank accounts for your business and personal activities, you should actually write a check from your personal account to the business account. If you reside in a state with a sales tax or use tax, pay the tax!

Use Taxes

State and local use taxes most often come into play when you, as a resident of State A, make a purchase in State B and delivery is made to State A.

Under most state and local sales tax laws the transaction is exempt from State B's tax since it is shipped to State A.

Those states with sales taxes generally require payment of use taxes on such out-of-state purchases. You may therefore be liable for a use tax in State A.

Although many states are diligent in collecting the use tax in connection with the out-of-state purchase of motor vehicles (you must pay the use tax in order to register), they are less rigorous in following up on use taxes.

If you reside in a jurisdiction with a use tax and you have made an out-of-state purchase of art which was shipped into the state, it is prudent to file and pay the use tax.

The failure to pay may not prove as fatal an omission as claiming unwarranted dealer status.

If, however, there is a chance that you may be deemed a dealer, or if you are a dealer acquiring for your investment portfolio, payment is objective evidence of your intent.

Several states, notably New York and New Jersey, have taken a more aggressive posture on use taxes during the past few years. It is safe to assume that they will be joined by other states. What has made enforcement feasible is the maintenance of sales records on computers by out-of-state vendors. Relying on tax cooperation agreements, New Jersey has obtained the records of all New Jersey purchasers from New York merchants. The purchaser then receives a tax bill from New Jersey. Although the program has thus far been limited to high profile merchants we predict that, in an effort to capture lost revenue, the program will be gradually expanded to all retail establishments including art, antique, and collectible dealers.

We are advised that in 1991 the United States Customs Service began to give information about traveler's overseas acquisitions to state tax authorities. Overseas art and antique purchases may result in a use tax bill from your home state! If you are a dealer you may claim an exemption from your state's use tax.

CHAPTER SIX

CHARITABLE GIFTS

Summary Of T.R.A.'86 Changes

For those who are conversant with the art of donating art, the following summary of changes made by T.R.A.'86 is set forth prior to proceeding to a full discussion.

While maintaining the basic structure providing a tax benefit arising from charitable giving, the benefit of some charitable giving was diminished by T.R.A.'86 in four ways.

1. The reduction in tax rates resulted in less of a tax saving that if the same gift had been made prior to 1987.

2. The charitable deduction for non-itemizers that had been permitted between 1981 and 1986 was eliminated. Donors who do not itemize their deductions lose the benefit of a post-1986 charitable gift.

3. Unrealized appreciation in gifts of property given to a charity is treated as a preference item when computing the Alternative Minimum Tax ("A.M.T.") (see Chapter 7). The result may be a diminished tax benefit for some, but not all, taxpayers. For the tax year 1991 the application of the A.M.T. to charitable gifts has been suspended.

4. Gifts of tangible personal property, including but not limited to works of art, antiques, and collectibles continue to be deductible if the property is used by the charity to carry out its exempt function. However, if the gift is non-related or is sold by the charity, T.R.A.'86 limits the deduction to the cost basis of the property, I.R.C.

§170(e)(1). Therefore a donation of a painting to an art museum or other charity for sale at a fund raising auction results in a non-related use, Reg. §1.170A-4(b)(3).

No Change In Distinction Between Long-Term And Short-Term Property For Purposes Of Charitable Deduction

T.R.A. '86 retained the distinction between long-term and short-term capital gain property for the purposes of the charitable deduction even though it temporarily eliminated the rate differential between long-term capital gains and ordinary income. In the area of charitable deductions the distinction is significant.

The Income Tax Deduction For The Charitable Gift Of Art

One major result of Congressional encouragement of philanthropy is the existence of the benefit of an income tax deduction for the charitable donation of art.

The dollar amount of that benefit, assuming gifts of equal value by different taxpayers, is variable. The dollar amount of the benefit is variable because it is calculated, for each taxpayer, using a formula which includes the following factors:

1. the status of the donor
    a. collector
    b. dealer
    c. investor
    d. artist

2. the length of time the donor owned the gift
3. the adjusted gross income of the donor
4. the application of the alternative minimum tax
    a. the amount, if any, by which the fair market value of the gift exceeds the basis of the donor
    b. the amount, if any, of other tax preferences of the donor

[*The application of the A.M.T. in relation to charitable gifts was suspended for the 1991 tax year. As we go to press it is uncertain as to whether the suspension will be extended to years beyond 1991.]*

5. the nature of the use to which the gift will be put by the donee

Even if a charitable income tax deduction is not of benefit to you or is unavailable, it may be important that the gift be a charitable gift so as to prevent the imposition of the gift tax. The majority of donors seem to be unaware that the income tax deduction is only part of the benefit.

The exemption from the application of the gift tax is a second and distinct benefit. The exemption is accomplished by permitting donors to deduct charitable gifts from the total of all gifts made during the calendar year, I.R.C. §2522.

The basic rules relating to the income tax deduction for charitable gifts are found in I.R.C. §170 and the regulations issued thereunder. That section permits you to deduct the value of certain types of contributions made to qualified charitable organizations from adjusted gross income in determining your taxable income.

The discussion in this chapter assumes that your gift is being made to a qualified "public type" charitable organization. That term embraces museums, universities and other teaching institutions, as well as churches, hospitals, and public foundations. The term also includes private foundations that distribute all their receipts each year.

Although it can be safely said that major museums such as *The Museum Of Modern Art* and *The Metropolitan Museum of Art* are qualified, it is prudent to verify status. Verification can be done by consulting the most recent edition of I.R.S. Publication 78 or obtaining a copy of a letter from the I.R.S. setting forth the donee's status.

Note that there is a difference between an organization's exemption ruling under §501(c)(3) and its ruling as a "public type" organization under § 509(a). A donee must have the latter in order for you to obtain the benefits of a deduction.

The discussion in this chapter also assumes that you itemize your deductions since, as previously noted, T.R.A. '86 eliminated the availability of a charitable deduction to non-itemizers.

Beginning in 1991 itemized deductions (other than medical expenses, investment interest and casualty theft losses) are limited for those with adjusted gross income of more than $100,000 ($50,000 for married couples filing separate returns). Specifically those deductions must be reduced by 3% of adjusted gross income (AGI) in excess of $100,000 I.R.C. §68.

For example, an individual with an AGI of $200,000 has $75,000 of itemized deductions that are subject to the reduction. Those deductions are reduced by $3,000 (3% of $100,00) [the AGI in excess of $100,000]). In no event will the reduction limit the itemized deduction by more than 80%.

Since your deductible gift reduces your taxable income, it therefore reduces your taxes by an amount equal to the value of the tax deduction multiplied by your marginal tax rate. Your true "cost" of making the gift is the value of the gift less the tax saving.

The balance of the gift, i.e. your tax savings, is in effect a subsidy to the donee from the federal government.

Example: If your taxable income is taxed at a marginal rate of 31%, a gift of a work of art to a museum with a fair market value of $10,000 will have the following result:

value of gift	$10,000.
marginal tax rate	31%
tax saving	$ 3,100.

The after tax cost of gift to you = ($10,000 - $3,100) = $ 6,900

The museum gets the benefit of the full $10,000 work of art notwithstanding the fact that your net cost is only $6,900; in effect the additional $3,100 comes from the $3,100 which the I.R.S. did not collect from you.

That example did not take into consideration the additional saving incurred over selling and then making a donation equal to the value of the art nor the possible application of the A.M.T. The mathematics of those procedures are illustrated later in this chapter.

Donative Intent

Your gift, in order to be deductible, must be made with donative intent and without consideration. You must not receive anything in exchange for the gift. The naming of a gallery or a building in your honor or the addition of your name to a bronze plaque of patrons is not deemed the type of consideration which would disqualify your gift as a charitable deduction.

Contingent Gifts

If your gift is made subject to a condition precedent (i.e. the happening of an event prior to the gift becoming effective), no deduction is allowed until the condition has been satisfied, Reg. §1.170A-1(e).

Thus if your gift is contingent on the museum's agreeing to exhibit the art permanently or temporarily, you may not take the deduction until the museum agrees.

Take care in making contingent gifts near year end. Allow sufficient time for the donee to respond to the contingency before December 31. Agreement may require a board meeting or the approval of a person who is away on holiday. In some instances the acquisitions committee may not have the authority to agree to a contingency and you must allow time for both the acquisitions committee and a separate decision maker to act.

If your tax planning requires that the gift be effective in the year in which it is offered, either eliminate the contingency or ascertain that sufficient time remains in the year for such action as may be required for agreement.

Partial Interests

With some significant exceptions, a gift of a partial interest in art is not deductible, I.R.C. §170(f)(3), 2055 (e)(2), 2522(c)(2). A loan of a work of art (see Permanent Loans), even for a year or more, does not result in a deductible gift.

One exception is a partial interest which represents your entire interest in the art. provided the partial interest was not created for the purpose of making the gift, Reg §1.170A-7(a)(2)(i).

A second exception is a partial interest which is your undivided portion of your entire interest in the art I.R.C. §170(f)(3)(B)(ii).

An example of the first exception would be a gift of your interest in a jointly owned painting or antique.

An example of the second would be a 50% interest in a painting. The donee must have the right to exclusive possession of the work for a portion of each year representing its interest. i.e. six months in the case of a 50% interest. The donee's initial possession must not be deferred more than one year. You retain partial enjoyment and must pay a proportionate part of the expense of maintenance. A recent Tax Court case sustained a deduction where there was a *right* to possession, as opposed to *actual physical* possession.

At a 1986 tax seminar, Stanley S. Weithorn, Esq. told of a gift of an undivided 25% interest he structured for a client. Physical possession of the art was given to the donee museum for three months each year. The three months coincided with his client's summer vacation at a second home. Mr. Weithorn suggested that the transfer of possession might even result in saving the donor the cost of insurance during the three month period.

Gifts of successive fractional interests can be used to extend the five-year carryover period for income tax purposes. The fractional interest technique may be particularly useful in with connection with single works and collections which have fair market values so high in relation to your contribution base that you will not be able to use up the deduction within the carry forward period.

One might speculate that, if the fractional interest is below the threshold for automatic referral to the Art Advisory Panel (see Chapter Ten), that a painting with an appraised value above the threshold might escape the automatic referral procedure.

In making a gift of an undivided fractional interest, you should take into account the possibility that the valuation of the fraction interest may have to reflect the fact that undivided interests may sell at a discount below an allocable portion of the value of the entire property, cf. *William R. Knapp*, 36 TCM 1576 (1977).

Remainder Interest

No deduction is available for the gift of remainder interest in works of art unless the interest is in a charitable remainder annuity trust, a charitable remainder unitrust or a pooled income fund, I.R.C. §170(f).

A special rule provides that for income tax purposes no contribution of a future interest will be considered to be made until the expiration of all intervening noncharitable interests or until all intervening noncharitable interests are no longer held by the donor or a related person, I.R.C. §170(a)(3).

For example, if you contributed a remainder interest in a painting to an art museum subject to a reserved right to keep the painting for 10 years, no income tax deduction would be allowed until the 10 year period expires or you relinquish your right to keep the painting.

In addition you would be subject to a gift tax on the contributed remainder interest because the reserved interest is not in a pooled income fund or charitable remainder trust.

If you died within the 10 year period without having relinquished the right to keep the painting, there would be no estate tax deduction on the donated interest, for the same reasons.

If the painting were given to a charitable remainder trust or a pooled income fund in which you retain an interest (or in which an interest is given to a related person) an estate and gift tax deduction will be available. An income tax deduction is available only if the income interest is given to a person who is unrelated to you.

Copyrights To Artworks

I.R.C. § 2055(e)(4) and 2522(c)(2) treat an original work of art and its related copyright as separate properties for purpose of the gift and estate tax charitable deductions. Thus, you may donate an original artwork to a museum while retaining the copyright without subjecting the gift to gift tax (or estate tax where the transfer is made on death). However, no income tax deduction is available for such a gift because for income tax purposes it is considered a gift of a non-deductible partial interest.

Valuable gifts may be made using those provisions while retaining the copyright for commercial exploitation. Commercial artists may find those provisions of great use.

Moreover if the work, in your hands, has a low basis because you obtained the work as a gift from the artist or you are the artist, the unavailability of the income tax deduction may not be a hardship.

Permanent Loans

One method of making a gift of artwork to a museum is to loan the work to the museum on either a "temporary" or "permanent" basis. A temporary loan runs for a fixed period whereas a permanent loan runs for an indefinite period.

A permanent loan creates a bailment, i.e. the property is held in trust for a specific purpose and is to be returned when that purpose is ended by demand of the owner. You, as the owner, can claim the work at any time. The statute of limitations does not begin to run against the donor until demand is made for return of the property.

The permanent loan creates a potential for confusion in cases where the lender dies, since it may be difficult to ascertain where title to the work resides. For example, in 1990 the *New York Times* reported on a dispute between the Museum of Modern Art (NY) and the Estate of Charlotte Steichen. Charlotte was the daughter of Edward Steichen. At issue was a Matisse valued at $800,000. It was a gift from Matisse to Edward. The museum had possession of the painting since 1974 and claimed that it had received it as a gift from Charlotte. Charlotte, however, bequeathed the painting to a grandniece and when the museum refused to return the Matisse, brought an action to recover it. MOMA returned the work prior to a court decision but both sides incurred substantial legal fees. The lesson to be learned is that the terms of permanent loans and/or gifts should be documented and signed by both the lender/donee and the museum.

Some, but not all, institutions have adopted policies of terminating all permanent loans which run for more than a pre-determined number of years (e.g. 15 years) unless such loans are renewed.

Bargain Sales

A bargain sale is a hybrid. It is part gift and part a sale of property to a charitable institution. It is used most often in connection with appreciated property since it permits the donor to recapture the original purchase price, make a gift, and obtain an income tax deduction. You must have an appraisal by a qualified appraiser (See Chapter 10) demonstrating a value in excess of the sale price.

In the case of a bargain sale which results in the allowance of a charitable deduction, the donor realizes a taxable gain which is computed by allocating a portion of the adjusted basis of the artwork to the sale in accordance with the ratio of the sale price to the fair market value, Reg. §1.1011-2(a)(2) and Reg. §170A-4-(c)(2).

> **Example:** You sell to a museum for $8,000 a painting which is long-term capital gain property having an adjusted basis of $4,000 with a fair market value of $20,000. Your contribution is $12,000 ($20,000 - $8,000). Your basis of $4,000 is allocated to the sale in accordance with the ratio of the sale price to the fair market value: (8,000/20,000) x $4,000 = $1,600. You have a recognized long-term capital gain of $6,400 ($8,000 - $1,600) on the bargain sale. The benefit is the $12,000 charitable deduction.
>
> Assuming a marginal tax rate of 28% the tax on the gain on an outright sale at fair market value would be $4,480. Your net cash in pocket is $15,520.
>
> Using the bargain sale technique your tax would be $1,792 (28% x $6,400). Your charitable deduction would be worth $3,360 (28% x $12,000). Your net cash in pocket would be $9,568 ($8,000 - $1,792 + $3,360).

The result is more favorable than selling the artwork, paying the capital gains tax and donating $12,000 to the museum out of the proceeds.

The $9,568 result is less favorable than under the pre-1987 rates which included a maximum capital gains tax rate of 20% and a maximum incremental bracket of 50%. The result using those percentages would be net cash in pocket of $12,720.

Since incremental tax rates change and the special treatment for long-term capital gains may be made more favorable, it may be helpful to remember that the lower the long-term capital gains rate and the higher your incremental tax bracket the more favorable the result in a bargain sale.

It should be noted that if you make a bargain sale of an artwork against which you owe money the amount of indebtedness must be included in the sale price thereby increasing your gain and the tax payable. The inclusion of the indebtedness is required even though the donee does not assume or pay the debt. The rationale for the rule arises from the concept that the forgiveness of indebtedness results in the recognition, for tax purposes, of income.

That problem rarely arises in connection with the gift of artwork but often arises in connection with mortgaged real estate.

The way to avoid the inclusion of the debt in the sale price is to agree to pay the debt or hold the donee harmless.

The bargain sale rules are applied only if the transaction involves a charitable deduction, Reg. §1.1011-2(a)(1). Using the last example you would pay a tax of $1,120 on the gain of $4,000 (28% x $4,000). You would have a net of $6,780, a result less favorable than reached by apportioning the gain and taking the deduction.

Effective Date Of The Gift

A gift of a physical object is effective and thus deductible when you have unconditionally parted with dominion and control over the object. Delivery to the donee is not required as long as you have relinquished all control over the object. Delivery to a third party who is the agent of the donee in accepting the object is effective, Reg.

§1.170A-1(b). Delivery to a third party acting as your agent is not effective until delivery is made to the donee or the donee's agent.

Your letter written to a museum director written on December 26th stating your intention to make a gift of the sculpture he recently admired is not the equivalent of parting with dominion and control. Delivering the work to a trucking firm hired by the museum is effective.

The acceptance of a cash gift is generally not required to make it effective, but the majority of museums do require approval of their acquisitions committee prior to the acceptance of artworks. If the charitable tax deduction is important to you the time for you to decide on specific gifts is in the spring or summer. You must allow time to make your offer and for the acquisitions committee to act prior to December 31 of that year.

Valuation

Your deduction for a work of art contributed to a qualified institution is based on the fair market value, which is generally defined as the price at which the property would change hands between a willing buyer and a willing seller, Reg.§1.170A-1(c).

The Dealer Limitation

While the investor and collector are permitted a deduction for the fair market value of a charitable contribution, the dealer who donates a work of art from inventory is limited to his cost basis because inventory is not a capital asset. If there has been substantial appreciation in the fair market value between acquisition and donation, the dealer receives substantially less of a tax benefit.

Dealers who anticipate making donations should carefully segregate their art investments from inventory.

Donations of appreciated property should be made from their investment portfolio (see Chapter Four).

A separate set of acquisition and inventory records should be maintained for the investment portfolio. A dealer should have a separate insurance policy, bank account, and storage space for the investment portfolio.

The concept of a dealer's having an investment portfolio is well established on Wall Street. There is no reason why an art dealer cannot adopt the same position as a stock broker or investment banker.

A second reason for physical segregation of the investment portfolio and the record keeping in connection therewith is to have a structure in place in the event of the return of the tax differential in the treatment of long-term capital gains.

The Artist Limitation

One of the most difficult concepts to absorb is that an artist, however well established and regardless of what his or her art brings in the open market, is limited to a charitable deduction equal to the cost of materials.

However unfair it appears, the reasoning among law makers is that the cost of materials is the cost basis to the artist, and the art is inventory. Artists are not singled out for this treatment. All copyrights and literary works, letters, memoranda or similar property in the hands of the author, or in the hands of any taxpayer whose tax basis is determined in whole or part by reference to the author's tax basis, do not constitute capital assets, I.R.C. §1221(3)(A).

Persistent efforts to amend the law have, so far, been in vain.

Beware Of Artists Bearing Gifts

If the rule concerning artists is a surprise to many people the rule concerning gifts from artists is a shocker. The rule is simply that your basis for a work of art which was a gift from the artist is the cost basis to the artist and is not changed however long you own the work or by an increase in fair market value.

The key to that result is I.R.C. §1221(3) which defines the term "capital asset". §1221(3)(C) states that the term "capital asset" does not include property held by a taxpayer "in whose hands the basis of such property is determined, for the purposes of determining gain from a sale or exchange, in whole or in part by reference to the basis of such property in the hands" of the taxpayer whose personal efforts created such property. Under §1015 I.R.C. covering the determination of basis on gifts, the basis of property in the hands of a donee is determined by the basis of such property in the hands of the donor. Thus artwork which is the gift of the artist is, because of statutory exclusion, prevented from becoming a capital asset in your hands.

If, for example, you accept the gift of a painting by a promising young artist with a cost basis to the artist of $100 [i.e. canvas + paint] your basis is not only $100 but the painting retains the character of "inventory" (i.e. a non-capital asset) in your hands.

The solution to avoiding the artist basis trap is to decline gifts of art from artists. Always make payment by check, or if by cash, obtain a receipt.

The sale to you, regardless of the price, breaks the chain which binds you to the artist's cost of materials basis. The sale converts the art to capital gain property. If there is a material difference between the fair market value of the painting and your payment the difference may be deemed a gift (see Chapter Eight).

Artwork obtained by inheritance or bequest from an artist does not fall within the foregoing rules. Your basis is the fair market value on the date of death.

An Overview Of Appraisals

If you claim a deduction in excess of $5,000 for a work of art you must obtain a qualified appraisal for the value of the work before you file the tax return on which the deduction is claimed Reg. §1.170A-13(c).

We will return to qualified appraisals in a Chapter Ten but in brief the following rules apply:

> The appraisal (which cannot be made more than sixty days prior to date of the contribution) must signed and dated by the qualified appraiser and set forth:
>
> 1. description of the work of art in detail,
> 2. its physical condition,
> 3. the date or expected date of the contribution,
> 4. a description of any agreement or understanding relating to the sale or disposition of the work or earmarking it for a particular need,
> 5. the name and taxpayer identification number of the appraiser,
> 6. the qualifications of the appraiser,
> 7. a statement that the appraisal was made for tax purposes,
> 8. the date of the appraisal
> 9. the appraised fair market value of the work,
> 10. the method of valuation used,
> 11. the specific basis for the valuation,

The appraisal requirements are in Reg. §1.170A-13(c)(3) and Publication 561 (see the Appendix).

You, as the donor, are required to provide the donee with a summary of the appraisal, obtain the donee's acknowledgement and file the acknowledged summary on Form 8283 with your tax return.

Form 8283, a copy of which is included in the Appendix, must be used to provide the necessary information. It includes, in Section B thereof, the "Appraisal Summary". The donee's acknowledgement of receipt of the property on Form 8283 *does not* represent the donee's concurrence on the issue of fair market value.

If the donee sells the work within two years after receipt, it is required to file an information Form 8282 with the I.R.S. and furnish a copy to the donor (see Form 8282, Appendix).

If you fail to obtain the required appraisal and to file a summary with your tax return, it will lead to a disallowance of the claimed deduction, unless the failure can be shown to be in good faith and an appraisal summary is furnished to the I.R.S. within 90 days after the I.R.S. requests the summary, Reg. §1.170A(c)(4)(iv)(H).

What constitutes a "good faith" failure to file has yet to be established. Regardless of the benefit to the donee the I.R.S. is a tax collection agency and looks upon any deduction as being in derogation of its mission. It is in your best interest to comply strictly with the appraisal and filing requirements.

A detailed discussion of appraisals is contained in Chapter 10 of this guide.

Contribution Of Property Which Has A Lower Fair Market Value Than Your Basis

The vagaries of the market are such that an object, at the time you desire to make a donation, may have a lower basis than your cost. That lower cost may arise from (i) your having purchased the work in a euphoric auction, or (ii) the particular school to which it belongs being in the doldrums.

Unless the donee desires that specific work or you desire the work to be in a specific institution, consideration should be given to a sale of the object instead of a donation. The proceeds can be given to the institution.

The reason for considering a sale is that a donation is not considered a sale, and you receive no loss deduction arising from the diminution in value of your investment property. This reasoning works for investors but not collectors!

If the work is sold and the proceeds donated, you (i) establish the tax loss, and (ii) obtain the charitable deduction.

Contribution Of Property Which Has Appreciated

If the object which is the subject of your gift has appreciated in value, your donation provides the benefits of (i) eliminating the tax payable if you had sold the work, and (ii) giving you a charitable deduction equal to the fair market value of the item.

Example: If your taxable income is taxed at a marginal rate of 31%, a gift of a work of art, purchased in 1984 for $2,500, with a fair market value of $10,000 has the following result:

value of gift	$10,000.
tax rate	31%
tax saving	$ 3,100.

If you first sell the work of art, instead of donating it, your federal tax is calculated as follows:

sale price	$10,000.
basis	(2,500.)
gain	$ 7,500.
marginal tax rate	31%
tax	$ 2,325.

If you make a gift of the proceeds, the donee receives $7,675 not the $10,000 work of art.

The government has pocketed the difference of $2,325.

In computing your tax savings in making a gift of the art you should consider the tax savings resulting from the fact that you did not have to recognize the gain and that you obtained a charitable deduction.

tax avoided on gain	$ 2,325.
tax benefit from deduction	3,100.
total tax benefit	$ 5,425.

amount of gift	$10,000.
tax savings	5,425.
after tax cost of gift	$ 4,575.

If you are a resident of a state and or city with an income tax, your aggregate tax will be greater, and you will have even less remaining to donate.

In the preceding example, the after tax cost, under pre-T.R.A.'86 maximum tax rates, would have been $3500.

T.R.A.'86 and subsequent adjustment to the rates has thus had the effect of increasing the cost of the $10,000 gift by $1075. While not insignificant, the increased cost is not so dramatic as to discourage individuals who take tax benefits into consideration when planning charitable donations.

The foregoing example does not take into consideration the possible application of the Alternative Minimum Tax ("A.M.T."). The reason the A.M.T. comes into play is that T.R.A.'86 made the amount of appreciation in the gift of art a tax preference item. The A.M.T. must be calculated separately for each individual and should not change the result if you have no other tax preference items. As previously mentioned the application of the A.M.T. has been suspended for the 1991 tax year. The application of the A.M.T. is discussed in Chapter Seven.

In the preceding example the date of acquisition was early enough to qualify the art as long-term gain property. In the event you donate a work of art which is not long-term property, your deduction is your basis, usually your cost. You lose the value of the appreciation in taking the charitable deduction.

It is therefore usually inadvisable, absent special circumstances, to donate appreciated short-term gain property.

Limits On Income Tax Deduction

In order to prevent taxpayers from reducing their income tax to zero, the I.R.C. contains percentage limits on the amount of charitable deductions. The dollar amount used to calculate the percentage is called the contribution base. Contribution base is adjusted gross income computed without any regard to net operating loss carryback to the taxable year under §172, §170(b)(1)(F).

Your contribution to a public-type charitable organization of a work of art which is capital gain property and meets the related use rule is allowable only to the extent of 30% of your contribution base.

The amount of the contribution which exceeds the 30% limitation may be carried forward for five years, retaining its character as capital gain property §170(d)(1)(A); 170 (b)(1)(C)(ii).

You may elect to increase the 30% limitation to 50% of the contribution base but in that event the amount of the deduction must be reduced to your cost basis, §170(b)(1)(C)(iii).

A calculation must be made for each taxpayer, but in instances where there has been substantial appreciation, it will generally be more beneficial to accept the 30% limitation.

The Interaction Of The 30% and the 50% Limit

The 30% limit and the 50% limit are not cumulative; the 30% limit is, in effect, a special limit within the 50% limit.

Gifts subject to the 30% limit are taken into account last, I.R.C. §170 (b)(1)(C)(i); Reg. §1.170A-8(d).

Therefore cash gifts made in or carried forward into the current year in excess of 20% of the contribution base will, in effect, reduce the 30% limit by the amount of such excess.

Example: Assume your contribution base is $100,000 and that you have made a cash gift of $22,000 and a gift of an appreciated painting worth $30,000. The limits are applied as follows:

contribution base	=	$ 100,000.
50% limit	=	50,000.
less cash gifts	–	22,000.
net remaining within the 50% limit	=	$ 28,000.
painting gift	=	$ 30,000.
deduction allowable for painting gift	–	28,000.
excess carried over to following year (subject to 30 % limit)	=	$ 2,000.

It is not permitted to make separate charitable gifts of appreciated property taking advantage of the 30% limit on one or more items and the 50% limit on others.

Once the 50% election is made it must be applied to all gifts of appreciated property made during the year. It will also be applied to any carryovers from and to the year in which the election is made. Any carryover from previous years must be recomputed as though the election had been in effect for those earlier years; however the deductions taken in earlier years are unaffected, Reg. §1.170A-8(d)(2)(i)(b).

Example: With a contribution base of $100,000 in 1986 you made a gift of a painting in that year worth $50,000 that you had purchased more than six months earlier for $20,000. For 1986 your deduction is limited and carried forward as follows:

value of painting	=	$50,000.
30% of contribution base	–	30,000.
excess to be carried forward	=	$20,000

If in 1987 your contribution base decreases to $80,000 and you make another gift of a painting worth $60,000 which you purchased more than 6 months earlier for $50,000, the effect of the special election to have the 50% limit apply will be as follows:

Recalculation of 1986 carryover:

value of 1986 gift	=	$50,000
basis	–	$20,000
appreciation "realized"	=	$30,000
		x40%
reduction of 1986 gift	=	$12,000
adjusted value of 1986 gift	=	$38,000
30% of '86 contribution base	=	$30,000
amount carried forward to 1987	=	$ 8,000

To calculate the 1987 deduction:

1987 gift	=	$60,000
basis	–	$50,000
appreciation	=	$10,000
		x40%
adjustment	=	$ 4,000

1987 gift	=	$60,000
adjustment	–	$ 4,000
1986 carryover as adjusted	+	$ 8,000
total		$64,000
1987 limit (50%)	=	$40,000
amount carried forward to 1988	=	$24,000

($8,000 is attributable to 1986)

Limit On Deduction When Art Is Sold Or Use Is Non-Related

If the object donated is non-related to the functions of the donee or is sold by the donee, T.R.A.'86 limits the deduction to your cost basis. The 30% limitation applies but since appreciation is not taken into consideration there is no option to take advantage of the 50% limitation.

The use test is applied by looking at the exempt purpose of the donee. If, for instance, a work of art is donated to a museum, the issue of use is satisfied if in fact the work is added to the collection or if it is reasonable for you to anticipate that it will be put to such use, I.R.C. §170(e)(1)(B)(i).

The test may be satisfied if the donee is a university and the work of art is hung in one of the university buildings or used in a course of instruction on art appreciation.

If your gift is of a collection , your deduction is not reduced if the donee sells or disposes of an insubstantial portion of the collection, Reg. §1.170A-4(b)(3)(i).

On the other hand, if you can reasonably expect that the donee will sell or lease your gift or a substantial portion thereof, or put it to a use which is not related to the donee's exempt purpose (e.g. an 18th century painting given to a museum of modern art and subsequently given to a curator for use in her apartment your tax deduction must be reduced.

Since the burden of proving that the gift is put to a related use (or that the donor can reasonably expect that it will be put to such use) is on the donor, it is advisable for any donor making a gift of a work of art to obtain a letter from the donee which indicates the use to which the donee expects to put the work. In order to insure that the donee is not required to keep the work indefinitely, any such letter may permit the donee to sell the property if in its judgment it is not longer advisable for the donee to retain the work. Note that a sale by the donee within two years of the gift must be reported to both the donor and the I.R.S. on Form 8282.

The most obvious "sale by donee situation" is encountered when you are requested to donate to a charity auction. If you donate appreciated property, your deduction is limited to your cost. This is true even if the art is sold at or above the fair market value.

Dealers who donate to a charity auction from inventory are limited to their cost basis in any event. They and others who do not care about the amount of charitable deduction are the only persons who should donate appreciated property to a charity auction.

Donating art work to a charity auction raises a second potential problem. Charity auctions are subject to the same realized price vagaries as commercial auctions. However they usually do not have the built in safety features of reserve prices (i.e. a price below which the work will not be sold).

It is therefore possible for the work to bring an abnormally low price. That low price may be the source of a problem in connection with a later appraisal of similar work by the same artist. The problem is particularly acute in connection with art which is produced in multiples, e.g. prints or photographs.

If an identical work which you believe to have a fair market value of $1000 realized $150 at a charity auction in July, it will give an appraiser making an appraisal in September pause in the valuation procedure unless there were both prior and subsequent market sales at higher prices.

It is therefore prudent to avoid gifts of multiples to charity auctions if you contemplate, in the future, the making of charitable gifts of artworks from the same set or even by the same artist.

QUICK REFERENCE CHART FOR CHARITABLE CONTRIBUTIONS

	Gifts To Public Charities[1]		Gifts to Private Foundations	
Type of Gift	Amount Deductible	% of AGI Deductible	Amount Deductible	% of AGI Deductible
Cash	all	50%	all	30%
Securities and real estate held over twelve months	FMV	30%	cost[2]	20%
Related tangible property[3]	FMV	50%	cost	30%
Securities and real estate held under twelve months	cost	50%	cost	30%
Unrelated tangible property[3]	cost	50%	cost	20%
Ordinary income property[4]	cost	50%	cost	30%

Cost means the lesser of tax basis or FMV. FMV must be reduced by depreciation capture, if any. [1]Includes private foundations called passthrough foundations and operating foundations. [2]Deductible amount is FMV if property is publicly traded. [3]Property is related if used by donee in its exempt function. [4]Includes inventory, some oil and gas assets, and depreciated business equipment, among others.

CHAPTER SEVEN

THE ALTERNATIVE MINIMUM TAX

The Alternative Minimum Tax ("A.M.T.") was made a factor in the calculation of income tax benefits arising from a charitable gift by T.R.A.'86.The A.M.T. has, as its purpose, the imposition of a minimum income tax on individuals who obtain large benefits under certain enumerated sections of the I.R.C.

> *The application of the A.M.T. to charitable gifts of appreciated property was suspended for the 1991 Tax Year. In Rev. Rul. 90-111 the IRS ruled that any carryover resulting from an unused deduction in 1991 will maintain its character in 1992, i.e. it will be free of A.M.T. in 1992 and any later carryover year. As we go to press it is uncertain as to whether the suspension will lapse, be extended, or made permanent. Before reading this Chapter it would be prudent to ascertain the status of the law for years subsequent to 1991.*

Insofar as the benefits from charitable gifts are concerned, the effect of T.R.A.'86 is to take back, under certain conditions, some or all of the benefits of the charitable gift deduction. *Contrary to the assertions in some of the mass media, the application of the A.M.T., in so far as it applies to charitable gifts, never increases your taxes unless it displaces a carryover deduction. If applicable the A.M.T., in the vast majority of instances, merely diminishes the expected benefit.*

It is important to remember that the A.M.T. applies only to income taxes and not estate taxes. The gift, by will, of appreciated property does not trigger the A.M.T. The application of the A.M.T. to you in connection with a charitable gift of appreciated property will depend on what other preference items you have and your adjusted gross income.

The majority of donors of appreciated property will find that the application of the A.M.T. has no effect on their ultimate income tax because of the exemptions which will be discussed in this Chapter.

Whether the A.M.T. affects you can only be determined by first calculating your tax in the ordinary manner and then performing a second calculation of the A.M.T. If the A.M.T. is greater than your regular tax you must pay the larger amount.

The charitable gift change was made by amending I.R.C. §57 to include appreciation in property donated to a charity as a item of tax preference. §57 now reads in relevant part:

> (a) General Rule - For purposes of this part, the items of tax preference determined under this section are-
>
> (6) Appreciated property charitable deduction.
> (A) In general.- The amount by which the deduction allowable under §170 or 642(c) would be reduced if all capital gain property were taken into account at its adjusted basis. (B) Capital gain property. - For purposes of subparagraph (A), the term "capital gain property" has the meaning given to such term by §170(b)(1)(C)(iv). Such term shall not include any property to which an election under §170(b)(1)(C)(iii) applies.

The result was a compromise from the Treasury Department's original proposal to eliminate all of the appreciation in determining the value of a charitable gift.

The A.M.T. applies only to the charitable deduction for income tax purposes and is not applicable to charitable deductions by estates.

Charitable Deduction Ceiling Limits Effect of A.M.T.

Since there is a charitable deduction ceiling of 30% of your adjusted gross income on gifts of capital gain property to public charities, if you do not have other A.M.T. preferences, the A.M.T. will probably not result in a higher tax unless the donated property is very highly appreciated and you have a very high income.

Tax Rates

For individuals the A.M.T. is presently 24%. For corporations the tax rate is 20%.

Exemptions From A.M.T.

There is a basic exemption of $40,000 for couples filing joint returns or a surviving spouse; $30,000 for single tax payers and; $20,000 for married persons filing separately, I.R.C. §55(d)(1). The exemption amount for corporations is $40,000.

The exemption, however, is phased out as adjusted gross income rises. Effective January 1, 1987 high-income individuals must reduce their exemption amount by 25¢ for each $1. by which their A.M.T. income exceeds a certain level, I.R.C.§55(d)(3).

For corporations and married persons filing jointly, the phase-out begins when A.M.T. income reaches $150,000 and the exemption is lost entirely when A.M.T. income exceeds $310,000. For singles and heads of households the phase-out begins at $112,500 and ends at $232,500. For married persons filing separately, it starts at $75,000 and ends at $155,000.

The net effect of the 30% limitation on charitable deductions and the exemption amount from the A.M.T. is such as to permit generous donations of substantially appreciated artwork without incurring an increased tax because of the A.M.T.

A married couple, with no other preference items and an adjusted gross income of $150,000, could donate a painting with a fair market value $45,000 without A.M.T. coming into play, so long as the appreciation did not exceed $40,000. Since $45,000 is 30% of their adjusted gross income, they would obtain the full benefit of the charitable income tax deduction.

The A.M.T. Computation

The determination of whether you are subject to the A.M.T. is made by completion of Form 6251 which along with its instruction sheet is reproduced in the Appendix. If you are subject to the A.M.T. Form 6251 is filed along with your income tax return. Even if you are not subject to the A.M.T. Form 6251 must be filed under certain circumstances (see Instruction for Form 6251).

Appreciation And Excess Charitable Gifts

If your charitable gift of appreciated property exceeds the 30% of your adjusted gross income you need not treat all of the appreciation as a preference in the year of the gift.

The A.M.T. is applied only to the proportionate amount of the appreciation from the portion of the gift deducted in each year. The remainder of the appreciation, like the remainder of the charitable deduction, carries over to future years.

> **Example:** In 1987 you donate a painting with a fair market value of $100,000 to a museum. Your cost basis is $50,000 and you have owned the painting in excess of six months. Your adjusted gross income is $175,000. The maximum charitable deduction you may take is $52,500 (30% x $175,000).
>
> In the absence of the A.M.T. your gift would reduce your taxable 1987 income by $52,500. Your taxable income would be $122,500 ($175,000 - $52,200).
>
> Applying the A.M.T., however, the appreciation of $26,500 in the $52,500 is treated as a preference (since the appreciation is ½ of the value, it is exactly ½ of the amount deducted).
>
> Your excess contribution of $47,500 ($100,000 - $52,500) can be carried over and deducted in future years. The portion of the carryover which is a preference will remain as a preference in calculating the A.M.T. in future years.

If you have a charitable deduction carryover from the period before August 16,1986, the A.M.T. is not applied to the appreciated portion of the carryover. The reason for the August 16th date is that certain provisions of T.R.A.'86 were made retroactive.

Bargain Sales

A bargain sale is part sale and part gift (see Chapter Six). You allocate your gain between the sale portion and the gift portion. The appreciation attributable to the sale portion is treated as income. The appreciation attributable to the gift portion is treated as a preference.

> **Example:** You sell a painting that you have owned for more than six months to a museum for $25,000. The F.M.V. is $125,000, and your cost basis is $25,000.
>
> Your contribution is $100,000 ($125,000 - $25,000). Your gain from the sale portion is $20,000 ($25,000 - $5,000). The $5,000 is the portion of basis allocated to the sale portion.It was arrived at by taking the same fraction (1/5) of the basis as the whole basis bore to the total F.M.V.
>
> You will treat as a preference the untaxed portion of the gain on the gift which is $80,000 ($100,000 - $20,000) [portion of basis allocated to gift portion].

Split Interest Gifts

If you are contemplating a split interest charitable gift (trusts, annuity trusts, pooled funds) you should most certainly involve your attorney and accountant. In general, however, only the untaxed appreciation attributable to the charity's remainder interest will be treated as a preference item.

CHAPTER EIGHT

THE GIFT TAX

The gift tax is an excise tax imposed on the exercise of your right to transfer property as a gift. The nature of the property under other tax law is not a factor. Thus the gift of tax exempt municipal bonds is not exempt from tax because the interest is exempt from the income tax. Works of art are property, and a gift tax may be payable when they are transferred by gift.

Who Pays The Gift Tax?

Unless you stipulate that the donee pay the gift tax, the tax is imposed on you as the donor, I.R.C. §2502(c), Rev. Rul. 75-72, 1975-1 CB 310. If you do not pay the tax the donee is liable for the tax up to the value of the gift, I.R.C. §6324(b), 6901(a).

What Is A Gift?

A gift, for gift tax purposes, is any transfer of money or property, whether made by sale or otherwise, without adequate and full consideration in money or otherwise.

A sale or other transfer of property made in the ordinary course of business will be considered as made for adequate consideration, Reg. §25.2512-8. Thus if you make a bad bargain in selling a work of art, you have not made a gift. The bad bargain rule assumes that the transaction is *bona fide*, arm's length, and free from donative intent.

When a work of art is transferred for less than fair market value in money or other value, absent the conditions set forth in the preceding paragraph, the amount by which the value of the artwork transferred exceeds the value of the consideration received is deemed a gift. The gift amount must be included in the total of gifts made by the donor during the year. As previously noted this does not apply in a *bona fide* arms length business deal where there is no donative intent.

The Relinquishment Of A Power As A Gift

A "power of appointment" is the right to name the persons who are to receive property from an estate. The power may be either a general or limited (special) power. The person who creates the power is the donor of the power. The person who has the right to exercise it is its possessor. Gift tax liability may arise from exercise or release of the power.

The complete release of a general power is subject to gift tax, I.R.C. §2514(b). A partial release of a general power is not taxable at that time, but a later exercise or release of the modified power during life which leaves the possessor no power to change the disposition of the property is a taxable gift.

A "qualified" disclaimer of a power can be used to avoid being liable for gift tax. "Qualified" means: (i) in writing; (ii) received by the transferor or legal representative within 9 months from the creation of the interest; (iii) no benefits were accepted by the donee before the making of the disclaimer; and (iv) the interest passes to a person other than the person who disclaimed, I.R.C. §2518

The disclaimer of a surviving spouse is not disqualified even though the property still passes to the spouse, e.g. after the spouse's disclaimer, the property may pass to a trust in which the surviving spouse has an income interest, I.R.C. §2514; 2518; Reg. §25.2518.

If the possessor of the power does not exercise the power, there is no gift tax liability with respect to the lapse in any year unless the amount of the authorized invasion exceeds the greater of $5,000 or 5% of the property out of which the power may be satisfied. If the authorized invasion exceeds this limit, the lapse will be treated as a taxable release of the power to the extent of the excess, I.R.C. §2514(e); Reg. §25.2514-3(c)(4).

Love and affection, not being capable of being reduced to a money value, are disregarded in calculating value received, as are all other considerations not capable of being reduced to a money value, Reg. §25.2512-8.

Property settlements in divorces are deemed to be for adequate consideration under certain conditions.

Timing

A gift is deemed to have been made, and taxable, when the donor has parted with dominion and control over the property and has no power to change the disposition of it, for his own benefit or another's. However, if on a transfer of property, whether or not in trust, the donor has reserved any power over its disposition, the gift may be wholly incomplete, or partially complete and partially incomplete. Thus, in order to determine gift tax liability, when a work of art has been transferred subject to a reserved power, the terms of the power must be examined, Reg. §25.2511-2.

A transfer from one individual to another, either directly or in trust, is not considered a complete taxable gift when the donor retains a power (i) to revest the beneficial title to the property in himself, or (ii) to divest the beneficiaries of their title, even though the donor himself may not get the property back, or (iii) to name new beneficiaries or change the interests of the beneficiaries, Reg. §25.2511-2(c). It is immaterial that the revocable transfer is made without consideration. A donor is considered as himself having the power when he can exercise it with any person not having a substantial adverse interest in the disposition of the transferred property, Reg. § 25.2511-2(e).

If a donor, after making a transfer subject to revocation, later and before death, parts with all dominion and control over the property transferred, and releases his right to revoke, the once incomplete gift becomes complete and taxable.

If the donor retains the power of revocation over a trust, there is no gift tax liability as to the trust corpus since the gift is incomplete. If the income is paid to a beneficiary other than the donor, the payment is a gift of income and taxable because the donor is deemed to have received the income and turned it over to the beneficiary.

How a trust should be structured and whether or not powers should be included or released can only be decided with reference to the particular circumstances of each individual.

Community Property

A gift of a painting which is community property to a third person is regarded as a gift by each spouse of his or her interest in the property. Normally each is regarded as having made a gift of one-half the property.

If separate property of one spouse is converted into community property, there is a gift by the original owner of the interest the other receives in the community property.

Exemption From The Gift Tax

Your gift or series of gifts may be exempt from the gift tax either because of the nature of the donee or because of the annual exclusion or the unified credit.

Exempt Gifts Arising From The Identity Of The Donee

The exemptions arising from the nature of the donee include gifts to or for the use of any of the following:

1. The United States, any state, territory, or political subdivision, or the District of Columbia, for exclusively public purposes.

2. A corporation, trust, community chest, fund or foundation, organized exclusively for religious, charitable, scientific, literary or educational purposes,...*including the encouragement of art* and...

3. A fraternal society, order, or association, operating under the lodge system, but only if such gifts are to be used exclusively for religious, charitable, scientific, literary or educational purposes, *including the encouragement of art* and prevention of cruelty to children or animals.

4. Posts or organizations of war veterans, or auxiliary units or societies of any such posts or organizations, if such posts, organizations, units, or societies are organized in the United States or any of its possessions, I.R.C. §2522(a); Reg. §25.2522(a)-1.

For a deduction to be allowed under paragraphs 2 or 4, no part of the net earnings may inure to the benefit of any private shareholder or individual.

The benefit of the deduction referred to in this section is a deduction of the amount of the gift from the total dollar amount of gifts so as to exclude the amount from taxation under the gift tax.

For a discussion of the income tax charitable deduction see Chapter Six.

An important deduction from gifts subject tax is the unlimited marital deduction for gifts to a spouse made after 1981. The deduction applies to transfers of community property between spouses and qualifying terminable interest property ("QTIP"), I.R.C. §2523; Prop. Reg. §25.2523(a)-1.

In connection with the marital deduction the donor must be (i) a citizen or resident of The United States; (ii) the spouse of the donee at the time of the gift; and (iii) the gift must be one of an outright interest. The later includes a transfer of QTIP.

QTIP means: (i) any property transferred by the donor spouse; (ii) the donee spouse has a right of income for life, payable at least annually; (iii) during the spouse's life no other person has the power to appoint any part of the property to any other person than the donee spouse; and (iv) the donor spouse, when filing the gift tax return,makes an irrevocable decision that such interest qualifies for the marital deduction. The election is due no later than April 15th of the calendar year after the gift is made for years before 1986. For transfers made after December 31, 1985, the QTIP election must be made on or before the date, including extensions, for filing a gift tax return as to the year in which the transfer was made. The election, once made, is irrevocable, I.R.C. §2523(f).

In connection with split interest trusts, a marital deduction is allowed for the value of the annuity or unitrust interest even though the only noncharity beneficiaries are the donor and spouse, I.R.C. §2056, 2523.

The gift of a life estate qualifies as an outright interest if the spouse is entitled for life to all of the income from all or a portion of the entire interest, with the power to appoint all or a portion of the entire interest to herself or her estate, I.R.C. 2523(e). A transfer to a spouse of a legal life estate with an unlimited power to invade corpus satisfies the requirement.

The requirement is not met if the donor gives his or her spouse a life estate or other terminable interest in the property and if, in addition, (i) the donor retains or transfers to anyone else, other than the spouse or the spouse's estate, for less than full consideration, an interest in the same property, making possible for the donor or the other person, their heirs or assigns to possess or enjoy any part of the property after the interest of the donee spouse ends, or if (ii) the donor, after the gift, has a power of appointment, the exercise of which makes it possible for anyone else to possess or enjoy any part of the property after the donee spouse's interest ends, I.R.C. §2523(e).

The marital deduction is allowed for gifts by one spouse to the other spouse as sole joint tenant or as a tenant by the entirety. Such an interest is not considered a "terminable interest" merely because the donor spouse may survive the donee spouse, I.R.C. §2523(d).

Note that to obtain the deduction you must report the amount of the gift on the gift tax return and the amount of the marital deduction is limited to the amount at which the gift is reported, I.R.C. §2524.

Annual Exclusion

When used systematically the annual gift exclusion is a valuable transfer device. Parents can transfer substantial assets, including collections to their children or grandchildren without payment of gift or estate taxes and without using any portion of their unified credit (see discussion of Unified Credit in this Chapter).

The first $10,000 of gifts made to each donee in a calendar year is excluded in calculating the gift tax, I.R.C. §2503(b); Reg. §25.2503-2.

A husband and wife may elect to treat a gift by either to a third party as though it were made one-half by each. They are then each taxed on one-half the gift, I.R.C. §2513; Reg. §25.2513-1.

The result is that the annual exclusion of $10,000 of gifts to each donee becomes in effect a $20,000 annual exclusion per married couple.

To qualify under the annual exclusion, the gift must be of an unqualified present interest. Thus in the case of a painting, the donee must obtain the present use, possession and enjoyment.

An unlimited deduction applies for medical and tuition costs paid for an individual donee. Thus you and your wife may make a gift of an artwork with a fair market value of $20,000 to a child even though you are also paying his or her college tuition and medical expenses. The tuition must be paid to a qualified educational institution and the medical expenses must be those which are not otherwise reimbursed to the donee. A qualified educational institution is essentially the same type of educational institution as would qualify for the income tax charitable deduction, see Chapter Six.

Because of the present use and enjoyment requirements the gift of a future interest in an artwork does not qualify for the annual exclusion, Reg. §25.2503-3. The time when enjoyment begins, and not when title vests, is controlling. An interest in property is not a future interest merely because there is a possibility that it may be diminished by the exercise of a power, if no part of the interest will at any time pass to any person besides the donee, I.R.C. §2503(b); Reg. §25.2503-3(b).

A gift to or for the benefit of a minor is not a gift of a future interest if (i) the gift property and the income from it may be spent for the minor's benefit during minority, and (ii) the balance not spent will pass outright to the minor at 21, or if the minor dies before 21, to the minor's estate or as the minor may appoint under a general power, I.R.C. §2503(c); Reg. §25.2503-4.

Gifts made pursuant to state laws known as the *Uniform Gifts To Minors Act* generally meet these requirements.

Each beneficiary of a trust is considered a separate donee, and the donor of a gift in trust is allowed an exclusion for each beneficiary with a present interest, Reg. §25.2503-2.

The Unified Credit

The unified credit is a concept which straddles the Estate Tax (see Chapter Nine). It applies to all transfers, whether made by lifetime gift or after death. In general, the unified credit used for gift taxes reduces the credit available for estate tax.

The unified credit for the year 1987 and subsequent years is $192,800, I.R.C. § 2505. It is used to reduce the gift tax due. You reduce the $192,800 by the amount of the gift tax calculated.

Thus, assuming no prior gifts which diminished the unified credit, gifts by you and your wife to a child of $20,000 in 1988 plus additional gifts which would result in a tax of $5,000, would result in your using first the $20,000 exclusion and then $5,000 of the lifetime unified credit. The credit would be reduced to $187,800. The reduction occurs whether or not you claim or use the credit, Rev. Rul. 55-278, 1955-1 CB 471.

Note that the exclusion amount refers to the F.M.V. of the gift. The unified credit refers to a dollar amount which directly offsets the tax which would otherwise be payable.

Although the unified credit for gift taxes is a separate provision apart from the unified credit from estate tax (I.R.C. §2010), it is, in effect, a "single credit". If you use all of the unified credit in your lifetime, none remains to be used after death.

The use in a single year of all the unified credit by a husband and wife with two children could permit the tax free transfer of an art collection with a fair market value of $1,744,324 to the children in equal shares .

Explanation: Referring to the tax rate schedule for estate and gift taxes you will find that a gift of $750,000 is taxed at $155,800. Any excess up to $1,000,000 is taxed at 37%. The unified credit is $192,800. Subtracting $155,800 from $192,800 you find that $37,000 of the credit is unused. Since the incremental tax rate is 37% you can make an additional gift of $100,000 for a total of $850,000. Multiply that amount by two to reflect gifts by both husband and wife and you get $1,700,000. Add $20,000 of gifts by each to each child (using the exclusion) and your total is $1,740,000.

In the next 15 years the $20,000 annual exclusion to each child would permit transfers of an additional $300,000 of fair market value of art to each for a total transfer of $2,340,000.

It can be readily seen that by use of the unified credit and the annual exclusion a substantial tax free transfers can be made from your collection .

To maximize the benefit of the annual exclusion it is necessary to commence annual gift giving at the earliest possible time consistent with your plan for your collection.

How To Calculate The Gift Tax

Gift taxes are reported on Form 709 or Short Form 709-A and calculated by using the Unified Rate Schedule (see Appendix for both Form 709 and 709-A).

The procedure is as follows, step by step:

1. Determine the amount of "taxable gifts" for the calendar year for which the return is being prepared.
2. Determine the amount of "taxable gifts" for all preceding periods.
3. Add the amounts in Steps (1) and (2) to find the cumulative total of taxable gifts.
4. Figure a tentative tax on the total in Step 3 by using the Unified Rate Schedule.
5. Figure a tentative tax on the amount in Step 2 (the aggregate gifts for preceding periods) by using the Unified Rate Schedule.
6. Subtract the result in Step 5 from the result in Step 4 to arrive at the tax before credit.
7. Subtract the unified credit you have unused.

If you have made prior taxable gifts, the procedure is complicated by the fact that you must know the amount of unified credit for each prior period.

Since this is a guide and not a text on how to prepare tax returns, we shall not attempt to teach you to do your own gift tax returns where there have been prior taxable gifts.

The Gift Tax Increases Basis Of The Gift

One of the little known and more interesting provisions of the I.R.C. is §1015(d)(6). It permits the donee, under certain circumstances, to increase his or her basis for the gift by all or a portion of the gift tax paid.

If the donor's basis is the same as fair market value at the time of the gift, all of the tax paid may be added. If there has been appreciation in value over the donor's basis, the amount that may be added is calculated by multiplying the tax by a fraction of which the numerator is appreciation and the denominator is the fair market value of the gift.

If gifts are made to more than one person in the same calendar year, the total gift tax paid by the donor in the taxable period is prorated over his gifts for that period. In determining the total gifts made, all deductions and allowable exclusions are taken into account with the exception of the pre-1977 $30,000 specific exemption.

If more than one gift is made in a calendar year to the same person, the allowable exclusion is applied against the gifts first in time to determine the gift tax to be used as an adjustment to the basis of each gift, I.R.C. §1015(d)(2). If third party gifts are split between a husband and wife, the gift tax of each is taken in account, I.R.C. §1015(d)(3).

Gift Tax Returns And Payment Of Gift Tax

Gift tax returns must be filed and gift tax paid on an annual basis, I.R.C. §2502(b), 6019.

Since an unlimited marital deduction is allowed for interspousal transfer, the gift tax filing requirements exempt all transfers eligible for the marital deduction except a timely elected QTIP.

No return need be filed in years where the only gifts are those within the annual exclusion and qualified charitable transfers.

A return must be filed in connection with (i) any gift of a future interest in property, regardless of amount, or (ii) a present interest in property in excess of the annual exclusion of $10,000, or (iii) a present interest in property which together with previous gifts of present interest to the same individual in the calendar years exceeds the annual exclusion of $10,000.

Returns are due annually by the April 15th following the close of the year. An extension of time to file your income tax return operates to extend the time to file a gift tax return, I.R.C. §6075(b)(2).

Married couples may file short Form 709-A to report nontaxable split gifts. If spouses elect to split gifts to a third party, the spouse who makes the gift is treated as the donor of the entire gift to determine whether a return must be filed. The other spouse is treated as the donor of one-half the gift to determine whether he or she must file a return. The short form may be used if the consenting spouse did not make (i) any gifts to any of the donees listed on the form, (ii) gifts of terminable interests to the donor spouse, (iii) gifts (other than gifts for tuition or medical care) of over $10,000 to any other donee, or (iv) any gifts of future interests.

The full amount of the gift tax is due and payable with the return. If you can show that payment by the due date would result in hardship, an extension of time for payment, not to exceed six months, may be granted. Interest at the current rate will be charged for the extension period.

If you do not pay the tax the donee is liable for the tax up to the value of the gift, I.R.C. §6324(b).

Assessments And Deficiencies

The I.R.S. ordinarily has three years from the date the return was filed to make an assessment. If the return omits 25% or more of the taxable gifts made during the year the period is extended to six years. The tax may be assessed at any time against you if you fail to file a return or file a false or fraudulent return, I.R.C. §6501.

CHAPTER NINE

ESTATE PLANNING

Estate planning is not high on the list of topics which most of us prefer to discuss. Nevertheless to ignore the topic often results in the payment of unnecessary estate taxes.

Estate planning involves not only the drafting of a will but the tax-free disposition of assets during your lifetime so as to lower the taxable portion of your estate.

Individual works of art and portions of collections are particularly suitable for lifetime gifts to children, grandchildren, and other persons to whom you plan to leave portions of your estate.

In connection with charitable donations, the I.R.C. does not impose as many limitations on estate gifts as it does on lifetime gifts, e.g. percentage limitations, A.M.T. and related use test.

If your estate will be subject to estate taxes, some thought should be given to lifetime gifts and charitable gifts.

The best estate planning accomplishes two goals. First, it provides for the disposition of assets to the persons for whom you have love and affection and to the charitable organizations you desire to assist. Second, it accomplishes the first goal with the payment of as small an estate tax as possible.

What Amount Triggers Filing The Estate Tax Return?

For persons dying after December 31,1986 a federal estate tax return must be filed if the sum of the following is greater than $600,000:

1. The adjusted taxable gifts (under I.R.C. §2001(b)) made by the decedent after 12/31/76; and
2. The total specific exemption allowed under §2521 (as in effect before repeal by the Tax Reform Act of 1976) with respect to gifts made by the decedent after 9/8/76; and
3. The decedent's gross estate valued at the date of death.

It is beyond the scope of this guide to provide a comprehensive discussion of what is included in the term "gross estate", but it should be noted that community property, property over which the decedent had a general power of appointment, transfers of life insurance within three years of death, proceeds of certain life insurance, and other less obvious items are included.

Municipal bonds, and other bonds, bills, notes, and certificates of indebtedness that may be exempt from income tax are nevertheless included in a calculation of gross estate.

For the majority of individuals, subparagraph 3. will the single most significant item in calculating whether an estate tax return must be filed.

In regard to an art collection, married persons living in community property states will find that all or a portion of an art collection owned by one spouse will be included in community property and will therefore increase the value of the decedent's gross estate.

The Unlimited Marital Deduction

The marital deduction is a deduction that is allowed for the value of property that passes at death to a surviving spouse, I.R.C.§2056; Reg. 20.2056(a)-1.

To qualify, the property for which the marital deduction is claimed must be included in the decedent's gross estate, and the surviving spouse must receive the property or interest.

The deduction is *unlimited* and applies to both lifetime gifts and property transferred from the estate.

The spouse must be a current spouse, i.e. a spouse at the time of the decedent's death. Thus a provision in a divorce agreement to leave an art collection to a surviving ex-spouse results in the inclusion of the art collection in the gross estate.

In contemporary society the custom of couples living together other than as husband and wife is widespread. The I.R.C. does not recognize the survivor of such a relationship as a spouse for purposes of the marital deduction.

If you are currently living with someone who is not your spouse, and you desire to leave him or her all or a portion of an otherwise taxable estate, the first piece of tax planning might involve a wedding ceremony!

A wedding ceremony is a particularly significant estate tax planning device if one or both persons are artists. While for charitable income tax deductions artists are limited to the cost of their materials, the estate tax values their artwork at fair market value!

Even if you plan to leave everything to your spouse, and thus hopefully avoid the imposition of an estate tax, you must plan for the eventuality that you may die in a common disaster.

Estate planning does not lend itself to a do-it-yourself project. Unless you have an extremely small estate we do not advise use of the various form books designed to assist those with a real or imagined aversion to legal counsel.

The Unified Credit

A unified credit applies to all otherwise taxable transfers, whether made during life or after death. The unified credit is a credit against the tax otherwise payable. Generally, the unified credit used for gift taxes reduces the credit available for estate tax. The gift tax unified credit is reflected as a reduction in subtracting the gift taxes payable for the estate tax computation. Because of this interrelationship between the separate estate tax unified credit and the computation of the estate tax payable, the separate estate tax unified credit does not operate to allow a double credit for both life and death transfers. Thus the credit is in effect a single "unified" credit for both the estate and gift taxes, I.R.C. §2010.

Commencing with 1987 the unified credit is $192,800.

The Charitable Deduction

A deduction from the gross estate is allowed for the value of property transferred for public, charitable, religious, education, or certain other uses.

The transfer must be to or for the use of any of the following:

1. The United States, any state, territory, or political subdivision, or the District of Columbia, for exclusively public purposes.

2. A corporation, trust, community chest, fund or foundation, organized exclusively for religious, charitable, scientific, literary or educational purposes,...*including the encouragement of art* and...

3. A trustee or trustees, or a fraternal society, order, or association, operating under the lodge system, but only if such gifts are to be used exclusively for religious, charitable, scientific, literary or educational purposes, *including the encouragement of art* and prevention of cruelty to children or animals.

4. Any veterans' organization incorporated by Act of Congress, or of its departments or local chapters or posts. I.R.C. §2055(a); Reg. §20.2055-1.(emphasis added)

For a deduction to be allowed under paragraphs 2 or 4, no part of the net earnings may inure to the benefit of any private shareholder or individual.

The deduction is not limited, in the estates of citizens or residents, to transfers to domestic corporations or associations, or to trustees for use in the United States, Reg. §20.2055-1.

If under the will or the law where the estate is administered or the law imposing the tax, all or part of the estate, succession, legacy, or inheritance tax is payable out of a deductible charitable transfer, the amount deductible is the balance after subtracting the tax, I.R.C. §2055(c), Reg. §20.2055-3.

Delayed gifts in connection with an aged spouse's power of appointment and charitable remainders are also deductible. The provisions are highly technical and beyond the scope of this guide.

A deduction is allowed for the transfer of a work of art to a qualified organization without the transfer of the copyright,if the use of the property by the organization is related to its function, I.R.C. §2055(e)(4). That deduction is particularly useful to artists whose work has commercial value separate and apart from the original.

The museum can own and display the original. The artist or copyright owner can continue commercial exploitation.

A significant difference between the estate tax charitable deduction and the income tax charitable deduction is *the absence of any percentage limitation in connection with the estate tax charitable deduction* (see Chapter Six).

Thus an art collection of any size or value can be donated to a qualified organization and an estate charitable donation deduction taken for the total fair market value, regardless of the size of the estate.

The A.M.T. has no application to the estate tax, and the gift of appreciated property does not require any special calculation or trigger the payment of an "alternate minimum estate tax".

Tax planning through (a) lifetime charitable gifts which result in income tax deductions; (b) lifetime gifts availing oneself of the annual exclusion; (c) the unlimited marital deduction from gross estate; (d) charitable bequests deductible from gross estate; and (e) other bequests, requires a careful examination of your assets, your goals, and your family needs. There is no single plan that is best for everyone nor even for two persons with identical assets.

The interplay of the various provisions of the I.R.C. is complex, but in general it is possible, over a period of years, to use the annual gift exclusion to pass assets, including but not limited to your collection, to children, grandchildren and others completely free of tax (see Chapter Eight).

Within the parameters imposed by the percentage limitations on charitable income deductions and the A.M.T. (see Chapters Six and Seven), it is possible to reduce your income tax by the judicious gifts of artwork.

The unlimited marital exclusion is a key element in some estate plans.

The nature of your collection is important in deciding whether to make lifetime gifts. Some thought, for instance, ought to be given to whether you envisage substantial appreciation in all or a portion of the collection. If the donee of the collection is to be a member of your family, other than your spouse, maximum use of the annual exclusion should be contemplated. Even though there is a unified credit of $192,800 for both taxable lifetime gifts and bequests commencing in 1987, you will be able to transfer, tax free, a larger portion of your collection prior to a period of great appreciation than subsequent thereto.

Estate planning cannot begin too early. No single plan can serve as a model for all those with an art collection nor even for the same person over a period of years. Tax laws change, your collection grows in size and value, and the needs of your family change.

Do your planning in conjunction with your accountant and lawyer, and be prepared to review the plan as your circumstances, tax rates, and the tax law change.

CHAPTER TEN

APPRAISALS

There are at least nine times when you may want or need an appraisal in connection with all of or a portion of an art collection:

1. prior to acquisition
2. prior to selling
3. prior to insuring
4. when filing an insurance claim
5. when making a lifetime gift
6. when making a charitable donation
7. when computing an estate tax
8. when claiming a casualty loss on your tax return
9. at the time of a tax-free swap

The valuation standard required in those instances when the appraisal is in connection with the payment or non-payment of taxes is fair market value ("F.M.V.").

Human nature being what it is, we find that when individuals are making lifetime gifts of works of art that may result in payment of a gift tax, they desire low appraisals. Should they be contemplating a charitable donation of the same works of art, they desire a high appraisal.

The beneficiaries under a will, seeking to minimize or avoid estate taxes, look to low appraisals on works of art. Should the same works of art be destroyed by a fire the following year, they would hope for a high appraisal in order to claim a casualty loss.

The I.R.S. functions through employees who tend to have mirror image aspirations of the taxpayer. Since their function is to collect taxes, they look for high F.M.V. in connection with lifetime gifts and a low F.M.V. in connection with charitable donations.

If determining F.M.V. were an exact science, the hopes and desires of taxpayers and their I.R.S. antagonists would not matter, for a computer could be programmed to compute F.M.V.

In connection with some real and personal property, there are mathematical formulae which assist in appraisal. Apartment buildings in a particular location of a city may have their F.M.V. in large part determined by a formula which says that the price at which they change hands is that which will permit the buyer to earn a yield of 10% on invested capital. Even when such formulae or rules of thumb exist, there is often a dispute as to F.M.V. when the issue is raised in connection with the payment of taxes. The dispute can be a good faith dispute because in any appraisal there is room for subjective judgment.

In the art world a large part of the appraisal process is subjective. That is particularly true when the work of art is unique, i.e. not a multiple. When a print, photograph, or sculpture is the subject of an appraisal there are often reasonable current auction or dealer sales of reasonably identical works. Nevertheless, condition, provenance, time of creation, and other factors enter into the appraisal.

Persons who are neither art collectors nor art connoisseurs generally tend to be skeptical about the value of art. Couple the general skepticism with the role of an I.R.S. employee and you have one-half of an adversarial contest.

The other half of the contest is the donor who believes that his or her gift is only slightly less valuable than the *Mona Lisa*.

Even when subjective factors do not enter into the appraisal, the concept of F.M.V., as is demonstrated in the following section, is elusive.

Fair Market Value Appraisals - Not So Simple

According to the American Society of Appraisers, appraising is, "The art and science of estimating the value, at any given time, of any sort of property...". Value may mean different things. For example, the IRS, in connection with charitable donations, desires "fair market value". An insurance policy may be concerned with "replacement cost".

The I.R.S. definition of "fair market value" is deceptively simple. In Publication 561 entitled *Determining the Value of Donated Property*, the I.R.S. states..."Fair market value generally is the price that property would sell for on the open market. It is the price that would be agreed on between a willing buyer and a willing seller, with neither being required to act, and both having reasonable knowledge of the facts."

In practice, fair market value is an elusive concept. For example, let us attempt to marshal the facts, not in relation to a work of art which involves subjective judgments, but to a one pound can of *Martinson* coffee. *Martinson* is a brand packed and distributed by *Tetley Inc.* Each can of *Martinson* coffee is fungible, i.e. any can replace another can of the same grind. During the past year, on any one day in New York City, you could have paid a retail price of as little as $1.89 and as much as $4.59. That is a variation of about 140%. Or to put it another way the $4.59 was in excess of 240% of $1.89.

The point is that if the F.M.V. of fungible goods can vary so widely in the same city, what is the probability of two different appraisers agreeing on the F.M.V. of a Rembrandt?

I.R.C. §6700, which concerns itself with abusive tax shelters, uses a relatively new term called "gross valuation overstatement". For purposes of that section, the term "gross valuation overstatement" means any statement as to the value of any property "...if...(A) the value so stated exceeds 200 percent of the amount determined to be the correct valuation, and (B) the value of such property...is directly related to the amount of any deduction or credit allowable...".

Our fungible can of coffee sells (presumably the best evidence of F.M.V.) at prices which exceed 200% of the lowest price!

Similar examples of retail price variations could be made of prices for television sets, cameras, jewelry, and even identical works of art. The determination of the F.M.V. of a work of art involves not only objective criteria but also subjective judgments. Thus, the process of appraising, when undertaken by different individuals, can result in wide variations.

Moreover, the purpose for which an appraisal is being made may affect the result. To go back to the coffee example, let us first assume that the person seeking the appraisal is not a dealer in coffee but is a donor with a warehouse full of cans of coffee which are going to be donated to the *Red Cross*. The donor wants to obtain the largest available deduction, and the appraiser is willing to give a high appraisal provided it can be supported by the facts. Can you guess what the price per can will be in the appraisal?

Suppose we have the same donor, but this time the gift is going to his children. He has already used up his annual exclusion. The gift may be taxable. Would you care to wager what the same appraiser will use as the price per can?

We are suggesting that the same person may have a different view of "fair market value" at different times when the only fact that has changed is the purpose of the appraisal. Now lest you think we are picking on taxpayers, look at the facts in a case recently before the U.S. Tax Court. It involved the appraisal of art in the estate of Alexander Calder. When Calder died in 1976, 1292 paintings in gouache (opaque water colors) were appraised and accepted by the I.R.S. at a value of $949,750.

Six weeks after his death, his widow received 1226 of the gouaches from the estate and divided them equally among four family trusts. She valued the gifts on the same basis as the estate and paid a gift tax.

The I.R.S. took the position that the gouaches were worth $2,300,000 not $897,230. It is a remarkable difference considering that only six weeks had elapsed. It is even more remarkable in view of the fact that the I.R.S. generally considers the cost to a donor to be of great weight in determining "fair market value" at the time of a charitable gift, particularly if the holding period was relatively short.

The I.R.S. does acknowledge that there are subjective elements in appraising art and has established an Art Advisory Panel ("Panel") and once had an independent Art Print Panel. The Panel meets periodically to help the IRS to determine fair market values of works (usually above $20,000) that have been the subject of bequests, gifts, or charitable donations. Although the Panel is not informed as to whether it is an estate valuation problem or a charitable deduction, they certainly, if well informed of the market and facts relating to who owns particular works of art, can make educated guesses as to the purpose for which their evaluation will be used.

The Art Print Panel came into being shortly after abuses appeared in the marketing of "fine art" print tax shelters.

The Panel cannot deal with all tax-related art appraisal problems. In an attempt to obtain realistic figures in connection with charitable donations of art, the Tax Reform Act of 1984 first included provisions requiring detailed written information relating to appraisals.

Statutory Appraisal Requirements

If you claim a charitable deduction in excess of $5,000 for a work of art, you must obtain a qualified appraisal for the value of the work before you file the tax return on which the deduction is claimed.

Failure to obtain the appraisal and to file a summary with the tax return will lead to a disallowance of the claimed deduction, unless the failure can be shown to be in good faith and an appraisal summary is furnished to the I.R.S. within 90 days after the I.R.S. requests a summary, I.R.C. §170(a)(1); Reg. §170A-13(c)(4).

A qualified appraisal is one which includes the information set forth in items 1 through 12 in the section on Elements of the Appraisal.

A separate qualified appraisal and a separate Form 8283 are required for each item of property except for an item which is part of a group of similar items. One appraisal may suffice for a group of similar items contributed in the same tax year, if it includes all the required information for each item. A separate Form 8283 is required for each donee.

If your total deduction for art donated is $20,000 or more, you must attach a complete copy of the signed appraisal to Form 8283. For individual object valued at $20,000 or more a photograph of a size and quality fully showing the object, preferably an 8 x 10 inch color photograph or transparency no smaller than 4 x 5 inches, must be provided upon request.

The Qualified Appraiser

A qualified appraisal must be done by a qualified appraiser, Reg. 1.170A-13(c)(5). The term "qualified" has a more encompassing meaning than "competent" or "expert".

A qualified appraiser must: (i) hold himself or herself out to the public as an appraiser or perform appraisals on a regular basis, (ii) be qualified (in the ordinary sense) to appraise the type of property being donated, and (iii) not be the donor or anyone claiming a deduction for the gift, a party to the transaction pursuant to which the donor acquired the property (i.e. the person who sold, exchanged, or gave the property to the donor, or any person who acted as an agent for the transferor or for the donor with respect to such sale, exchange or gift), unless the property is donated within 2 months of the date of acquisition and its appraised value does not exceed the acquisition price, the donee, any person employed or related to any of the foregoing persons (e.g. if the donor acquired the painting from an art dealer, neither the art dealer nor persons employed by the dealer can be qualified appraisers with respect to that painting). Spouses of any of the foregoing are also deemed to be unqualified as are any other persons who may be deemed related pursuant to I.R.C. §267(b). An appraiser the majority of whose business comes from a person or entity who is not "qualified" is also "not qualified" (e.g. Jean Smith, an independent appraiser, performs appraisals for anyone willing to pay but the majority of her appraisals are for Gallery XYZ. Gallery XYZ sold the donated painting to the donor. Jean Smith may not serve as the qualified appraiser.). In addition, a person is not a qualified appraiser for a particular donation if the donor had knowledge of facts that would cause a reasonable person to expect the appraiser to falsely overstate the value of the donated property (e.g. If a donor makes an agreement with the appraiser that the property will be valued at more than its F.M.V., the appraiser is not a qualified appraiser for the donation.)

The appraisal fee cannot be based on a percentage of the appraised value of the artwork or the amount allowed as a deduction, except for certain fees paid to a generally recognized association that regulates appraisers. One such association is the *Art Dealers Association of America, Inc.*

It is not unreasonable to eliminate the donor, the donee, and the dealer who sold the artwork to the donor from the appraisal process. The vested interests of the dealer in the appraised value, the donor in obtaining the deduction, and the donee in obtaining the work, do seem to obviate any claim of objectivity.

It is category (iii) that presents the most difficulty for donors. It has been criticized because it has the potential to eliminate the most knowledgeable experts from the appraisal process. It is most restrictive where the field itself is specialized and the number of experts willing to perform appraisals is small. Often the most knowledgeable experts have close ties to both the donors and donees. This is particularly so when the objects to be appraised fall within a narrow spectrum of the art, antiques, and collectibles world.

Under the regulations you may find that the most knowledgeable experts are not, in so far as your gift is concerned, qualified appraisers!

Elements Of An Appraisal

The appraisal (which cannot be made more than sixty days prior to date of the contribution) must contain the following elements:

1) A description of the property in sufficient detail for a person who is not generally familiar with the type of property to determine that the property appraised is the property that was (or will be) contributed,

2) The physical condition of any tangible property,

3) The date (or expected date) of contribution,

4) The terms of any agreement or understanding entered into (or expected to be entered into) by or on behalf of the donor,

5) The name, address, and taxpayer identification number of the qualified appraiser and, if the appraiser is a partner, an employee, or an independent contractor engaged by a person other than the donor, the name, address, and taxpayer identification number of the partnership or the person who employs or engages the appraiser,

6) The qualifications of the qualified appraiser who signs the appraisal, including the appraiser's background, experience, education, and any membership in professional appraisal associations,

7) A statement that the appraisal was prepared for (income) (estate) tax purposes,

8) The date (or dates) on which the property was valued,

9) The appraised fair market value on the date (or expected date) of contribution,

10) The method of valuation used to determine F.M.V. such as the income approach, the comparable sales or market data approach, or the replacement cost less depreciation approach,

11) The specific basis for the valuation such as any specific comparable sales transaction, and

12) A description of the fee arrangement between the donor and appraiser.

The appraisal requirements set forth may be found in Reg. §1.170A-13(c).

You, as the donor, are required to provide the donee with a summary of the appraisal, obtain the donee's acknowledgment, and file the acknowledged summary with your tax return on Form 8283.

The Cost Of The Appraisal Is A Separate Deduction

The cost of the appraisal is not added to the charitable deduction but is a separate deduction under I.R.C. §212(3). Rev. Rul. 67-461, (1967-2 C.B. 125).

The advantage to the cost being a separate deduction is that it does not count against the limitation on charitable deductions.

Penalties

The I.R.C. imposes various civil and criminal penalties when you or your tax preparer fail to properly account to the IRS as required by the tax law. Unlike interest (which is an addition to tax intended to compensate the IRS for late payments), penalties are intended to punish you for unreasonably failing to file or pay taxes. Fines and penalties paid are nondeductible.

The Omnibus Budget Reconciliation Act of 1989 (OBRA '89) made major changes to the Revenue Code's penalty provisions. Collectively the new provisions are known as IMPACT, an acronym for Improved Penalty Administration and Compliance Tax Act. The new code sections are intended to streamline the system and make it fairer and easier to understand. IMPACT applies to tax years beginning after December 31,1989. It is organized into four penalty categories: (1) document and information reporting penalties; (2) accuracy-related penalties; (3) preparer, promoter and protester penalties; and (4) delinquency (failure to file or make timely deposits) penalties.

In regard to appraisals and the deductions based on deductions or the tax paid on transfers we are concerned with over valuation and undervaluation. An overstatement of value can result in an understatement of tax liability in connection with a gift to a museum while an understatement of value can result in an understatement of tax liability with regard to gift or estate taxes.

Accuracy Related Penalties

Prior to 1990, there were a multitude of accuracy penalties that sometimes overlapped. This was quite confusing and often caused administrative problems. The current law revised and consolidated these penalties into one umbrella penalty. It is equal to 20% of the portion of the underpayment attributable to the inaccuracy, I.R.C. §6662(a).

In addition to simplifying the overall structure, the change makes the penalty more equitable. The new penalty applies only to the portion of the underpayment of tax resulting from the inaccuracy. Under prior law, the penalty applied to the entire underpayment in some situations, not merely the portion attributable to the negligence. The result of this change is that a slightly negligent taxpayer will now be treated more leniently than one who is more culpable.

The 20% accuracy-related penalty applies to the portion of any underpayment that is attributable to one or more of the following I.R.C. §6662 (a),(b):

1. Negligence or disregard of rules or regulations.
2. Substantial understatement of income tax.
3. Substantial valuation overstatement.
4. Substantial overstatement of pension liabilities.
5. Substantial estate or gift tax valuation understatement.

Negligence is defined as any failure to make a reasonable attempt to comply with the tax law, and includes the careless, reckless, or intentional disregard of rules or regulations I.R.C. §6662(b),(c).

An understatement of income tax is basically the difference between the tax shown on your return and the correct tax due. It is considered to be substantial (and thus subject to the 20% umbrella accuracy related penalty) if it exceeds the greater of (1) 10% of the tax required to be shown on the return for the taxable year or (2) $5,000 ($10,000 in the case of a corporation other than an S-corporation or a personal holding company), I.R.C. §6662(b),(d). The penalty does not apply to the tax treatment of a particular item if (1) you have substantial authority for that tax treatment or (2) the item's tax treatment was adequately disclosed on the return or in a statement attached to your return,I.R.C. §6662(d)(2)(B).

The 200% Rule

The 20% accuracy-related penalty applies to the portion of an underpayment of tax that is attributable to a substantial valuation overstatement. A substantial valuation overstatement exists if the value or adjusted basis of any property claimed on a return is 200% or more of the correct value or adjusted basis. The rate of the penalty is doubled (to 40%) for gross overstatements. This is where the value or adjusted basis claimed is 400% or more than the correct value or adjusted basis, I.R.C. §6662(e).

This 20% penalty applies to all taxpayers (not just individuals, personal service corporations and closely-held corporations, as under prior law). But the penalty applies only if the amount of the underpayment attributable to a valuation overstatement exceeds $5,000 ($10,000 in the case of most corporations), I.R.C. §6662(e), (f).

Special Rule For Overstatement Of Charitable Deductions

A special rule applies in instances of substantial or gross overstatements of charitable deduction. The 20% penalty does not apply if you can show there was a reasonable cause for the underpayment and you acted in good faith. However, to qualify for this break (1) the claimed value of the property must have been based on a qualified appraisal made by a qualified appraiser and (2) you made a good faith investigation of the value of the contributed property in addition to getting the appraisal, I.R.C. §6664(c)(2), (3).

Substantial Estate Or Gift Tax Valuation Understatement

The 20% accuracy-related penalty applies if you value any property claimed on an estate or gift tax return at 50% or less than the amount determined to be correct. The penalty applies only if the underpayment attributable to the understatement exceeds $5,000. The penalty is doubled if the valuation claimed is 25% or less of the amount determined to be correct, I.R.C. §6662(g), (h)(2)(C).

Exceptions

There is a general exception that precludes the application of the accuracy-related penalty. The general rule is that the penalty does not apply if there was reasonable cause for an underpayment and the taxpayer acted in good faith with respect to the underpayment, I.R.C. §6664(c). A special rule applies to the substantial understatement of income tax component, I.R.C. §3722(b). Substantial authority or adequate disclosure is required. A special rule applies to the negligence component. The position taken on a tax return must be nonfrivolous and you must make a "complete, item-specific" disclosure of that position. Disclosure must be full and substantial.

The special rule for charitable valuation overstatements was previously mentioned.

Fraud Penalty

If any part of an underpayment of tax is due to fraud, the entire underpayment is treated as attributable to fraud. A 75% fraud penalty is imposed, I.R.C. §6663(a),(b)]. However, if you can establish that part of the underpayment is not attributable to fraud, that portion is not subject to the 75% penalty, although it may be subject to the 20% accuracy-related penalty. The portion coming under the 75% fraud penalty is not also subject to the 20% accuracy-related penalty, I.R.C. §6663(b)].

The I.R.S. has the burden of proving fraud by clear and convincing evidence. The taxpayer, on the other hand, is only required to establish that items are not attributable to fraud by a preponderance of the evidence, a much lower standard, I.R.C. §6663(b).

Appraisers May Be Penalized

Appraisers are now subject to the same penalties that may be imposed upon tax return preparers including fines ranging from $1,000 to $10,000, I.R.C. §6701. An appraiser who has been penalized may be barred from presenting evidence before the I.R.S. or the Treasury Department, 31 U.S.C. § 330.

Required Records

In connection with each charitable contribution of property, regardless of value, you must maintain a receipt from the donee charitable organization containing the following information: (i) the name of the donee; (ii) the date and location of the contribution; and (iii) a description of the property in detail reasonably sufficient under the circumstances, Reg. §170A-13(b). A letter or other written communication from the donee charitable organization acknowledging receipt of the contribution, showing the date of the contribution, and containing the required description of the property contributed constitutes a receipt.

The Appraisal Summary

The appraisal summary previously referred to is submitted on Form 8283, a copy of which is included in the Appendix.

In fact Form 8283 is more than an Appraisal Summary since it includes information that is not required to be in the appraisal. The required additional information includes your date of acquisition, manner of acquisition (e.g. purchase, exchange, gift or bequest), and cost or adjusted basis. The regulations, in detailing the "manner of acquisition" requirement state, "...if the property was created, produced,or manufactured by or for the donor, a statement to that effect and the approximate date the property was substantially completed."

It would appear that the later requirement is less directed at gifts by artists than artwork which was manufactured for the purpose of later donation.

Note that the Appraisal Summary is signed by both the donor and the appraiser. The donee acknowledges receipt of the gift on one copy of the Appraisal Summary.

Internal Revenue Service Review of Appraisals

In reviewing a tax return, the I.R.S. may accept the claimed value of property, based on information or appraisals sent with the return, or may make its own determination of F.M.V. In either case, the I.R.S. may: (a) contact you to get more information, (b) refer the valuation problem to an I.R.S. appraiser or valuation specialist, (c) refer the issue to the Commissioner's Art Advisory Panel, or (d) contract with an independent dealer, scholar, or appraiser to appraise the property when the objects require appraisers of highly specialized experience and knowledge.

The Service is responsible for reviewing appraisals, but it is not responsible for making them. Supporting the fair market value listed on your return is your responsibility.

The I.R.S. does not give recognition to any appraiser or organization of appraisers and does not accept their appraisals without question. The I.R.S. does not approve valuations or appraisals before the actual filing of the tax return to which the appraisal applies. The Service does not issue advance rulings approving or disapproving such appraisals.

The Art Advisory Panel

The Art Advisory Panel is a group of outside experts, selected by the I.R.S., to pass on contested valuations of artworks in the $20,000+ category.

The decisions of the Art Advisory Panel are not binding on the I.R.S., but the I.R.S. almost always abides by the panel's decisions unless new evidence is presented by the taxpayer.

The panel is used in connection with income, gift, and estate tax returns. Supposedly the panel is unaware of the purpose of the valuation (i.e. a charitable deduction, estate tax, or gift tax). The panel members are prominent dealers, museum directors, and curators. They are well aware of who owns what and what museum received a major work of art. It would not seem unreasonable that they have some idea of the position that the taxpayer has taken.

The panel has been functioning since 1968. Item by item results are not published, but the I.R.S. does announce the dollar amounts of the upward and downward revisions.

The only distinct pattern that has emerged is that there is usually an increase in valuations that turn out to have been made in connection with estate and gift taxes and a decrease in valuations that were made in connection with income tax deductions.

In 1985 the panel reviewed valuations placed on 1,266 works of art donated by 173 taxpayers in 1983 and 1984. 74% of the valuations were adjusted, 20% were accepted, and 6% required further study. The results were announced in 1986 and did not reflect the effect of the appraisal regulations which were adopted in 1985.

In terms of dollars the taxpayers claimed an aggregate valuation of $47,659,241. The panel adjusted that figure to $30,082,124, a 37% reduction.

On the estate and gift side the taxpayers claimed valuations of $17,048,916, but the panel found their value to be $19,383,316, an increase of 14%. 272 items were appraised in 53 different cases. An upward adjustment was made in 66% of the cases.

In 1989, the last year for which figures were available as of press time, the panel reviewed 1031 items with an aggregate taxpayer valuation of $109,307,000 in 136 different cases. The claimed value of the average charitable contribution item was $92,000 and the average estate and gift item was $135,000. The Panelists recommended total adjustments of $17,727,000 claimed on the reviews now concluded for these meetings. On the adjusted items, the Panel recommended adjustments amounting to a 53% reduction on the overvalued items in charitable contribution claims and a 101% increase on the undervalued items in estate and gift appraisals.

It is interesting that according to the 1989 statistics taxpayers overvalued items donated by roughly 100% and undervalued estate items by roughly 50%!

The Panel recommended acceptance of 45% of the appraisals reviewed. Adjustments were recommended on 52% of the reviewed appraisals. 3% percent of the appraisals reviewed by the Panel were indicated as requiring additional staff development before a value decision could be made.

The Panel reconsidered 65 charitable contribution items in 8 cases valued at $4,636,000 by the taxpayer and $2,347,000 by the Panel. After reviewing the additional information subsequently submitted by the taxpayer, the Panel recommended $3,636,000 as the fair market value on these reconsidered items. The Panel also reconsidered 65 estate items in 7 cases valued at $6,338,000 by the taxpayer and $9,197,000 by the Panel. After reviewing the additional information, the Panel recommended $8,409,000 on these items.

In addition to the Panel items, 38 taxpayer cases with a claimed value of $5,860,000 were reviewed by the National Office Art Appraisal Office appraisers. These cases involved the valuation of various objects such as furniture, prints, photographs, decorative arts, antiquities, musical instruments, and historical properties. Eight cases were accepted. Adjustment of $5,173,000 were recommended on the remaining cases.

As of the date of the report relating to 1989 (September 1990) responses had been received in 45% of the cases reviewed by the Art Advisory Panel in 1988. 40% of the cases were agreed (36% at the examination level). The remaining five percent of the responses were unagreed.

The *Practising Law Institute* handbook, *Representing Artists, Collectors, and Dealers*, is the course manual for a two day program that was chaired by Ralph E. Lerner,Esq. The outline of the presentation by Karen E. Carolan on the workings of the Art Advisory Panel is the most informative we have found. Ms. Carolan is Chairwoman, Commissioner's Art Advisory Panel, and Chief of the I.R.S. Art Evaluation Group.

The Panel, composed of 25 members, is divided into three different groups. Each group represents specialization in particular areas of art.

The Panel meetings are closed to the public, but a summary report is issued each year. The purpose of the Panel meetings is to discuss and make recommendations regarding the acceptability of taxpayer appraisals.

The staff of the Art Evaluation Group, prior to each Panel meeting, provides the members with photographs and written materials concerning each work of art to be considered. The written materials incorporate information from both the taxpayer's appraisal and the results of staff research. The information supplied in reference to each work includes the title, date of creation, size, medium, substrate, physical condition, history of ownership, public exhibitions, and citations in literature. Information regarding public and private sales of works by the same artist is provided together with the valuation date and the value claimed by the taxpayer.

The materials supplied do not identify the taxpayer, appraiser or the tax consequences of adjusting the valuation. Ms. Carolan noted that even though the taxpayer's name is not disclosed, the prominence in the art world of many of the works, or discussed as comparable sales, often results in identification of taxpayers and even other art buyers being recognized by the Panelists.

In an attempt to minimize taxpayer identities, the items are arranged in alphabetical order by artist name; or for non-western art, by category or culture, thus reducing the possibility of recognizing specific collections.

The Panel members discuss each work and express a conclusion as to the fair market value on the valuation date.

Panelists aware of any conflict of interest in connection with a particular item are expected to excuse themselves from the discussion.

Subsequent to the Panel meeting the appraisers from the National Office prepare valuation reports in those instances where the taxpayer appraisal has been rejected. Those reports are returned to the District Office which initiated the referral, and the taxpayer is notified and provided with both a copy of the report and a list of the Panelists.

If the proposed appraisal regulations work well, the adjustments to the valuations of charitable income tax deductions should diminish.

The penalties which apply to income, gift, and estate taxes should further diminish over and undervaluations.

A third factor tending to diminish overvaluations will be the application of the A.M.T., imposed by T.R.A. '86 to the appreciated portion of the value of the gift.

The valuation of gifts with a claimed value below $20,000 is often settled in field offices.

One technique to be considered to avoid the automatic Art Advisory Panel procedure is to donate undivided fractional interests over a period of years. Possession of the artwork can be given to the donee in the first year but the gift staggered. If, for instance, the work of art is worth $75,000, you might consider 5 annual donations of interests each worth $15,000.

If you are making a gift of 5 works, each worth less than $20,000, you should consider making five separate gifts, each of an individual work over a period of five years. A permanent loan to the donee can serve to provide the donee with immediate possession.

These techniques are suggested not because you need fear a change in a valid appraisal but because it is generally not in the interests of taxpayers to trigger the automatic selection of their tax returns for special attention.

In addition to the Art Advisory Panel, the I.R.S. has a permanent staff of appraisers in what is known as the National Office Art Valuation Group. The members of the National Office Group provide support to other staff members and review some of the appraisals submitted in connection with cases not referred to the Art Advisory

Panel. The National Office Group does not initiate reviews. They work on cases sent in from District Offices which have already been selected for audit.

The Panel's decision is not binding on the taxpayer, and all the remedies open in any contested tax matter are open to the taxpayer.

The Art Print Advisory Panel

The Art Print Advisory Panel was established in 1980 to deal with abusive tax shelters in the area of prints and other multiples. In 1984 it was merged with the Art Advisory Panel subsequent to a sharp decrease in the number of contested print valuation cases.

During its separate existence its reductions in valuations were more dramatic than those of the Art Advisory Panel. As of June 1985 the total taxpayer claimed valuations considered by the Print Panel were $219,758,000. That number was reduced by $216,881,000!

It must be remembered that the majority of prints examined by the Print Panel had been recently "manufactured" for the purpose of creating a "tax shelter".

The reductions reflect less on print collectors and dealers than they do on the promoters of tax shelter and "investors" in tax shelters.

A Look At A Contested Appraisal Case

A 1989 United States Tax Court decision relating to a major collection now residing at the California Museum of Photography, University of California, Riverside ("UCR") provides a rare view of the Court's analysis of differing appraisals. The appraisals were presented in a contested charitable donation case. The collection, whose value was in question, is the famous Mast Collection of stereographic negatives and cards. There were several issues before the Court but the primary issue was the "fair market value of the collection."

The appraisers involved on behalf of the taxpayers were (1) Mead B. Kibbey, a collector of photographica who made the original appraisal for the donors, (2) Marjorie Neikrug, the owner of the Neikrug Gallery and a professional appraiser, and (3) John Waldsmith, a co-founder of the National Stereoscopic Association and long time editor of Stereo World Magazine. The Court noted that Waldsmith had been originally retained by the government to appraise the collection. The government's only expert was Penelope A. Dixon, a full-time appraiser of photographs. Both Dixon and Neikrug are senior members of the American Society of Appraisers. In their field, each appraiser was eminently qualified.

The starting point of the dispute was the $1,427,253 set by Kibbey as the fair market value and which served as the basis for the deductions taken by the taxpayers. The government contested that figure as being too high.

Although one could hardly fault the credentials of the appraisers they could not even agree on the question of how many negatives were in the collection. The testimony varied as follows: 105,000 (Dixon); 129,732 (Kibbey) [later increased 150,000]; 149,900 (Neikrug); 159,2000 (Waldsmith). According to the Court a UCR "audit estimate" was 163,135. We find the juxtaposition of "audit" and "estimate" to be inimical.

It was undisputed that the source of the negatives was primarily the collection amassed by the Keystone View Company in the course of its business and by Keystone's acquisition of other stereograph publishers including Kilbur, White Berry, Kelly and Chadwick, Graves and Underwood. The Court described the subject matter of the collection as "images ranging from portraits of Presidents and other famous individuals to landscapes and panoramas from various locations around the world".

Kibbey arrived at his figure of $1,427,253 by estimating a replacement cost of $11 for each negative discounted by 60% and $5 for the retail value of each stereo card. He based the valuation on his study of comparable retail sales as listed in two catalogs. When he updated his count, he raised his estimate to $1,544,368.

Neikrug used a market data comparison approach to reach her estimate. Therefore her valuation of $1,592,166 was based on "comparisons with reported sales, offers to sell by catalog, showroom or gallery pricing, and historical data".

Waldsmith stated that the fair market value was $1,207,500. He "made his valuation by breaking the collection up into component parts and then assigning average per unit values for the items in each segment".

Dixon took a bulk sale approach and "determined the fair market value of the Collection by estimating the price at which a comparable collection could be sold, in its entirety. She cited four collections of negatives and prints of which only two were of stereographs. One collection was all stereocards and the second a combination of stereocards and negatives. The sales prices were all private sales and the major player was George Rinhart. Dixon's fair market value was $450,000 (less than 1/3 of the highest valuation). Because Dixon's had been retained by the government on the eve o[trial, her report and testimony was not submitted 15 days prior to the trial as required by Court rules. It was admitted into evidence over the objections of the taxpayers, but the Court seemed to factor the rule violation into the consideration of her appraisal. The Court did not dispute her qualifications but basically rejected the bulk sale valuation and the use of sale prices of collections which were not similar. It remarked on the similarity of the approach taken by the taxpayer's three appraisers, i.e. "a per unit method". The result was that the testimony of each reinforced the testimony of the other two. The Court arrived at a valuation of $1,250,000 which was almost the same as the Waldsmith appraisal (the lowest of the taxpayers' three appraisals). It did not detail the formula used but stated that it did give some weight to the government's expert witness. For those interested, the decision is reported in Tax Court Memo 1989-111 under the title *Gifford M. Mast Jr. and Judith A. Mast et. al. v. Commissioner*. It is reprinted in the Appendix.

Our own view of the case is based in part on reading between the lines and a knowledge of the arguments usually made in other tax cases. First, it would appear that the Court was influenced by the fact that the government had initially hired Waldsmith and then chose not to use him as a witness. The unspoken assumption is that his appraisal was too high for the government to accept, even though they had chosen him and paid him. We find it strange that the Court did not explore the bulk sale theory in greater depth. When taxpayers desire to minimize the value of a collection, particularly in connection with the estate of a noted artist, they claim a large discount is due because the amount realized in a single bulk sale is always substantially lower than the aggregate of individual sales made over a period of time. On the other hand, the Court did not spend much time discussing that the Mast collection might have had a high value because it was (1) so complete and (2) so unique that a duplicate collection could not be assembled in the contemporary market.

Summary

In connection with the income tax deduction for charitable gifts, the possible inclusion of appreciation as a tax preference, other than for tax year 1991, and the penalties for overvaluation should diminish any inclination to seek inflated appraisals.

In connection with the gift and estate taxes the penalties for undervaluation should deter those with the inclination to lowball appraisals.

Appraisers should be wary of having penalties imposed on them in connection with overvaluation and undervaluation.

Take advantage of tax benefits, do not abuse them!

APPENDIX

Form 8283	Noncash Charitable Contributions
Instructions	Instructions for Form 8283
Form 8282	Donee Information Return with Instructions
Publication 526	Charitable Contributions
Publication 561	Determining the Value of Donated Property
Form 6251	Alternative Minimum Tax - Individuals
Instructions	Instructions for Form 6251
Form 709-A	Short Form Gift Tax Return with Instructions
Form 709	Gift (and Generation-Skipping Transfer) Tax Return
Instructions	Instructions for Form 709
Publication 529	Miscellaneous Deductions
Case	Wrightsman v. United States
Case	Mast v. Commissioner
Statement	Standards Of Professional Appraisal Practice

Note: The I.R.S. Forms and Publications are those available as we go to press. They are included for information purposes only. Obtain the most recent versions prior to using any form or relying on any publication.

Form **8283**
(Rev. March 1990)
Department of the Treasury
Internal Revenue Service

Noncash Charitable Contributions

▶ **Attach to your tax return if the total claimed deduction for all property contributed exceeds $500.**
▶ **See separate Instructions.**

OMB No. 1545-0908
Expires 2-28-93

Attachment Sequence No. **55**

Name(s) shown on your income tax return | **Identification number**

Note: *Compute the amount of your contribution deduction before completing Form 8283. (See your tax return instructions.)*

Section A Include in Section A **only** items (or groups of similar items) for which you claimed a deduction of $5,000 or less per item or group, and certain publicly traded securities (see Instructions).

Part I Information on Donated Property

1	**(a)** Name and address of the donee organization	**(b)** Description of donated property (attach a separate sheet if more space is needed)
A		
B		
C		
D		
E		

Note: *If the amount you claimed as a deduction for the item is $500 or less, you do not have to complete columns (d), (e), and (f).*

	(c) Date of the contribution	**(d)** Date acquired by donor (mo., yr.)	**(e)** How acquired by donor	**(f)** Donor's cost or adjusted basis	**(g)** Fair market value	**(h)** Method used to determine the fair market value
A						
B						
C						
D						
E						

Part II Other Information—If you gave less than an entire interest in property listed in Part I, complete lines 2a–2e. If restrictions were attached to a contribution listed in Part I, complete lines 3a–3c.

2 If less than the entire interest in the property is contributed during the year, complete the following:

a Enter letter from Part I that identifies the property ________. (If Part II applies to more than one property, attach a separate statement.)

b Total amount claimed as a deduction for the property listed in Part I for this tax year ________________; for any prior tax year(s) ________________

c Name and address of each organization to which any such contribution was made in a prior year (complete only if different than the donee organization above).

Name of charitable organization (donee)

Address (number and street)

City or town, state, and ZIP code

d The place where any tangible property is located or kept ________________

e Name of any person, other than the donee organization, having actual possession of the property ________________

3 If conditions were attached to any contribution listed in Part I, answer the following questions and attach the required statement (see Instructions):

		Yes	No
a	Is there a restriction, either temporary or permanent, on the donee's right to use or dispose of the donated property?		
b	Did you give to anyone (other than the donee organization or another organization participating with the donee organization in cooperative fundraising) the right to the income from the donated property or to the possession of the property, including the right to vote donated securities, to acquire the property by purchase or otherwise, or to designate the person having such income, possession, or right to acquire?		
c	Is there a restriction limiting the donated property for a particular use?		

Name(s) shown on your income tax return | Identification number

Section B **Appraisal Summary**—Include in Section B only items (or groups of similar items) for which you claimed a deduction of more than $5,000 per item or group. *(Report contributions of certain publicly traded securities only in Section A.)*

If you donated art, you may have to attach the complete appraisal. See the **Note** in Part I below.

Part I **Information on Donated Property** *(To be completed by the taxpayer and/or appraiser.)*

1 Check type of property:

☐ Art* (contribution of $20,000 or more) ☐ Real Estate ☐ Gems/Jewelry ☐ Stamp Collections
☐ Art* (contribution of less than $20,000) ☐ Coin Collections ☐ Books ☐ Other

*Art includes paintings, sculptures, watercolors, prints, drawings, ceramics, antique furniture, decorative arts, textiles, carpets, silver, rare manuscripts, historical memorabilia, and other similar objects. **Note:** *If you donated art after December 31, 1987, and your total art contribution deduction was $20,000 or more, you must attach a complete copy of the signed appraisal. See Instructions.*

2	(a) Description of donated property (attach a separate sheet if more space is needed)	(b) If tangible property was donated, give a brief summary of the overall physical condition at the time of the gift	(c) Appraised fair market value
A			
B			
C			
D			

	(d) Date acquired by donor (mo., yr.)	(e) How acquired by donor	(f) Donor's cost or adjusted basis	(g) For bargain sales after 6/6/88, enter amount received	See Instructions: (h) Amount claimed as a deduction	See Instructions: (i) Average trading price of securities
A						
B						
C						
D						

Part II **Taxpayer (Donor) Statement**—List any item(s) included in Part I above that is (are) separately identified in the appraisal as having a value of $500 or less. See Instructions.

I declare that the following item(s) included in Part I above has (have) to the best of my knowledge and belief an appraised value of not more than $500 (per item). *(Enter identifying letter from Part I and describe the specific item)*: ____________

Signature of taxpayer (donor) ▶ Date ▶

Part III **Certification of Appraiser** *(To be completed by the appraiser of the above donated property.)*

I declare that I am not the donor, the donee, a party to the transaction in which the donor acquired the property, employed by, married to, or related to any of the foregoing persons, or an appraiser regularly used by any of the foregoing persons and who does not perform a majority of appraisals during the taxable year for other persons.

Also, I declare that I hold myself out to the public as an appraiser or perform appraisals on a regular basis; and that because of my qualifications as described in the appraisal, I am qualified to make appraisals of the type of property being valued. I certify that the appraisal fees were not based upon a percentage of the appraised property value. Furthermore, I understand that a false or fraudulent overstatement of the property value as described in the qualified appraisal or this appraisal summary may subject me to the civil penalty under section 6701(a) (aiding and abetting the understatement of tax liability). I affirm that I have not been barred from presenting evidence or testimony by the Director of Practice.

Please Sign Here Signature ▶ Title ▶ Date of appraisal ▶

Business address | Identification number

City or town, state, and ZIP code

Part IV **Donee Acknowledgment** *(To be completed by the charitable organization.)*

This charitable organization acknowledges that it is a qualified organization under section 170(c) and that it received the donated property as described in Part I on ____________ (Date).

Furthermore, this organization affirms that in the event it sells, exchanges, or otherwise disposes of the property (or any portion thereof) within 2 years after the date of receipt, it will file an information return (**Form 8282,** Donee Information Return) with the IRS and furnish the donor a copy of that return. This acknowledgment does not represent concurrence in the claimed fair market value.

Name of charitable organization (donee)	Employer identification number	
Address (number and street)	City or town, state, and ZIP code	
Authorized signature	Title	Date

*U.S. GPO:1991-518-933/20355

Department of the Treasury
Internal Revenue Service

Instructions for Form 8283

(Revised March 1990)

Noncash Charitable Contributions

(Section references are to the Internal Revenue Code, unless otherwise noted.)

General Instructions

Paperwork Reduction Act Notice

We ask for this information to carry out the Internal Revenue laws of the United States. We need it to ensure that taxpayers are complying with these laws and to allow us to figure and collect the right amount of tax. You are required to give us this information.

The time needed to complete and file this form will vary depending on individual circumstances. The estimated average time is:

Recordkeeping	20 min.
Learning about the law or the form	26 min.
Preparing the form	35 min.
Copying, assembling, and sending the form to IRS	35 min.

If you have comments concerning the accuracy of these time estimates or suggestions for making this form more simple, we would be happy to hear from you. You can write to either IRS or the Office of Management and Budget at the addresses listed in the instructions of the tax return with which this form is filed.

Purpose

Use Form 8283 to report certain required information about noncash charitable contributions. Do not report on Form 8283 out-of-pocket expenses for volunteer work or amounts you gave by check or credit card. Treat these items as cash contributions.

Additional Information

Do not use this form to figure your charitable contribution deduction. For information on computing the amount of the deduction, see your tax return instructions. You may also want to get **Pub. 526,** Charitable Contributions (for individuals), and **Pub. 561,** Determining the Value of Donated Property. If you contribute depreciable property, get **Pub. 544,** Sales and Other Dispositions of Assets.

Who Must File

You must file Form 8283 if the amount of your deduction for all noncash gifts is more than $500. (For this purpose, "amount of your deduction" means your deduction BEFORE applying any income limitations that could result in a carryover. The carryover rules are explained in Pub. 526.)

If you must complete Form 8283, you may need to complete Section A, Section B, or both, depending on the type of property and the amount claimed as a deduction. See **Which Sections To Complete.**

Form 8283 is filed only by:

- Individuals
- Partnerships
- S corporations
- Closely held corporations
- Personal service corporations
- Other C corporations

Note: *C corporations, other than personal service corporations and closely held corporations, must file Form 8283 only if the amount claimed as a deduction is over $5,000 and the property was donated after June 6, 1988.*

Reductions to Fair Market Value (FMV).—Make any required reductions to FMV before you determine if you must file Form 8283. Attach a computation to your tax return showing the reduction. The amount of the reduction (if any) depends on whether the property is ordinary income property or capital gain property. See the FMV discussion below.

When To File

File Form 8283 with your tax return for the tax year you contribute the property and first claim a deduction.

Fair Market Value (FMV)

Although the **amount** of your deduction determines if you have to file Form 8283, you also need to have information about the **value** of your contribution to complete the form.

Fair market value (FMV) is the price a willing buyer would pay a willing seller when neither has to buy or sell, and both are aware of the sale conditions.

You may not always be able to deduct the FMV of your contribution. Depending on the type of property donated, you may have to reduce the FMV to get to the deductible amount, as explained below.

Ordinary income property is property that would result in ordinary income or short-term capital gain if it were sold on the date it was contributed. Examples of ordinary income property are inventory, works of art created by the donor, and capital assets held for 1 year or less (6 months or less if acquired before January 1, 1988). The deduction for a gift of ordinary income property is limited to the FMV less the amount that would be ordinary income or short-term capital gain if the property were sold at its FMV.

Capital gain property is property that would result in long-term capital gain if it were sold at its FMV on the date it was contributed. It includes certain real property and depreciable property used in your trade or business, and generally held for more than 1 year (more than 6 months if acquired before January 1, 1988). You usually may deduct gifts of capital gain property at their FMV. However, you must reduce the FMV by the amount of the appreciation if:

- the capital gain property is contributed to certain private nonoperating foundations;
- you choose the 50% limit instead of the special 30% limit; or
- the contributed property is tangible personal property that is put to an unrelated use by the charity.

Qualified Conservation Contribution.—If your donation qualifies as a "qualified conservation contribution" under section 170(h), attach a statement that shows the claimed FMV of the underlying property before and after the gift and the conservation purpose furthered by the gift.

Which Sections To Complete

Section A

Include in Section A only items (or groups of similar items as defined on page 2) for which you claimed a deduction of $5,000 or less per item (or group of similar items). Also include certain publicly traded securities even if the deduction exceeds $5,000.

The publicly traded securities you should report in Section A even if the deduction claimed exceeds $5,000 are:

1. Securities listed on an exchange in which quotations are published daily;

2. Securities regularly traded in national or regional over-the-counter markets for which published quotations are available; or

3. Securities that are shares of a mutual fund for which quotations are published on a daily basis in a newspaper of general circulation throughout the United States.

Section B

Include in Section B only items (or groups of similar items) for which you claimed a deduction of more than $5,000 (except for certain publicly traded securities reportable in Section A).

Similar Items of Property

Similar items of property are items of the same generic category or type, such as stamp collections, coin collections, lithographs, paintings, books, nonpublicly traded stock, land, or buildings.

Example. *You claimed a deduction of $400 for clothing, $7,000 for publicly traded securities (quotations published daily), and $6,000 for a collection of 15 books ($400 for each book). Report the clothing and the securities in Section A and the books (a group of similar items) in Section B.*

With certain exceptions, items reported in Section B will require information based on a written appraisal by a qualified appraiser.

Special Rule for Contributions of Inventory and Scientific Equipment by Certain C Corporations

A special rule applies for deductions taken by certain C corporations under section 170(e)(3) or (4) for contributions of inventory or scientific equipment. To determine if you must file Form 8283, or which section to complete, take into account only the amount claimed as a deduction in excess of the amount you would have deducted as cost of goods sold (COGS) had you sold the property instead. This rule is **only** for purposes of Form 8283. It does not change the amount or method of computing your contribution deduction.

You must attach a statement to your tax return (similar to the one in the example below) if, because of this rule, you do not have to file Form 8283. Also attach a statement if, because of this rule, you must complete Section A instead of Section B.

Example. *You donated clothing from your inventory for the care of the needy. The clothing cost you $5,000 and your claimed charitable deduction is $8,000. Complete Section A instead of Section B since the excess of the deduction over what would have been your COGS deduction is $3,000 ($8,000 − $5,000). Attach a statement to Form 8283 similar to the following:*

Form 8283—Inventory

$8,000	contribution deduction
−$5,000	COGS (if sold, not donated)
=$3,000	for Form 8283 filing purposes.

Specific Instructions

Identification Number

Donors who are individuals must enter their social security number. All other donors should enter their employer identification number.

Partnerships and S Corporations

A partnership (S corporation) that claims a contribution deduction of over $500 must file Form 8283 with Form 1065 (1120S). If the total deduction of any item or group of similar items exceeds $5,000, the partnership (S corporation) must complete Section B of Form 8283 even if the amount allocated to each partner (shareholder) does not exceed $5,000.

The partnership (S corporation) must give a completed copy of Form 8283 to each partner (shareholder) who receives an allocation of the contribution deduction shown in Section B of the partnership's (S corporation's) Form 8283.

Partners and Shareholders

The partnership (S corporation) will provide information about your share of the contribution on your Schedule K-1 (Form 1065 or Form 1120S).

In some cases, the partnership (S corporation) must give you a copy of its Form 8283. In these cases, attach a copy of the Form 8283 you received to your tax return. Deduct the amount shown on your Schedule K-1, not the amount shown on the Form 8283.

If the partnership (S corporation) is not required to give you a copy of its Form 8283, combine the amount of noncash contributions shown on your Schedule K-1 with your noncash contributions to see if you must file Form 8283. If you need to file Form 8283, you do not have to complete all the information requested in Section A for your share of the partnership's (S corporation's) contributions. Do not complete line 1, columns (a)–(f) and (h). Instead, write "From Schedule K-1 (Form 1065 or 1120S)" across columns (c)–(f). Enter your share of the contribution on line 1, column (g).

Section A

Part I, Information on Donated Property

Line 1

Column (b).—Describe the property in sufficient detail. The greater the value, the more detail is needed. For example, a car should be described in more detail than pots and pans.

For securities, include the following:

- name of the issuer,
- kind of security,
- whether it is regularly traded on a stock exchange or in an over-the-counter market, and
- whether it is a share of a mutual fund.

Note: *Columns (d), (e), and (f) do not have to be completed if the amount you claimed as a deduction for the item is $500 or less.*

Column (d).—Enter the approximate date you acquired the property. If it was created, produced, or manufactured by or for you, enter the date it was substantially completed.

Column (e).—State how you acquired the property (i.e., by purchase, gift, inheritance, or exchange).

Column (f).—Do not complete for:

- Publicly traded securities; or
- Property held 12 months or more (6 months or more if donated in tax years beginning before June 7, 1988).

Keep records on cost or other basis.

Note: *If you have reasonable cause for not providing the acquisition date in column (d), or the cost basis when required in column (f), attach an explanation.*

Column (g).—Enter the fair market value (FMV) of the property on the date you gave it. If you were required to reduce the FMV of your deduction, or if you gave a qualified conservation contribution, you must attach a statement. FMV, reductions to FMV, and the type of statement you may have to attach are explained on page 1.

Column (h).—Enter the method(s) used to determine the FMV of your donation. FMV of used household goods and clothing is usually much lower than when new. For this reason, standard formulas or methods to value this kind of property are generally not appropriate.

A good measure of value might be the price that buyers of these used items actually pay in consignment or thrift shops.

Examples of entries to make include "Appraisal," "Thrift shop value" (for clothing or household goods), "Catalog" (for stamp or coin collections), or "Comparable sales" (for real estate and other kinds of assets). See Pub. 561.

Part II, Other Information

Attach a separate statement if Part II applies to more than one property. Give the required information for each property separately. Identify which property listed in Part I the information relates to.

Lines 2a–2e

Complete lines 2a–2e only if you contributed less than the entire interest in the donated property during the tax year. Enter on line 2b the amount claimed as a deduction for this year and in any earlier tax years for gifts of a partial interest in the same property. If the organization that received the prior interest in the property is the same as the one listed on line 1, column (a), do not complete line 2c.

Lines 3a–3c

Complete lines 3a–3c only if you attached restrictions to the right to the income, use, or disposition of the donated property. Attach a statement explaining:

- The terms of any agreement or understanding regarding the restriction; and
- Whether the property is designated for a particular use.

An example of a "restricted use" is furniture that you gave only to be used in the reading room of an organization's library.

Section B

Note: *Section B was revised after the 1989 Pub. 526 and Pub. 561 were printed. Therefore, the references in those publications to the various parts of Section B are incorrect. Also, the rules regarding the submission of photographs for art valued at $20,000 or more were changed after the 1989 Pub. 561 was printed. The new rules are discussed under* ***Art Valued at $20,000 or More*** *in the instructions for Part I below.*

Part I, Information on Donated Property

You must have a written appraisal from a qualified appraiser that supports the information in Part I. However, see the **Exception** below.

Use Part I to summarize your appraisal(s). Generally, you do not need to attach the appraisals, but you should keep them for your records. But, see **Art Valued at $20,000 or More** below.

Exception.—You do not need a written appraisal if the property is:

1. Nonpublicly traded stock of $10,000 or less;

2. Securities for which market quotations are readily available (see Regulations section 1.170A-13(c)(7)(xi));

3. Property donated by C corporations (other than closely held corporations or personal service corporations) after June 6, 1988; or

4. Inventory and other property donated by closely held corporations and personal service corporations after November 9, 1988, which are "qualified contributions" for the care of the ill, the needy, or infants within the meaning of section 170(e)(3)(A).

Although a written appraisal is not required for the types of property listed above, you must provide certain information in Part I of Section B (see Regulations section 1.170A-13(c)(4)(iv)) and have the donee organization complete Part IV.

Art Valued at $20,000 or More.—If your total deduction for art donated after 1987 is $20,000 or more, you must attach a complete copy of the signed appraisal. For individual objects valued at $20,000 or more, a photograph of a size and quality fully showing the object, preferably an 8 × 10 inch color photograph or a color transparency no smaller than 4 × 5 inches, must be provided upon request.

Appraisal Requirements

The appraisal must be made not earlier than 60 days before the date you contribute the property. You must receive it before the due date (including extensions) of the return on which you first claim a deduction for the property. For a deduction first claimed on an amended return, the appraisal must be received before the date the amended return was filed.

A separate qualified appraisal and a separate Form 8283 are required for each item of property except for an item which is part of a group of similar items. Only one appraisal is required for a group of similar items contributed in the same tax year, if it includes all the required information for each item.

The appraiser may select any items whose aggregate value is appraised at $100 or less for which a group description rather than a specific description of each item will suffice.

If you gave similar items to more than one donee for which you claimed a deduction of more than $5,000, you must attach a separate form for each donee.

Example. *You claimed a deduction of $2,000 for books given to College A, $2,500 for books given to College B, and $900 for books given to a public library. You must attach a separate Form 8283 for each donee.*

See Regulations section 1.170A-13(c)(3)(i)–(ii) for the definition of a "qualified appraisal" and information to be included in the appraisal.

Line 2

Note: *You* ***must*** *complete at least column (a) of line 2 (also column (b) if applicable) before submitting Form 8283 to the donee. You may then complete the remaining columns.*

Column (a).—Describe the property in enough detail so that a person not familiar with it could tell that the property appraised is the property that was contributed.

Column (c).—Include the FMV from the appraisal. If one was not required, include the FMV you determine to be correct.

Columns (d)–(f).—If you have reasonable cause for not providing the information asked for in any of these columns, attach an explanation so that your deduction won't be automatically disallowed.

Column (g).—A bargain sale is a transfer of property which is in part a sale or exchange, and in part a contribution. Enter the amount received ("consideration") for bargain sales after June 6, 1988.

Column (h).—Complete column (h) only if you were not required to get an appraisal, as explained earlier.

Column (i).—Complete column (i) only if you donated securities for which market quotations are considered to be readily available because the issue satisfies the 5 requirements described in Regulations section 1.170A-13(c)(7)(xi)(B).

Part II, Taxpayer (Donor) Statement

If you (the donor) complete Part II, the donee is relieved of filing Form 8282 for items valued at $500 or less. (See the **Note** in the Part IV instructions on page 4 for more information on the filing of Form 8282 by the donee.)

Complete Part II only for items included in Part I that have an appraised value of $500 or less per item. Be sure to clearly identify these items in Part II. This is necessary because the donee may not know the value of the donated property, since you are not required to show it in Part I on the donee's copy of Form 8283.

The amount of information you give in Part II depends on the description of the donated property you enter in Part I. If you separately show a single item as "Property A" in Part I, and that item is appraised at $500 or less, then the entry "Property A" in Part II is enough. However, if "Property A" consists of several items and the total appraised value is over $500, list in Part II any item(s) you gave that is (are) valued at $500 or less.

All shares of nonpublicly traded stock, or items in a set, are considered one item. For example, a book collection by the same author, components of a stereo system, or six place settings of a pattern of silverware are one item for the $500 test.

Example. *You donated books valued at $6,000. The appraisal states that one of the items, a collection of books by author "X" is worth $400. On the Form 8283 that you are required to give the donee, you decide not to show the appraised value of all of the books. But you also don't want the donee to have to file Form 8282 if the collection of books is sold. If on line 2 of Part I your description of Property A includes all the books, then specify in Part II the "collection of books by X included in Property A." But if in Part I your Property A description is "collection of books by X," the only required entry in Part II is "Property A."*

In the above example you may have instead chosen to give a completed copy of Form 8283 to the donee. The donee would then be aware of the value. If in Part I you include all the books as Property A, and thus enter $6,000 in column (c), you may still want to describe the specific collection in Part II so the donee can sell it without filing Form 8282.

Part III, Certification of Appraiser

If you had to get an appraisal, the appraiser MUST complete Part III to be considered qualified. See Regulations section 1.170A-13(c)(5) for a definition of a qualified appraiser.

Persons who cannot be qualified appraisers are listed in the Certification of Appraiser (Part III) of Form 8283. Usually, a party to the transaction will not qualify to sign the certification. But a person who sold, exchanged, or gave the property to the donor may sign the certification if the property is donated within 2 months of the date the donor acquired it and the property's appraised value does not exceed its acquisition price.

An appraiser may not be considered qualified if the donor had knowledge of facts that would cause a reasonable person to expect the appraiser to falsely overstate the value of the property. An example of this is an agreement between you and the appraiser about the property value when you know that the agreed amount exceeds the actual FMV.

Usually, appraisal fees cannot be based on a percentage of the appraised value unless the fees were paid to certain not-for-profit associations. See Regulations section 1.170A-13(c)(6)(ii).

Part IV, Donee Acknowledgment

The donee organization must complete Part IV. Before submitting page 2 of Form 8283 to the donee for acknowledgment, complete at least your name, identification number, and description of the donated property (line 2, column (a)). If tangible property is donated, also describe its physical condition (line 2, column (b)) at the time of the gift. Complete the Taxpayer (Donor) Statement in Part II, if applicable, before submitting the form to the donee. See the instructions for Part II.

The person acknowledging the gift must be an official authorized to sign the tax returns of the organization, or a person specifically designated to sign Form 8283. After completing Part IV, the organization must return Form 8283 to you, the donor. A copy of Section B of this form must be provided to the donee organization. You may then complete any remaining information required in Part I. Also, Part III may be completed at this time by the qualified appraiser.

In rare and unusual circumstances, it may be impossible to get the donee's signature on the appraisal summary. The deduction will not be disallowed for that reason if you attach a detailed explanation why it was impossible.

Note: *If the donee (or a successor donee) organization disposes of the property within 2 years after the date the original donee received it, the organization must file **Form 8282**, Donee Information Return, with IRS and send a copy to the donor. An exception applies to items having a value of $500 or less if the donor identified the items and signed the statement in Part II (Section B) of Form 8283. See the instructions for Part II.*

Failure To File Form 8283, Section B

If you donate property required to be reported in Section B and you fail to attach the form to your return, the deduction will be disallowed unless your failure was due to a good faith omission. If IRS asks you to submit the form, you have 90 days to send a completed Section B of Form 8283 before your deduction is disallowed.

☆U.S. Government Printing Office: 1990-262-151/00082

Form **8282**
(Rev. March 1990)
Department of the Treasury
Internal Revenue Service

Donee Information Return

(Sale, Exchange, or Other Disposition of Donated Property)

▶ See instructions on back.

OMB No. 1545-0908
Expires 2-28-93

Give Copy to Donor

Please Print or Type

Name of charitable organization (donee) | Employer identification number

Address (number and street)

City or town, state, and ZIP code

Note: *If you are the original donee,* ***DO NOT*** *complete Part II, or column (c) of Part III.*

Part I Information on ORIGINAL DONOR and DONEE YOU GAVE THE PROPERTY TO

1a **Name of the original donor** of (first person to give) the property | **1b** Identification number

Note: *Complete lines 2a–2d only if you gave this property to another charitable organization (successor donee).*

2a **Name of charitable organization** | **2b** Identification number (EIN)

2c Address (number and street)

2d City or town, state, and ZIP code

Part II Information on PREVIOUS DONEES—Complete this part only if you were not the first donee to receive the property.

If you were the second donee, leave lines 4a–4d blank. If you were a third or later donee, complete lines 3a–4d. On lines 4a–4d give information on the preceding donee (the one who gave you the gift).

3a **Name of original donee** | **3b** Identification number (EIN)

3c Address (number and street)

3d City or town, state, and ZIP code

4a **Name of preceding donee** | **4b** Identification number (EIN)

4c Address (number and street)

4d City or town, state, and ZIP code

Part III Information on DONATED PROPERTY

(a) Description of donated property sold, exchanged, or otherwise disposed of (attach a separate sheet if more space is needed)	**(b)** Date you received the item(s)	**(c)** Date the first donee received the item(s) (if you weren't the first)	**(d)** Date item(s) sold, exchanged, or otherwise disposed of	**(e)** Amount received upon disposition

For Paperwork Reduction Act Notice, see instructions on back.

General Instructions

(Section references are to the Internal Revenue Code.)

Paperwork Reduction Act Notice

We ask for this information to carry out the Internal Revenue laws of the United States. We need it to ensure that taxpayers are complying with these laws and to allow us to figure and collect the right amount of tax. You are required to give us this information.

The time needed to complete this form will vary depending on individual circumstances. The estimated average time is:

Recordkeeping . . . . 3 hrs., 7 min.

Learning about the law or the form . . . . 30 min.

Preparing and sending the form to IRS . . . . . . 34 min.

If you have comments concerning the accuracy of these time estimates or suggestions for making this form more simple, we would be happy to hear from you. You can write to the **Internal Revenue Service,** Washington, DC 20224, Attention: IRS Reports Clearance Officer, T:FP; or the **Office of Management and Budget,** Paperwork Reduction Project (1545-0908), Washington, DC 20503.

Purpose

Donee organizations use Form 8282 to report information to the Internal Revenue Service about dispositions of certain charitable deduction property made within 2 years after the donor contributed the property.

Definitions

Note: *For purposes of Form 8282 and instructions, the term "donee" includes all donees, unless specific reference is made to "original" or "successor" donees.*

Original Donee.—The first donee to or for which the donor gave the property. The original donee is required to sign an appraisal summary presented by the donor for charitable deduction property.

Appraisal Summary.—Section B of **Form 8283,** Noncash Charitable Contributions.

Successor Donee.—Any donee of property other than the original donee.

Charitable Deduction Property.—Property (other than money or certain publicly traded securities) contributed after 1984 for which the original donee signed, or was presented with for signature, an appraisal summary on Form 8283.

Generally, only items or groups of similar items for which the donor claimed a deduction of more than $5,000 are included on an appraisal summary. There is an exception if a donor gives similar items to more than one donee organization and the total deducted for these similar items exceeds $5,000. For example, if a donor deducts $2,000 for books given to a donee organization and $4,000 for books to another donee organization, the donor must present a separate appraisal summary to each organization. For more information, see the Instructions for Form 8283.

Who Must File

Form 8282 must be filed by original and successor donee organizations who sell, exchange, consume, or otherwise dispose of (with or without consideration) charitable deduction property within 2 years after the date the original donee received the property. For successor donees, the form must be filed only for property transferred by the original donee after July 5, 1988.

Exceptions.—There are two situations where Form 8282 does not have to be filed.

1. Items valued at $500 or less.—You do not have to file Form 8282 if, at the time the original donee signed the appraisal summary, the donor had signed a statement on Form 8283 that the appraised value of the specific item was not more than $500. If Form 8283 contains more than one similar item, this exception applies only to those items that are clearly identified as having a value of $500 or less. However, for purposes of the donor's determination of whether the appraised value of the item exceeds $500, all shares of nonpublicly traded stock, or items that form a set, are considered one item. For example, a collection of books written by the same author, components of a stereo system, or six place settings of a pattern of silverware, are considered one item.

2. Items consumed or distributed for charitable purpose.—You do not have to file Form 8282 if an item is consumed or distributed without consideration. The consumption or distribution must be in furtherance of your purpose or function as a tax-exempt organization. For example, no reporting is required for medical supplies consumed or distributed by a tax-exempt relief organization in aiding disaster victims.

When To File

If you dispose of charitable deduction property within 2 years of the date the original donee received it and you do not meet exception **1** or **2** above, you must file Form 8282 within 125 days after the date of disposition.

Exception: *If you did not file because you had no reason to believe the substantiation requirements applied to the donor, but you later become aware that they did apply, file Form 8282 within 60 days after the date you become aware you are liable.*

The above exception would apply if you were never given an appraisal summary, and it was reasonable to believe that the property you received was worth $5,000 or less.

Missing Information

If Form 8282 is filed by the due date, you must enter your organization's name, address, and EIN and complete at least Part III, column (a). You do not have to complete the remaining items if the information is not available. For example, you may not have the information necessary to complete all entries if the donor's appraisal summary is not available to you.

Where To File

Mail Form 8282 to the Internal Revenue Service Center, Cincinnati, OH 45944.

Penalties

You may be subject to a penalty if you fail to file this form by the due date, fail to include all of the information required to be shown on this form, or fail to include correct information on this form (see Missing Information above). For Forms 8282 required to be filed after 1989 (determined without regard to extensions), the penalty is generally $50 for each such failure. For more details, see sections 6721 and 6723.

Other Requirements

Information You Must Give a Successor Donee.—If the property is transferred to another charitable organization within the 2-year period discussed earlier, you must give your successor donee the following information:

1. The name, address, and EIN of your organization;

2. A copy of the appraisal summary (the Form 8283 that you received from the donor or a preceding donee); and

3. A copy of this Form 8282 within 15 days after you file it.

You must furnish items 1 and 2 within 15 days after the latest of:

- The date you transferred the property,
- The date the original donee signed the appraisal summary, or
- If you are also a successor donee, the date you received a copy of the appraisal summary from the preceding donee.

Note: *The successor donee organization to whom you transferred this property is required to give you their organization's name, address, and EIN within 15 days after the later of:*

- *The date you transferred the property, or*
- *The date they received a copy of the appraisal summary.*

Information You Must Give the Donor.—You must give a copy of your Form 8282 to the donor of the property.

Appraisal Summary.—You must keep a copy of the appraisal summary in your records.

☆U.S. Government Printing Office: 1990-262-151/00081

Department of the Treasury
Internal Revenue Service
Catalog Number 15050A

Publication 526

Charitable Contributions

For use in preparing

1990 Returns

Introduction

You may deduct charitable contributions as an itemized deduction on Schedule A (Form 1040), subject to certain limits. A charitable contribution is a contribution or gift to, or for the use of, a qualified organization. This publication discusses:

- Qualified organizations,
- Deductible and nondeductible contributions,
- Limits on deductibility,
- Figuring your deduction,
- Recordkeeping, and
- Reporting your deduction.

Checklist of Contributions

Use the following lists for a ***quick check*** of the kinds of contributions you may or may not deduct. More examples are found later in this publication.

You May Deduct Contributions to:

- Churches, Salvation Army, Red Cross, CARE, Goodwill Industries, United Way, Boy Scouts, Girl Scouts, Boys and Girls Club of America, etc.
- Veterans' groups.
- Nonprofit schools and hospitals.
- Federal, state, and local governments, if the gifts are solely for public purposes.
- Civil defense organizations.
- Public parks and recreation facilities.

You May Not Deduct as Contributions:

- Dues, fees, or bills paid to country clubs, lodges, fraternal orders, or similar groups.
- Cost of raffle, bingo, or lottery tickets.
- Tuition.
- Value of your time or services.
- Value of blood given to a blood bank.
- Donations to homeowners associations.
- Gifts to individuals.
- Political contributions.

Free Publications and Forms

If you need information on a subject not covered in this publication, you may check our other free publications. To order publications and forms, call our toll-free telephone number 1-800-TAX-FORM (829-3676) or write the IRS Forms Distribution Center for your area as shown in the income tax package.

Qualified Organizations

Any organization can tell you if it is a qualified organization. Most qualified organizations are listed in IRS Publication 78, *Cumulative List of Organizations*. You may deduct a contribution you made to, or for the use of, the following qualified organizations.

A state, a U.S. possession (including Puerto Rico), a political subdivision of a state or possession, the United States, or the District of Columbia, if the contribution is made for public purposes only. An Indian tribal government and any of its subdivisions that are recognized by the Secretary of the Treasury as performing substantial government functions will be treated as a state for purposes of the charitable contributions deduction.

A community chest, corporation, trust, fund, or foundation organized or created in or under the laws of the United States, any state, the District of Columbia, or any possession of the United States. The organization must be organized and operated only for charitable, religious, educational, scientific, or literary purposes. It may also be for the prevention of cruelty to children or animals. Certain organizations that foster national or international amateur sports competition are also included.

Examples of qualified organizations. Qualified organizations include:

- Nonprofit volunteer fire companies.
- Civil defense organizations.
- Public parks and recreation facilities.
- Nonprofit hospitals and medical research organizations.
- Churches or other religious organizations.
- Most nonprofit educational organizations, including day care centers if substantially all the child care provided is to enable individuals (the parents) to be gainfully employed and the services are available to the general public. However, if your contribution is a substitute for tuition or other enrollment fee, it is not deductible as a charitable contribution, as explained later under *Nondeductible Contributions.*
- Utility company emergency energy programs, if the utility company is an agent for a charitable organization that assists individuals with emergency energy needs.
- Most nonprofit charitable organizations.
- War veterans' organizations, including posts, auxiliaries, trusts, or foundations, organized in the United States or its possessions.
- Domestic fraternal societies operating under the lodge system, if the contribution is to be used only for charitable, religious, scientific, literary, or educational purposes, or for the prevention of cruelty to children or animals.
- Nonprofit cemetery companies, if the contribution can be used only for the perpetual care of the cemetery as a whole, and not for a particular lot or mausoleum crypt.

Deductible Contributions

Generally, you may deduct your contributions of money or property that you make to, or for the use of, qualified organizations. If you give property to a qualified organization, you generally may deduct the fair market value of the property at the time of the contribution. See *Gifts of Property*, later.

Your deduction for charitable contributions is generally limited to 50% of your adjusted gross income, but in some cases 20% and 30% limits may apply. See *Limit on Deductions*, later.

Benefits Received

If you contribute to a charitable organization and also receive a benefit from it, you may deduct only the amount that is more than the value of the benefit you receive. If you pay more than fair market value to a qualified organization for merchandise, goods, or services, the amount you pay that is more than the value of the item may be a charitable contribution.

Example 1. You pay $75 for a dinner-dance at a church. All the proceeds of the function go to the church. If the dinner, plus any entertainment or other services provided, has a fair market value of $25, the excess paid, $50, is a contribution to the church.

Example 2. At a fund-raising auction conducted by a charity, you pay $600 for a week's occupancy of a house at the beach. The amount you pay is no more than the fair rental value. You have not made a deductible charitable contribution.

Athletic events. If you make a payment to or for the benefit of a college or university and as a result, you receive the right to buy tickets for an athletic event in the athletic stadium of the college or university, you can deduct 80% of the payment as a charitable contribution.

If any part of your payment is for tickets (rather than the right to buy tickets), that part is not deductible, but 80% of the remaining part is deductible.

Example. You pay $300 annually for membership in an athletic scholarship program maintained by a university (a qualified organization). The only benefit of membership is that you are entitled to buy one season ticket to the university's home football games for a seat in a designated area of the stadium, for a stated price of $120. 80% of the $300 payment or $240 is deductible.

Benefit performances, etc. If you pay more than fair market value to a qualified organization for charity balls, banquets, shows, sporting events, etc., you may deduct only the amount that is more than the value of the privileges or other benefits you receive.

If there is an established charge for the event, that charge will determine the value of your benefit. If there is no set charge, only that part of your payment that is more than the reasonable value of your benefit is a gift. Whether you use the tickets or other privileges has no effect on the amount you may deduct. However, if you return the ticket to the qualified organization for resale, you may deduct the amount you paid.

The fact that the ticket or other evidence of payment indicates that the payment is a "contribution" does not mean you can deduct the entire amount. If the ticket shows the price of admission and the amount of the gift, you can deduct the gift amount.

Example. You pay $40 to see a special showing of a movie for the benefit of a qualified organization. Printed on the ticket is "Contribution—$40." If the regular price for the movie is $8, your contribution is $32.

Token items. If you receive only token items (such as bookmarks, calendars, mugs, or caps) in connection with your payment, you may be able to deduct the entire payment as a charitable contribution. You must be notified by the charity that the item you received is of insubstantial value and that the payment can be deducted in full.

Dues, fees, or assessments are deductible if you pay them to qualified organizations. However, you may deduct only the amount that is more than the value of the benefits you receive. You may not deduct dues, fees, or assessments paid to country clubs and other social organizations.

Student Living With You

If you pay the costs of a student who lives in your home, you may deduct up to $50 a month of the amount you pay. The student may be foreign or American, but must not be your dependent or relative. The student must be a member of your household under a written agreement between you and a qualified organization. The purpose of the agreement must be to provide educational opportunities for the student.

A qualified organization is any organization described earlier, in *Qualified Organizations* except it does not include any state or other governmental body that may enter into an agreement with you to provide a home for a student. For example, if you are providing a home for a child through a state or local agency, you may not deduct amounts you spend as charitable contributions.

You may deduct up to $50 of your expenses for each full calendar month of your tax year during which the student is:

1) A member of your household, and
2) A full-time student in the 12th or lower grade at a school located in the United States.

A period of 15 or more days in a month counts as a full calendar month for this purpose.

Qualifying expenses include the cost of books, tuition, food, clothing, transportation, medical and dental care, entertainment, and other amounts you actually spend for the well-being of the student. Depreciation on your home and the fair market value of lodging or any similar item is not considered an amount spent by you. In addition, general household expenses, such as taxes, insurance, repairs, etc., do not qualify for the deduction.

If you are compensated or reimbursed for any part of the costs of having a student living with you, none of the costs may be deducted. However, if you are reimbursed for only an extraordinary or nonrecurring item, such as a hospital bill or vacation trip, that you paid in advance at the request of the student's parents or the sponsoring organization, you may deduct your other expenses for the student.

For a list of what you must file with your return if you deduct expenses for a student living with you, see *Maintaining certain students as members of your household*, under *Recordkeeping and How to Report*, later.

Mutual exchange program. You may not deduct the costs of a foreign student living in your home under a mutual exchange program whereby your child will live with a family in a foreign country.

Out-of-Pocket Expenses

You may deduct some amounts you pay in giving services to a charitable organization. However, you may not deduct the value of your time or services.

The contributions must be made to a qualified organization and not set aside for use by a specific person. However, you may deduct reasonable unreimbursed out-of-pocket expenses you pay for underprivileged juveniles to attend athletic events, movies, or dinners, if they are selected by a charitable organization whose goal is to reduce juvenile delinquency. Your own similar expenses in accompanying the juveniles are not deductible.

Conventions. If you are a chosen representative attending a convention of a qualified organization, you may deduct unreimbursed expenses for travel and transportation, including a reasonable amount for meals and lodging, while away from home overnight in connection with the convention. However, see *Travel*, later.

You may not deduct personal expenses for sightseeing, fishing parties, theater tickets, or nightclubs. You also may not deduct travel, meals and lodging, and other expenses for your spouse or children.

You may not deduct your expenses in attending a church convention if you go only as a member of your church rather than as a chosen representative. You may deduct unreimbursed expenses that are directly connected with giving services for your church during the convention.

Uniforms. You may deduct the cost and upkeep of uniforms that you must wear while performing donated services for a charitable organization if they are not suitable for everyday use.

Foster parents. If you are a foster parent (foster care provider) and have no profit motive in providing foster care, you may deduct expenses you pay that exceed any nontaxable payments you receive to provide foster care for individuals placed in your home by a charitable organization. The expenses must be amounts spent to provide support for the individual. For more information, see *Foster Child or Adult* in Publication 501, *Exemptions, Standard Deduction, and Filing Information*.

Permanent diaconate programs. You may deduct as a charitable contribution any unreimbursed expenses you have while in a permanent diaconate program established by your church. These expenses include the cost of vestments, books, and transportation required in order to serve in the program as either a deacon candidate or as an ordained deacon.

Car expenses. You may deduct unreimbursed out-of-pocket expenses, such as the cost of gas and oil, that are directly related to the use of your car in giving services to a charitable organization. You may not deduct general repair and maintenance expenses, depreciation, or insurance.

If you do not want to deduct your actual expenses, you may use a standard rate of ***12 cents a mile*** to figure your contribution.

You may deduct parking fees and tolls, whether you use your actual expenses or the standard rate.

Travel. You may claim a charitable contribution deduction for travel expenses while you are away from home performing services for a charitable organization only if there is ***no significant element*** of personal pleasure, recreation, or vacation in such travel. This applies whether you pay the expenses directly, or indirectly through reimbursement by the charitable organization. An arrangement whereby you make a payment to the charitable organization and the organization pays for your travel expenses is treated as a reimbursement.

The deduction will not be denied simply because you enjoy providing services to the charitable organization.

Example 1. You are a troop leader for a tax-exempt youth group and take the group on a camping trip. You may qualify to take a charitable deduction for your own travel expenses if you are on duty in a genuine and substantial sense throughout the trip, even though you enjoyed the trip. However, if you have only nominal duties relating to the performance of services for the charity, or for significant portions of the trip you are not required to render services, you may not take a charitable deduction for travel expenses.

Example 2. You sail from one island to another and spend 8 hours a day counting whales and other forms of marine life. The project is sponsored by a charitable organization. In most circumstances, no charitable deduction is allowed for the expenses you incur.

Example 3. You work for several hours each morning on an archeological excavation sponsored by a charitable organization. The rest of the day is free for recreation and sightseeing. No charitable deduction is allowed even though you work during the morning hours.

Example 4. You spend the entire day attending a charitable organization's regional meeting. In the evening you go to the theater. You may qualify to claim your travel expenses as charitable contributions.

Daily allowance (per diem). If you provide services for a charitable organization and receive a daily allowance to cover reasonable travel expenses, including meals and lodging while away from home overnight, include in income the amount that is more than your actual travel expenses. You may deduct your necessary travel expenses that are more than the allowance.

Deductible travel expenses include:

- Air, rail, and bus transportation,
- Out-of-pocket expenses for your car,
- Taxi fares or other costs of transportation between the airport or station and your hotel,
- Lodging costs, and
- The cost of meals.

For more information, see *Travel Expenses* in Publication 463, *Travel, Entertainment, and Gift Expenses.*

When Deductible

To deduct your contributions, you must make them in cash or other property before the close of your tax year. This applies whether you use the cash or accrual method of accounting.

Usually, you make a contribution at the time of its unconditional delivery. For example, a check that you mail to a charity is considered delivered on the date you mail it. If you use a pay-by-phone account, the date reported on the statement of the financial institution showing when payment was made is the date of payment.

The gift to a charity of a properly endorsed stock certificate is completed on the date of mailing or other delivery to the charity or to the charity's agent. However, if you give a stock certificate to your agent or to the issuing corporation for transfer to the name of the charity, your gift is not completed until the date the stock is transferred on the books of the corporation.

If you issue and deliver a promissory note to a charitable organization as a contribution, it is not a contribution until you make the note payments. Similarly, if you grant an option to buy real property at a bargain price to a charitable organization, no deduction is allowed until the organization exercises the option.

If you make a contribution with borrowed funds, a deduction is allowed in the year you make the contribution, regardless of when you repay the loan. Contributions charged on your bank credit card are deductible in the year you make the charge.

Nondeductible Contributions

This section of the publication provides information about a number of contributions that are not deductible.

Nonqualified organizations. Some organizations are not qualified to receive tax-deductible contributions. Contributions to the following organizations, for example, are not deductible:

- Chambers of commerce and other business leagues or organizations,
- Civic leagues,
- Communist organizations,
- Country clubs and other social clubs,
- Homeowners associations,
- Most foreign organizations, and
- Political organizations and candidates.

Appraisal fees that you pay to find the fair market value of donated property are not deductible as contributions. You may claim them, subject to the 2% of adjusted gross income limit, as miscellaneous deductions on Schedule A (Form 1040). See *Deductions Subject To the 2% Limit* in Publication 529, *Miscellaneous Deductions*, for more information.

Blood donated to the Red Cross or to blood banks is not deductible.

Child care expenses while you perform services for a qualified organization are not deductible.

Contributions to fraternal societies are not deductible if they are used to pay sickness or burial expenses of members.

Contributions to a state bar by members and other donors are not deductible. Membership dues that apply to all members of the bar as a condition of membership are deductible as business expenses.

Contributions used to influence legislation are not deductible. Even if an organization is a qualified organization, no deduction is allowed for contributions to the organization that are earmarked for use in, or in connection with, attempting to influence the general public on legislative matters, elections, or referenda.

Direct contributions made to a foreign organization are not deductible. However, you may deduct contributions to a U.S. organization that transfers funds to a charitable foreign organization if the U.S. organization controls the use of the funds or if the foreign organization is only an administrative arm of the U.S. organization.

Exception. Under an income tax treaty with Canada, you may be able to deduct contributions to certain Canadian charitable organizations. See Publication 597, *Information on the United States-Canada Income Tax Treaty*, for information on how to figure your deduction.

Direct contributions to needy or worthy individuals are not deductible. The contributions must be made to or for the use of a qualified organization and not earmarked by you for the use of a specific person.

A donation of the right to use property, such as a rent-free lease, is not deductible because it is considered a contribution of less than your entire interest in the property. However, see *Partial interest in property*, later for exceptions and more information.

Dues to fraternal orders and similar groups are not deductible.

Dues to labor unions are not deductible as charitable contributions. You may deduct them as a miscellaneous expense, subject to the 2% of adjusted gross income limit, on Schedule A (Form 1040). See Publication 529.

Payments to a hospital for care of particular patients or for services provided to those patients are not deductible as contributions, even if the hospital is operated by a city, state, or qualified organization.

Pre-adoption expenses. The costs of keeping a child in your home before the child is adopted may not be deducted as a contribution. However, you may be able to claim an exemption for the child. See *Adoption* in Publication 501.

Raffles, bingo, etc. You may not deduct as charitable contributions amounts you pay to a charitable organization to buy raffle tickets or to play bingo or other games of chance. They are gambling losses, which may be deducted as an itemized deduction only to the extent of gambling winnings. See *Deductions Not Subject To the 2% Limit* in Publication 529.

Sustainer's gift to retirement home. You may not deduct a sustainer's gift you pay when being admitted to a retirement home that is operated by a qualified organization. Generally, such a gift entitles you to the benefit of occupying a certain type of apartment.

Tuition, or amounts you pay instead of tuition, are not deductible as contributions, even if they are paid for children who attend parochial schools or qualifying nonprofit day care centers. A fixed amount, designated as a "donation," that is required to be paid to a private school in addition to the tuition fee as a condition of enrollment is not deductible.

Gifts of Property

If you donate property to a qualified organization, you generally may deduct the fair market value of the property at the time of the contribution. However, if the property has increased in value, you may have to make some adjustments. See *Giving Property That Has Increased in Value*, later.

For information about the records you must keep and the information you must furnish with your return if you donate property, see *Recordkeeping and How to Report*, later.

Property subject to a debt. If you contribute property subject to a debt obligation, you must reduce the fair market value of the property by the amount of the outstanding obligation. In addition, the debt obligation is treated as an amount realized on the sale or exchange of property. See *Bargain sales* under *Giving Property That Has Increased in Value*, later.

If you paid (or will pay) interest that is attributable to any period after the contribution, the fair market value must be further reduced by the amount of your allowable deduction for the interest. (For 1990, your allowable deduction for personal interest is 10% of the interest paid.)

Partial interest in property. Generally, no deduction is allowed for a charitable contribution of less than your entire interest in property. A contribution of the right to use property is a contribution of less than your entire interest in that property and is not deductible.

Example. You own a 10-story office building of which you donate rent-free use of the top floor to a charitable organization. Since you retain ownership, you have a partial interest in the property and may not take a deduction for the contribution.

Exception. You may deduct a charitable contribution of a partial interest in property only if that interest represents:

1) An undivided part of your entire interest,
2) A remainder interest in your personal home or farm,
3) A partial interest that would be deductible if transferred to a trust, or
4) A qualified conservation contribution.

In addition, you may deduct a partial interest in property if the charitable contribution meets the requirements for a transfer in trust.

For more information about the valuation of a gift of a partial interest in property, see *Partial Interest in Property* in Publication 561, *Determining the Value of Donated Property.*

Future interests in tangible personal property. You may deduct the value of a charitable contribution of a future interest in tangible personal property only after all intervening interests in and rights to the actual possession or enjoyment of the property have either expired or been turned over to someone other than yourself or a related person or a related organization.

A ***future interest*** is any interest that is to begin at some future time, regardless of whether it is designated as a future interest under state law.

Example. You own an antique car that you donate to a museum in 1990. You relinquish ownership, but retain the right to keep the car in your garage with your personal collection. Since you have an interest in the property, you may not take a deduction for the contribution in 1990. If you turn the car over to the museum in 1991, giving up all rights to its use, possession, and enjoyment, you may take a deduction for the contribution in 1991.

Inventory. If you donate inventory (property that you sell in the course of your business), the amount of your contribution deduction is limited to the inventory's cost or other basis. See *Giving Property That Has Increased in Value*, later. Any costs or expenses you had in earlier tax years and properly included in your opening inventory for the year of the contribution must be removed from opening inventory. They are not a part of the cost of goods sold for purposes of figuring gross income for the year of the contribution. Instead, they are used to figure the basis of the contributed inventory.

However, any costs or expenses for the contributed inventory in the year of the contribution that would be properly included in the cost of goods sold should be included in cost of goods sold. They are not considered in arriving at the contributed inventory's basis.

Determining Fair Market Value

This section discusses general guidelines for determining the fair market value (FMV) of various types of donated property. A more comprehensive discussion can be found in Publication 561, *Determining the Value of Donated Property*.

Fair market value (FMV) is the price at which property would change hands between a willing buyer and a willing seller, neither being required to buy or sell, and both having reasonable knowledge of all the necessary facts.

Used clothing. The fair market value of used clothing and other personal items is usually far less than the price you paid for them. Valuation of items of clothing does not lend itself to fixed formulas or methods.

You should claim as the value the price that buyers of used items actually pay in used clothing stores, such as consignment or thrift shops.

Household goods. The fair market value of used household goods, such as furniture, appliances, and linens, is usually much lower than the price paid when new. Such used property may have little or no market value because of its worn condition. It may be out of style or no longer useful. For these reasons, formulas, such as 15% of the replacement cost new, are not acceptable in determining value.

You should support your valuation with photographs, canceled checks, or receipts from your purchase of the items. Magazine or newspaper articles and photographs that describe the items and statements by the recipients of the items are also useful. None of these items need to be included with your tax return.

If the property is valuable because it is old or unique, see the discussion under *Paintings, Antiques, and Other Objects of Art* in Publication 561.

Cars, boats, and aircraft. If you donate a car, boat, or aircraft to a charitable organization, its fair market value must be determined.

Certain commercial firms and trade organizations publish monthly or seasonal guides, for different regions of the country, containing complete dealer sale prices or dealer average prices for recent model years. These guides also provide estimates for adjusting for unusual equipment, unusual mileage, and physical condition. The prices are not "official" and these publications are not considered an appraisal of any specific donated property. But they do provide clues for making an appraisal and suggest relative prices for comparison with current sales and offerings in your area.

These publications are sometimes available from the loan officer at a bank, credit union, or finance company.

Except for inexpensive small boats, the valuation of boats should be based on an appraisal by a marine surveyor because the physical condition is critical to the value.

Example. You donate your car to a local high school for use by their students studying automobile repair. Your credit union told you that the "blue book" value of the car is $1,600. However, your car needs extensive repairs and, after some checking, you find that you would not be able to sell it for more than $750. You may deduct $750, the ***true*** fair market value of the car, as a charitable contribution.

Large quantities. If you contribute a large number of the same item, fair market value is the price at which comparable numbers of the item are being sold.

Example. You purchase 500 bibles for $1,000. The retail value of these bibles is $3,000. If you contribute these bibles to a qualified organization, you may claim a deduction only for the price at which similar numbers of the same bible are currently being sold. Your charitable contribution would be $1,000, unless you could show that similar numbers of that bible at the time of the contribution were selling at a different price.

Giving Property That Has Increased in Value

If you donate property with a fair market value that is more than your basis in it, you may have to reduce the fair market value by the amount of appreciation (increase in value) when you figure your deduction. Different rules apply, depending on whether the property is ordinary income property or capital gain property.

Ordinary income property. Property is ordinary income property if its sale at fair market value on the date it was contributed would have resulted in ordinary income or in short-term capital gain. Examples of ordinary income property are inventory, works of art created by the donor, manuscripts prepared by the donor, and capital assets held one year or less.

The deduction for a gift of ordinary income property is its fair market value less the amount that would be ordinary income or short-term capital gain if the property were sold at its fair market value. Generally, this rule limits the deduction to your basis in the property.

Example. You donate stock that you held for 5 months to your church. The value of the stock is $1,000, but you paid only $800 (your basis). Because the $200 of appreciation would be short-term capital gain if you sold the stock, your deduction is limited to $800 (fair market value less the appreciation).

Property used in a trade or business is considered ordinary income property to the extent of any gain that would have been treated as ordinary income because of depreciation had the property been sold. See *Dispositions of Depreciable Property* in Publication 544, *Sales and Other Dispositions of Assets*, for the kinds of property to which this rule applies.

Capital gain property. Property is capital gain property if its sale at fair market value on the date of the contribution would have resulted in long-term capital gain. It includes capital assets held more than one year, as well as certain real property and depreciable property used in your trade or business and, generally, held more than one year. For more information, see *Ordinary or Capital Gain or Loss* in Publication 544.

You usually may deduct a gift of capital gain property at its fair market value. However, in certain situations, the fair market value is reduced to the property's cost or other basis. You must reduce the fair market value by any increase in value if:

1) The property (other than ***qualified appreciated stock***) is contributed to certain private nonoperating foundations,
2) You choose the 50% limit instead of the special 30% limit, discussed later, or
3) The contributed property is tangible personal property that is put to an ***unrelated use*** by the charity.

Contributions to private nonoperating foundations. The reduced deduction for contributions to certain private nonoperating foundations does not apply to contributions of qualified appreciated stock. ***Qualified appreciated stock*** is any stock of a corporation that is capital gain property and for which market quotations are readily available on an established securities market on the day of the contribution. This exception does not apply, however, to the extent you contribute more than 10% of the value of all of the outstanding stock of a corporation.

Tangible personal property put to an unrelated use. The term ***unrelated use*** means a use that is unrelated to the exempt purpose or function of the charitable organization. For a governmental unit, it means the use of the contributed property for other than exclusively public purposes.

Example. If a painting contributed to an educational institution is used by that organization for educational purposes by being placed in its library for display and study by art students, the use is not an unrelated use. But if the painting is sold and the proceeds are used by the organization for educational purposes, the use is an unrelated use.

Alternative minimum tax. If you deduct a gift of capital gain property at its fair market value, the difference between that value and the adjusted basis of the property is a tax preference item subject to the alternative minimum tax rules. For more information, see Publication 909, *Alternative Minimum Tax for Individuals*.

Exception. You do not reduce your charitable contribution if you include the ordinary or capital gain income in your gross income in the same year as the contribution. This may happen when you transfer installment or discount obligations or when you assign income to a charitable organization. If you contribute an obligation received in a sale of property that is reported under the installment method, see Publication 537, *Installment Sales*.

Bargain sales. A bargain sale of property to a qualified organization (a sale or exchange at less than the property's fair market value) is partly a charitable contribution and partly a sale or exchange. The charitable contribution part is the difference between the fair market value at the time of sale and the amount received.

A bargain sale may result in a taxable gain. For more information on determining your taxable gain, see *Other Dispositions* in Publication 544.

You determine the amount of your charitable contribution by allocating the adjusted basis of the property between the part contributed and the part sold. The adjusted basis of the contributed part is figured as follows:

$$\text{Adjusted basis of entire property} \times \frac{\text{Fair market value of contributed part}}{\text{Fair market value of entire property}}$$

Then you apply the ordinary income property and capital gain property rules (discussed earlier) to determine the amount of your charitable contribution.

Example. You sell ordinary income property with a fair market value of $10,000 to a church for $2,000. Your basis is $4,000 and your adjusted gross income is $20,000. You make no other contributions during the year. The fair market value of the contributed part of the property is $8,000 ($10,000 − $2,000). The adjusted basis of the contributed part is $3,200 ($4,000 × [$8,000 ÷ $10,000]). Because you must reduce the fair market value by the amount that would be ordinary income, or $4,800 ($8,000 − $3,200), your charitable contribution deduction is $3,200.

Penalty. You may be liable for a penalty if you overstate the value or adjusted basis of donated property.

The penalty is 20% of the underpayment of tax related to the overstatement if:

The value or adjusted basis claimed on the return is 200% or more of the correct amount, and

You underpaid your tax by more than $5,000 because of the overstatement.

The penalty is 40% of the underpayment of tax related to the overstatement if:

The value or adjusted basis claimed on the return is 400% or more of the correct amount, and

You underpaid your tax by more than $5,000 because of the overstatement.

Limit on Deductions

If your total contributions for the year are 20% or less of your adjusted gross income (line 32, Form 1040), they are fully deductible (provided they otherwise qualify), and it is not necessary to figure whether the limits discussed here apply.

If your contributions are more than 20% of your adjusted gross income, the amount of your deduction may be limited to either 20%, 30%, or 50% of your adjusted gross income, depending on the type of property you give and the type of organization you give it to.

Your maximum charitable contribution deduction is 50% of your adjusted gross income for the year (line 32, Form 1040). Adjusted gross income is not reduced by net operating loss carrybacks due to losses you have in later tax years. See *How to Figure Your Deduction*, later, if your contributions are more than the applicable limits or total more than 50% of your adjusted gross income.

The 50% limit applies to gifts (other than capital gain property deducted at fair market value) ***to*** organizations listed later under *50% limit organizations.*

The 30% limit applies to:

- Gifts ***for the use of*** any organization, and
- Gifts (other than capital gain property) to all qualified organizations other than 50% limit organizations. This includes gifts to veterans' organizations, fraternal societies, nonprofit cemeteries, and certain private nonoperating foundations.

A special 30% limit applies to gifts of capital gain property (if deducted at fair market value) to 50% limit organizations (but see the rules for electing the 50% limit under *How to Figure Your Deduction*, later).

The 20% limit applies to gifts of capital gain property to all qualified organizations other than 50% limit organizations.

50% limit organizations. The following are 50% limit organizations:

1) Churches, or conventions or associations of churches.
2) Tax-exempt educational organizations with a regular faculty and curriculum and a regular student body attending resident classes.
3) Tax-exempt hospitals and, under certain circumstances, organizations directly engaged in continuous medical research with these hospitals.
4) Organizations that receive substantial support from the United States or any state or their political subdivisions, or from the general public, and that are operated only to hold and administer property for state and municipal colleges and universities.
5) A state, a possession of the United States, or any political subdivision of any of the foregoing, or the United States, or the District of Columbia, if the contribution is made for public purposes only.
6) Corporations, trusts, or community chests, funds, or foundations organized and operated exclusively for charitable, religious, educational, scientific, or literary purposes, or to prevent cruelty to children or animals, or to foster certain national or international amateur sports competition. These organizations normally must receive a substantial part of their support, other than income from their exempt activities, from direct or indirect contributions from the general public or from governmental units. The public support received must be from a representative number of persons within the community, not from a few individuals or families.
7) Qualified organizations that normally receive more than one-third of their support from persons other than disqualified persons or from organizations described in (1) through (6), if such charitable organizations receive not more than one-third of their support from gross investment income and the excess of unrelated business taxable income over the tax on such income.
8) Most organizations operated or controlled by, and operated for the benefit of, those organizations described in (1) through (7).
9) Private operating foundations.
10) Private nonoperating foundations that make qualifying distributions of 100% of contributions within 2½ months following the year they receive the contribution. (A deduction for charitable contributions to any of these private nonoperating foundations must be supported by evidence from the foundation confirming that it made the qualifying distribution timely. Attach a copy of this supporting data to your tax return.)
11) A private foundation whose contributions are pooled into a common fund, if the foundation would be described in section 509(a)(3) of the Internal Revenue Code but for the right of substantial contributors to name the public charities that receive contributions from the fund. Distributions of income must be made within 2½ months following the tax year in which it was realized and corpus must be distributed not later than one year after the donor's death or after the death of the donor's surviving spouse if the spouse can name the recipients of the corpus.

Student living with you. Amounts you spend on behalf of a student living with you are subject to the 30% limit. These amounts are considered a contribution **for the use of** a qualified organization.

Out-of-pocket expenses. Amounts you spend performing services for a charitable organization are subject to the limit of the organization. For example, the 50% limit applies to amounts you spend on behalf of a church, a 50% organization. These amounts are considered a contribution **to** a qualified organization.

How to Figure Your Deduction

If your contributions are more than the limits just discussed, deduct them in the following order (up to 50% of your adjusted gross income):

1) Contributions qualifying for the 50% limit.
2) Contributions qualifying for the 30% limit to the extent of the ***lesser*** of:
   - 30% of adjusted gross income, or
   - 50% of adjusted gross income minus contributions to 50% limit organizations (including contributions of capital gain property subject to the special 30% limit).
3) Contributions qualifying for the special 30% limit (up to 30% of adjusted gross income).
4) Contributions qualifying for the 20% limit to the extent of the ***lesser*** of:
   - 20% of adjusted gross income, or
   - 30% of adjusted gross income minus contributions to which the special 30% limit applies.

Example. Your adjusted gross income is $50,000 for 1990. During the year, you gave your church $2,000 cash and land with a fair market value of $30,000. You had purchased the land in 1988 and its basis is $22,000. You held the land for investment purposes. The deduction for the gift of land does not have to be reduced by the appreciation in value. You also gave $5,000 cash to a private foundation to which the 30% limit applies.

The $2,000 cash donated to the church is considered first and is fully deductible. Your contribution to the private foundation is considered next. However, because your contributions to 50% limit organizations ($2,000 + $30,000) are more than $25,000 (50% of $50,000), your contribution to the private foundation is not currently deductible. It may be carried over to later years. See *Carryovers*, later. The deduction for the gift of land is limited to $15,000 (30% × $50,000). The unused part of the land ($15,000) may be carried over. Therefore, in 1990, your deduction is limited to $17,000 ($2,000 + $15,000).

Capital gain property election. You may choose the 50% limit for gifts of capital gain property to 50% limit organizations, but you must reduce the fair market value of the property by the appreciation in value that would be long-term capital gain if the property had been sold. If you make this choice, it applies to all 30% capital gain property. You must make the choice on your original return or on an amended return filed by the due date for filing the original return.

Example. In the previous example, if you choose to disregard the special 30% limit for the land given to your church, you must reduce the fair market value of the property by the appreciation in value. Therefore, your deduction for the land would be its basis to you of $22,000. You add this amount to the $2,000 cash contributed to the church. You may now deduct $1,000 of the amount donated to the private foundation because your contributions to 50% limit organizations ($24,000) are $1,000 less than 50% of adjusted gross income. Your total deduction for 1990 is $25,000: $2,000 cash to your church, $22,000 for property donated to your church, and $1,000 cash to the private foundation. The excess contribution ($4,000) to the private foundation may be carried over.

Carryovers. You may carry over your contributions that you are not able to deduct in the current year because they exceed your adjusted-gross-income limit. The excess may be deducted in each of the 5 succeeding years until it is used up, but not beyond that time. Your total contributions deduction for the year to which you carry your contributions cannot exceed 50% of your adjusted gross income for that year.

Contributions you carry over are subject to the same percentage limits in the year to which they are carried. For example, contributions subject to the 20% limit in the year in which they are made are 20% limit contributions in the year to which they are carried. For each category of contributions, you deduct carryover contributions only **after** deducting all allowable contributions in that category for the current year.

Example 1. During 1989, you contributed $11,000 to a 50% limit organization, but because of the limit you deducted only $10,000 and carried over $1,000 to 1990. In 1990 your adjusted gross income is $20,000 and you contribute $9,500 to a 50% limit organization. You may deduct $10,000 (50% of $20,000), using your 1990 contribution of $9,500 plus $500 of your 1989 carryover. The $500 balance of your 1989 carryover is carried over to 1991.

Example 2. In 1990 your adjusted gross income is $24,000. You make contributions of $6,000 to which the 50% limit applies and $3,000 to which the 30% limit applies. You have a contribution carryover from 1989 of $5,000 for capital gain property contributed to a 50% organization and subject to the special 30% limit.

Your 1990 contribution deduction is limited to $12,000 (50% of $24,000). Your 50% limit contributions of $6,000 are fully deductible. The deduction for your 30% limit contributions of $3,000 is limited to $1,000. This is the lesser of:

1) $7,200 (30% of $24,000), or
2) $12,000 (50% of $24,000) minus $11,000 (the sum of your current and carryover contributions to 50% organizations).

Because your $5,000 carryover subject to the special 30% limit does not exceed $7,200 (30% of $24,000), it is deducted in full. Your deduction is $12,000 ($6,000 + $1,000 + $5,000) and you carry over the $2,000 balance of your 1990 30% limit contributions to 1991.

If you carry over contributions of capital gain property subject to the special 30% limit and you choose in the next year to use the 50% limit and take appreciation into account, you must refigure the carryover. You reduce the fair market value of the property by the appreciation and reduce that result by the amount actually deducted in the previous year.

Example. In 1989 your adjusted gross income was $50,000 and you contributed capital gain property valued at $30,000 to a 50% organization and did not choose to use the 50% limit. Your basis in the property was $20,000. Your deduction was limited to $15,000 and $15,000 was carried over. In 1990 your adjusted gross income is $80,000 and you contribute capital gain property valued at $25,000 to a 50% limit organization. Your basis in the property is $20,000 and you choose to use the 50% limit. You must refigure your carryover as if you had taken the appreciation into account in 1989 as well as in 1990. Because your deduction in 1989 would have been $20,000 instead of the $15,000 you actually deducted, your refigured carryover is $5,000 ($20,000 − $15,000). Your total deduction in 1990 is $25,000 (your $20,000 current contribution plus your $5,000 carryover).

If you do not itemize deductions in any of the carryover years, you must reduce the carryover by the amount that would have been deductible had you itemized your deductions.

Example. You have a contributions carryover of $500 from 1989 to 1990. In 1990 your adjusted gross income is $10,000, your deductible contributions are $300, and you do not itemize deductions. If you had itemized your deductions, the total of your contributions paid during 1990 plus the carryover from 1989 would have fallen below 50% of your adjusted gross income and would have been deductible. Therefore, you must consider that your carryover is used up in 1990.

Recordkeeping and How to Report

You are required to keep records to prove the amount of the cash and noncash contributions you make during the year. The kind of records you must keep depends on the amount of your contributions and whether they are cash or noncash contributions.

Cash contributions. If you make a charitable contribution of money (including out-of-pocket expenses when donating your services), you must keep one of the following for each contribution you make:

1) A canceled check,
2) A receipt (or a letter or other written communication) from the charitable organization showing the name of the organization, the date of the contribution, and the amount of the contribution, or
3) Other reliable written records that include the information described in (2). Records may be considered reliable if they are of a contemporaneous nature, if you regularly keep records, or if, in the case of small donations, you have items such as buttons, tokens, or emblems that are given to contributors.

Form 1040. Enter on line 14, Schedule A (Form 1040), the contributions you made in cash or by check (including out-of-pocket expenses).

Enter on line 15, Schedule A (Form 1040) your contributions other than cash or check.

Maintaining certain students as members of your household. If you claim amounts paid to maintain a student as a member of your household, as described earlier under *Student Living With You*, you must submit with your return:

1) A copy of your agreement with the organization sponsoring the student placed in your household,
2) A summary of the various items you paid to maintain the student, and
3) A statement of:
   a) the date the student became a member of your household,
   b) the period of his or her full-time attendance at school, and
   c) the name and location of the school.

Noncash contributions. The records you must keep and the forms you must file depend on whether your deductions for contributions of property other than money total:

1) $500 or less,
2) Over $500 but not more than $5,000, or
3) Over $5,000.

Deductions of $500 or less. If you make a noncash contribution, you must get and keep a receipt from the charitable organization showing:

1) The name of the charitable organization,
2) The date and location of the charitable contribution, and
3) A reasonably detailed description of the property.

A letter or other written communication from the charitable organization acknowledging receipt of the contribution and containing the information in (1), (2), and (3) will serve as a receipt. You are not required to have a receipt where it is impractical to get one. In all cases, you must keep reliable written records for each item of donated property.

Your written records must include the following:

1) The name and address of the organization that you contributed to.
2) The date and location of the actual contribution.
3) A description of the property in detail reasonable under the circumstances. For a security, give the name of the issuer, the type of security, and whether it is regularly traded on a stock exchange or in an over-the-counter market.
4) The fair market value of the property at the time of the contribution and how you figured the fair market value. If it was determined by appraisal, you should also keep a signed copy of the appraisal.
5) The cost or other basis of the property if you must reduce its fair market value by appreciation, the amount of the reduction, and how you figured it. If you choose the 50% limit instead of the special 30% limit on certain capital gain property (discussed under *Capital gain property election* earlier, you must keep a record showing the years for which you made the choice, contributions for the current year, and carryovers from preceding years to which the choice applies.
6) The amount you claim as a deduction for the tax year as a result of the contribution. If you contribute less than your entire interest in the property during the tax year, your records must include the amount you claimed as a deduction in any earlier years for contributions of other interests in this property. They must also include the name and address of each organization to which you contributed the other interests, the place where any such tangible property is located or kept, and the name of the person or organization in possession of the property, if it is other than the one to which you contributed.
7) The terms of any conditions attached to the gift of property.

If the gift was a "qualified conservation contribution," your records must also include the fair market value of the underlying property before and after the gift, the type of legal interest donated, and the conservation purpose furthered by the gift. See *Qualified conservation contribution* in Publication 561 for more information.

Deductions over $500 but not more than $5,000. If you claim a deduction over $500 but not over $5,000 for noncash charitable contributions, you must complete Section A of ***Form 8283***, *Noncash Charitable Contributions*, and attach it to your income tax return.

You must get and keep a receipt from the charitable organization, and your written records must include the information in the preceding list. You must also keep written records that include the following information:

1) How you acquired the property, for example, by purchase, gift, bequest, inheritance, or exchange.
2) The approximate date you got the property or, if created, produced, or manufactured by or for you, the approximate date the property was substantially completed.
3) The cost or other basis, and any adjustments to the basis, of property held less than 12 months and, if you have the information, the cost or other basis of property held 12 months or more. This requirement, however, does not apply to publicly traded securities.

If you are not able to provide information on either the acquisition date or the cost basis of the property and you have a reasonable cause for not being able to provide this information, attach a statement of explanation to your return.

Deductions over $5,000. If you claim a deduction over $5,000 for charitable contributions of one item or a group of similar items (other than money or certain publicly traded securities), you must complete Section B of Form 8283 for each item or group. The claimed deductions for all similar items of property donated to any charitable organization during the year are aggregated. The organization that received the property must complete and sign Part IV of Section B.

Your written records must include the information listed in the items under *Deductions of $500 or less* and in the three items under *Deductions over $500 but not more than $5,000.* In addition, you are generally required to obtain a qualified written appraisal of the donated property from a qualified appraiser.

See *Deductions of More Than $5,000* in Publication 561 for more information.

If an organization, within 2 years after the date of receipt of a contribution of property for which it was required to sign a Form 8283, sells, exchanges, transfers, consumes, or otherwise disposes of the property, the organization must file an information return with the Internal Revenue Service on ***Form 8282***, *Donee Information Return,* and send you a copy of the form. However, if you have informed the organization that the appraised value of the donated item, or a specific item within a group of similar items, is $500 or less, the organization is not required to make a report on its sale of that item. For this purpose, all shares of non-publicly traded stock, or items that form a set, are considered to be one item.

Form 1040. Enter your noncash contributions on line 15, Schedule A (Form 1040). If your deductions for noncash contributions are over $500, you must attach Form 8283 to your return. The Internal Revenue Service will disallow the noncash portion (if more than $500) of your charitable contribution deduction if a required Form 8283 is not submitted with the return.

Index

*U.S. Government Printing Office: 1990-282-015/20005

Department of the Treasury
Internal Revenue Service
Catalog Number 15109Q

ublication 561
Rev. Dec. 1990)

Determining the Value of Donated Property

ote: This publication has not been updated, but u can still use it to answer your questions. If ere are any significant changes affecting the ntents, they are explained in an addendum cluded with the publication. If you do not find all of ur answers in this publication, please call the toll-e number for tax help shown in your phone ectory under U.S. Government, Internal Revenue ervice. If there is no number listed, call 1-800-9-1040.

The toll-free phone number for requesting free S forms and publications has changed. The new umber is 1-800-TAX-FORM (1-800-829-3676).

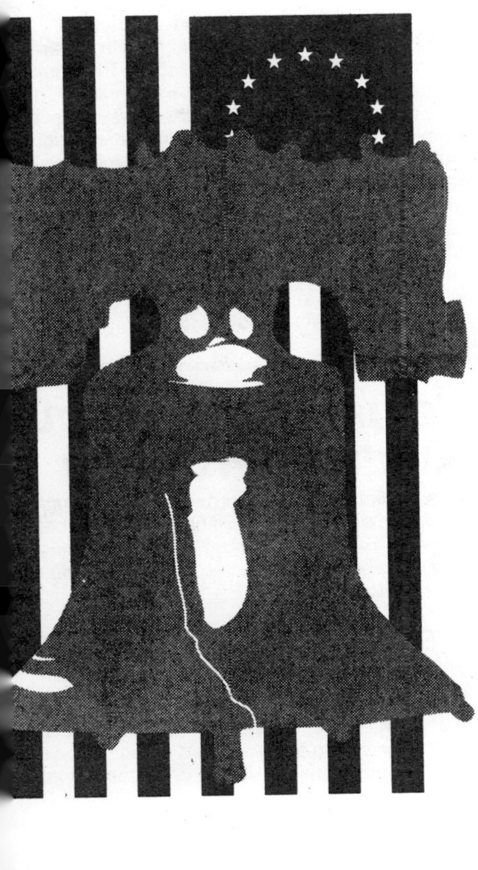

Introduction

This publication is designed to help donors and appraisers determine the value of property (other than cash) that is given to qualified organizations. It includes the kind of information you must have to support the charitable contribution deduction you claim on your return.

Topics discussed in this publication include:

- Fair market value, and how it is determined
- Valuation of various kinds of property
- Recordkeeping
- Appraisals

For more information on charitable contributions, see Publication 526, *Charitable Contributions.*

Penalty. You may be liable for a penalty if you overstate the value or adjusted basis of donated property. The penalty is 30% of the underpayment of tax related to the overstatement. In general, you are liable for the penalty if:

- The value or adjusted basis claimed on the return is 150% or more of the correct amount, and
- You underpaid your tax by at least $1,000 because of the overstatement.

Free Publications and Forms

If you need information on a subject not covered in this publication, you may check our other free publications. To order publications and forms, call our toll-free telephone number 1–800–829–FORM (3676) or write the IRS Forms Distribution Center for your area as shown in the income tax package.

What Is Fair Market Value?

To figure how much you may deduct for property that you contribute, you must first determine its fair market value on the date of the contribution.

Fair market value generally is the price that property would sell for on the open market. It is the price that would be agreed on between a willing buyer and a willing seller, with neither being required to act, and both having reasonable knowledge of the relevant facts.

For example, if you give used clothing to the Salvation Army, the fair market value would be the price that typical buyers actually pay for clothing of this age, condition, style, and use. Usually, such items are worth far less than what you paid for them.

In making and supporting the valuation of property given to a qualified organization, all relevant factors affecting its value must be considered. These include the cost or selling price of the item, sales of comparable properties, replacement cost, and opinions of experts.

If you put a restriction on the use of property you donate, the fair market value must reflect that restriction. For example, if you donate land and restrict its use to agricultural purposes, you must value the land at its value for agricultural purposes, even though it would have a higher fair market value if it were not restricted.

Date of contribution. Ordinarily, the date of a contribution is the date that the transfer of the property takes place.

Stock. If you deliver, without any conditions, a properly endorsed stock certificate to a qualified organization, or the organization's agent, the date of the contribution is the date of delivery. If the certificate is mailed and received through the regular mail, it is the date of mailing. If you deliver the certificate to a bank or broker acting as your agent, or to the issuing corporation or its agent, for transfer into the name of the organization, the date of the contribution is the date the stock is transferred on the books of the corporation. This, in effect, is the date of delivery to the organization.

Options. If you grant an option to a qualified organization to purchase real property, you have not made a charitable contribution until the organization exercises the option. The amount of the contribution is the fair market value of the property on the date the option is exercised minus the exercise price.

Example. You grant an option to a local university, which is a qualified organization, to purchase real property. Under the option, the university could purchase the property at any time during a 2-year period for $40,000. The fair market value of the property on the date the option is granted is $50,000.

In the following tax year, the university exercises the option. The fair market value of the property on the date the option is exercised is $55,000. Therefore, you have made a charitable contribution of $15,000 ($55,000, the fair market value, minus $40,000, the exercise price) in the tax year the option is exercised.

Cost or Selling Price of the Donated Property

The cost of the property or the actual selling price may be the best indication of its fair market value. However, because conditions in the market change, the cost or selling price of property may have less weight if the property was not bought or sold reasonably close to the date of contribution.

The cost or selling price is a good indication of the property's value if:

- The purchase or sale took place close to the valuation date in an open market,
- The purchase or sale was at "arm's length,"
- The buyer and seller knew all relevant facts,
- The buyer and seller did not have to act, and
- The market did not change between the date of purchase or sale and the valuation date.

Example. In 1987, Tom Morgan, who is not a dealer in gems, bought an assortment of gems for $5,000 from a promoter. The promoter claimed that the price was "wholesale" even though he and other dealers made similar sales at similar prices to other persons who were not dealers. The promoter said that if Tom kept the gems for more than one year and then gave them to charity, Tom could claim a charitable deduction of $15,000, which, according to the promoter, would be the value of the gems at the time of contribution. Tom gave the gems to a qualified charity 13 months after buying them and claimed a charitable deduction of $15,000.

The best evidence of fair market value depends on actual transactions and not on some artificial estimate. The $5,000 charged Tom and others is, therefore, the best evidence of the maximum fair market value of the gems.

The terms of the purchase or sale should be considered in determining fair market value if they influenced the price.

Unusual circumstances. Unless you can show that there were unusual circumstances, it is assumed that the increase or decrease in the value of your donated property from your cost has been at a reasonable rate. For time adjustments, an appraiser may consider published price indexes for information on general price trends, building costs, commodity costs, securities, and works of art sold at auction in arm's-length sales.

Example. Bill Brown bought a painting for $10,000. Thirteen months later he gave it to an art museum, claiming a charitable deduction of $15,000 on his tax return. The appraisal of the painting should include information showing that there were unusual circumstances that justify a

50% increase in value for the 13 months Bill held the property.

Arm's-length offer. An arm's-length offer to buy the property close to the valuation date may help to prove its value if the person making the offer was willing and able to complete the transaction. To rely on an offer, you should be able to show proof of the offer and the specific amount to be paid. Offers to buy property other than the donated item will help to determine value if the other property is reasonably similar to the donated property.

Sales of Comparable Properties

The sales prices of properties similar to the donated property are often important in determining the fair market value. The weight to be given each sale depends on the following:

The degree of similarity between the property sold and the donated property.

The time of the sale—whether it was close to the valuation date.

The circumstances of the sale—whether it was at arm's length with a knowledgeable buyer and seller, with neither having to act.

The conditions of the market in which the sale was made—whether unusually inflated or deflated.

See the discussion of the comparable sales method of valuing real estate, later, under *Valuation of Various Kinds of Property.*

Example 1. Mary Black, who is not a book dealer, paid a promoter $10,000 for 500 copies of a single edition of a modern translation of the Bible. The promoter had claimed that the price was considerably less than the "retail" price, and gave her a statement that the books had a total retail value of $30,000. The promoter advised her that if she kept the Bibles for more than one year and then gave them to a qualified organization, she could claim a charitable deduction for the "retail" price of $30,000. Thirteen months later she gave all the Bibles to a church that she selected from a list provided by the promoter. At the time of her donation, wholesale dealers were selling similar quantities of Bibles to the general public for $10,000.

The fair market value of the Bibles is $10,000, the price at which similar quantities of Bibles were being sold to others at the time of the contribution.

Example 2. Assume the same facts as in Example 1, except that the promoter gave Mary Black a second option. The promoter said that if Mary wanted a charitable deduction within one year of the purchase, she could buy the 500 Bibles at the "retail" price of $30,000, paying only $10,000 in cash and giving a promissory note for the remaining $20,000. The principal and interest on the note would not be due for 12 years. According to the promoter, Mary could then, within one year of the purchase, give the Bibles to a qualified organization and claim the full $30,000 retail price as a charitable contribution. She purchased the Bibles under the second option and, 3 months later, gave them to a church, which will use the books for church purposes.

At the time of the gift, the promoter was selling similar lots of Bibles for either $10,000 or $30,000. The difference between the two prices was solely at the discretion of the buyer. The promoter was a willing seller for $10,000. Therefore, the value of Mary's contribution of the Bibles is $10,000, the amount at which similar lots of Bibles could be purchased from the promoter by members of the general public.

Replacement Cost

The cost of buying, building, or manufacturing property similar to the donated item should be considered in determining fair market value. However, there should be a reasonable relationship between the replacement cost and the fair market value.

The replacement cost is the amount it would cost to replace the donated item on the valuation date. Often there is no relationship between the replacement cost and the fair market value. If the supply of the donated property is more or less than the demand for it, the replacement cost becomes less important.

To determine the replacement cost of the donated property, find the "estimated replacement cost new." Then subtract from this figure an amount for depreciation due to the physical condition and obsolescence of the donated property. You should be able to show the relationship between the depreciated replacement cost and the fair market value, as well as how you arrived at the "depreciated replacement cost new."

Opinions of Experts

Generally, the weight given to an expert's opinion on matters such as the authenticity of a coin or a work of art, or the most profitable and best use of a piece of real estate, depends on the knowledge and competence of the expert and the thoroughness with which the opinion is supported by experience and facts. For an expert's opinion to deserve much weight, the facts must support the opinion. For additional information, see *Appraisals,* later.

Problems in Determining Fair Market Value

There are a number of problems in determining the fair market value of donated property.

Fixed Formulas, Rules, or Methods

Determining the value of donated property would be a simple matter if the appraiser could rely only on fixed formulas, rules, or methods. Usually it is not that simple. Using such formulas, etc., seldom results in an acceptable determination of fair market value. There is no single formula that always applies when determining the value of property.

This is not to say that a valuation is only guesswork. The appraiser must consider all the facts and circumstances connected with the property, such as its desirability, use, and scarcity.

For example, donated furniture should not be evaluated at some fixed rate such as 15% of replacement cost new. When the furniture is contributed, it may be out of style or in poor condition, therefore having little or no market value. On the other hand, it may be an antique whose value could not be determined by using any formula.

Unusual Market Conditions

The sale price of the property itself in an arm's-length transaction in an open market is often the best evidence of its value. When you rely on sales of comparable property, the sales must have been made in an open market. If those sales were made in a market that was artificially supported or stimulated so as not to be truly representative, the prices at which the sales were made will not indicate the fair market value.

For example, liquidation sale prices usually do not indicate the fair market value. Also, sales of stock under unusual circumstances, such as sales of small lots, forced sales, and sales in a restricted market, may not represent the fair market value.

Careless Selection of Comparable Sales

Using sales of comparable property is an impor tant method for determining the fair market valu of donated property. However, the amount of weight given to a sale depends on the degree o similarity between the comparable and the donated properties. The degree of similarity mu be close enough so that this selling price would have been given consideration by reasonably w informed buyers or sellers of the property.

Example. You give a rare old book to your f mer college. The book is a third edition and is ir poor condition because of a missing back cove You discover that there was a sale for $300, ne the valuation date, of a first edition of the book that was in good condition. Although the conter are the same, the books are not at all similar because of the different editions and their physi condition. The selling price of the $300 property would be given little consideration by knowledge ble buyers or sellers.

Future Events

You may not consider unexpected events happening after your donation of property in making the valuation. You may consider only th facts known at the time of the gift, and those th could be reasonably expected at the time of the gift.

Example. You give farmland to a qualified charity. The transfer provides that your mother w have the right to all income and full use of the property for her life. Even though your mother d one week after the transfer, the value of the pro erty on the date it is given is its present value, subject to the life interest as estimated from act arial tables. You may not take a higher deductio because the charity received full use and possession of the land only one week after the transfer.

Using Past Events to Predict the Future

A common error is to rely too much on past events to predict future earnings and fair marke value.

Example. You give all your rights in a successful patent to your favorite charity. Your records show that before the valuation date the were three stages in the patent's history of earnings. First, there was rapid growth in earnin when the invention was introduced. Then, there was a period of high earnings when the inventio was being exploited. Finally, there was a decline earnings when competing inventions were introduced. While the entire history of earnings may relevant in estimating the future earnings, the appraiser must not rely too much on the stage o rapid growth in earnings, or of high earnings. Th market conditions at those times do not represe the condition of the market at the valuation date What is most significant is the trend of decline ir earnings up to the valuation date.

Valuation of Various Kinds of Property

This section contains information on determining the fair market value of ordinary kinds of donate property. For information on records you must keep and on appraisals, see *Recordkeeping* and *Appraisals,* later.

Household Goods

The fair market value of used household goods, such as furniture, appliances, and linens, is usua much lower than the price paid when new. Such used property may have little or no market value because of its worn condition. It may be out of style or no longer useful. For these reasons, formulas, such as 15% of the replacement cost new, are not acceptable in determining value.

You should support your valuation with photographs, cancelled checks, or receipts from your purchase of the items. Magazine or newspaper articles and photographs that describe the items and statements by the recipients of the items are also useful. None of these items needs to be included with your tax return.

If the property is valuable because it is old or unique, see the discussion under *Paintings, Antiques, and Other Objects of Art.*

Used Clothing

Used clothing and other personal items are usually worth far less than the price you paid for them. Valuation of items of clothing does not lend itself to fixed formulas or methods.

You should claim as the value the price that buyers of used items actually pay in used clothing stores, such as consignment or thrift shops.

For valuable furs or very expensive gowns, an appraisal summary may have to be sent with your tax return.

Jewelry and Gems

Jewelry and gems, other than "costume" jewelry, are of such a specialized nature that it is almost always necessary to get an appraisal by a specialized jewelry appraiser. The appraisal should describe, among other things, the style of the jewelry, the cut and setting of the gem, and whether it is now in fashion. If not in fashion, the possibility of having the property redesigned, recut or reset should be reported in the appraisal. The stone's coloring, weight, cut, brilliance, and flaws should be reported and analyzed. Sentimental personal value has no effect on fair market value. But if the jewelry was owned by a famous person, its value might increase.

Paintings, Antiques, and Other Objects of Art

Your deduction should be supported by a written appraisal from a qualified and reputable source, unless the item has a value of $500 or less. Examples of information that should be included in appraisals of art objects—paintings in particular—are found later under *Qualified Appraisal.*

Art valued at $20,000 or more. If you claim a deduction of $20,000 or more for donations of art made after 1987, you must attach a complete copy of the signed appraisal to your return. Include either a color photograph (no smaller than 8 inches × 10 inches) or a color transparency (no smaller than 4 inches × 5 inches).

The authenticity of the donated art must be determined by the appraiser. Certificates of authenticity may be useful, but this depends on the genuineness of the certificate and the qualifications of the authenticator.

Important items in the valuation of antiques and art are physical condition and extent of restoration. These have a significant effect on the value and must be fully reported in an appraisal. An antique in damaged condition, or lacking the "original brasses," may be worth much less than a similar piece in excellent condition.

Art appraisers are not experts on all art. More weight will usually be given to an appraisal prepared by an individual specializing in the kind and price range of the art being appraised. Certain art dealers or appraisers specialize, for example, in old masters, modern art, bronze sculpture, etc. Their opinions on the authenticity and desirability of such art would usually be given more weight than the opinions of more generalized art dealers or appraisers. They can report more recent comparable sales to support their opinion.

To identify and locate experts on unique, specialized items or collections, you may wish to use the current *Official Museum Directory* of the American Association of Museums. It has both a subject category and geographic index.

The *Encyclopedia of Associations,* Gale Research Company, is another useful starting point, particularly section 5, which describes educational organizations. Section 6 describes cultural organizations. Section 13 describes national hobby and avocational organizations, including various highly specialized private collector groups. It also has an alphabetical and key word index. These books may be available at state, city, college, or museum libraries.

To help you locate a qualified appraiser for your donation, you may wish to ask an art historian at a nearby college or the director or curator of a local museum. The Yellow Pages often list specialized art and antique dealers, auctioneers, and art appraisers. Associations of dealers also may be contacted for guidance.

Collections

So many kinds of hobby collections may be the subject of a charitable donation that it is not practical to discuss them all in this publication. Most common are rare books, autographs, manuscripts, stamps, coins, guns, phonograph records, and natural history items. Many of the elements of valuation that apply to paintings and other objects of art, discussed earlier, also apply to miscellaneous collections.

Reference material. Publications available to help you determine the value of many kinds of collections include catalogs, dealers' price lists, and specialized hobby periodicals. However, these sources are not always reliable indicators of fair market value.

For example, a dealer may sell an item for much less than is shown on a price list, particularly after the item has remained unsold for a long time. The price an item sold for in an auction may have been the result of a rigged sale or a mere bidding duel. The appraiser must analyze the reference material, and recognize and make adjustments for misleading entries. If you are donating a valuable collection, you should get an appraisal. If your donation appears to be of little value, you may be able to make a satisfactory valuation using reference materials available at a state, city, college, or museum library. If your local library does not have the necessary material, your librarian can often borrow it from the city or state library system.

Stamp collections. Most libraries have catalogs or other books that report the publisher's estimate of values. Generally, two price levels are shown for each stamp: the price postmarked and the price not postmarked. Stamp dealers generally know the value of their merchandise and are able to prepare satisfactory appraisals of valuable collections.

Coin collections. Many catalogs and other reference materials show the writer's or publisher's opinion of the current value of coins. Like many other collectors' items, the value of a coin depends on the demand for it, its age, and its rarity. Another important factor is the coin's condition. For example, there is a great difference in the value of a coin that is in mint condition and a similar coin that is only in good condition.

Catalogs indicate the physical condition of a coin—mint or uncirculated, extremely fine, very fine, fine, very good, good, fair, or poor—with a different valuation for each category.

Books. The value of books is usually determined by selecting comparable sales and adjusting the prices according to the differences between the comparable sales and the item being evaluated. This is difficult to do and, except for a collection of little value, should be done by a specialized appraiser. Within the general category of literary property, there are dealers who specialize in certain areas, such as Americana, foreign imports, Bibles, and scientific books.

If the collection you are donating is of modest value, not requiring a written appraisal, the following information may help you in determining the fair market value.

A book that is very old, or very rare, is not necessarily valuable. There are many books that are very old or rare, but that have little or no market value.

The condition of a book may have a great influence on its value. Collectors are interested in items that are in fine, or at least good, condition. When a book has a missing page, a loose binding, tears, stains, or is otherwise in poor condition, its value is greatly lowered.

Some other important factors in the valuation of a book are the kind of binding (leather, cloth, paper), page edges, and illustrations (drawings and photographs). Collectors usually want first editions of books. However, because of changes or additions, other editions are sometimes worth as much as, or more than, the first edition.

Manuscripts, autographs, diaries, and similar items that are handwritten, or at least signed, by famous people often are in demand and are valuable. The writings of unknowns also may be of value if they are of unusual historical or literary importance. Determining the value of such material is difficult. For example, there may be a great difference in value between two diaries that were kept by a famous person—one kept during childhood and the other during a later period in his or her life. The appraiser determines a value in these cases by applying knowledge and judgment to such factors as comparable sales and conditions.

Signatures, or sets of signatures, that were cut from letters or other papers usually have little or no value. But complete sets of the signatures of U.S. Presidents are in demand.

Cars, Boats, and Aircraft

If you donate a car, a boat, or an aircraft to a charitable organization, its fair market value must be determined.

Certain commercial firms and trade organizations publish monthly or seasonal guides for different regions of the country, containing complete dealer sale prices or dealer-average prices for recent model years. Prices are reported for each make, model, and year of used car, aircraft, truck, recreational vehicle, and boat. These guides also provide estimates for adjusting for unusual equipment, unusual mileage, and physical condition. The prices are not "official," and these publications are not considered an appraisal of any specific donated property. But they do provide clues for making an appraisal and suggest relative prices for comparison with current sales and offerings in your area.

These publications are sometimes available from the loan officer at a bank, credit union, or finance company.

Except for inexpensive small boats, the valuation of boats should be based on an appraisal by a marine surveyor because the physical condition is so critical to the value.

Example. You donate your car to a local high school for use by students studying automobile repair. Your credit union told you that the "blue book" value of the car is $1,600. However, your car needs extensive repairs and, after some checking, you find that you would not be able to sell it for more than $750. You may deduct $750, the true fair market value of the car.

Inventory

If you donate inventory (property that you hold for sale in the course of your business), the fair market value is the price that you would have received if you had sold the contributed property in the market in which you usually sell at the time and place of the contribution. For a donation of goods in quantity, the fair market value is the price for the quantity contributed. The usual market of a manufacturer or other producer is the group of wholesalers or other distributors to or through whom sales are usually made. However, if sales are made only at retail, the usual market is the retail customer.

If you donate inventory at a time when you reasonably could not expect to get its usual selling price, the value of the gift is not the usual selling price but is the amount that you could have sold the property for at the time of the contribution.

Stocks and Bonds

The value of stocks and bonds is the fair market value of a share or bond on the valuation date. See *Date of contribution,* earlier, under *What Is Fair Market Value?*

Based on selling prices. If there is an active market for the contributed stocks or bonds on a stock exchange, in an over-the-counter market, or elsewhere, the fair market value of each share or bond is the mean of the highest and lowest quoted selling prices on the valuation date. For example, if the highest selling price for a share was $11, and the lowest $9, the mean is $10 (($11 + $9) ÷ 2).

If there were no sales on the valuation date, but there were sales within a reasonable period before and after the valuation date, the fair market value is determined by taking a weighted average of the means between the highest and lowest sales prices on the nearest date before and the nearest date after the valuation date. The average is to be weighted in ***inverse*** order by the respective number of trading days between the selling dates and the valuation date.

Example. On the day you gave stock to a qualified organization, there were no sales of the stock. Sales of the stock nearest the valuation date took place two trading days before the valuation date at a mean selling price of $10 and three trading days after the valuation date at a mean selling price of $15. The fair market value on the valuation date was $12, figured as follows:

$$[(3 \times \$10) + (2 \times \$15)] \div 5 = \$12$$

Stocks or bonds listed on more than one stock exchange are valued based on the prices of the exchange where they are principally dealt in. If these prices are not published in a generally available listing or publication of general circulation, and the stocks or bonds are reported on a composite listing of combined exchanges in a publication of general circulation, the composite list is used. See also *Unavailable prices or closely held corporation,* later.

Based on bid and asked prices. If there were no actual sales within a reasonable period before and after the valuation date, the fair market value is the mean between the bona fide bid and asked prices on the valuation date. If there were no prices available, the value may be determined by taking a weighted average of the means between the bona fide bid and asked prices on the closest trading date before and after the valuation date. Both dates must be within a reasonable period. The average should be weighted in ***inverse*** order by the respective number of trading days between the bid and asked dates and the valuation date.

Example. Although there were no sales of Blue Corporation stock on the valuation date, bona fide bid and asked prices were available on that date of $14 and $16, respectively. The fair market value is $15, the mean between the bid and asked prices.

If no actual selling prices or bona fide bid and asked prices are available on a date within a reasonable period before the valuation date, but are available on a date within a reasonable period after the valuation date, or vice versa, then the mean between the highest and lowest of such available prices may be treated as the value.

Large blocks of stock. When a large block of stock is put on the market, it may lower the selling price of the stock if the supply is greater than the demand. On the other hand, market forces may exist that will afford higher prices for large blocks of stock. Because of the many factors to be considered, determining the value of large blocks of stock usually requires the help of experts specializing in underwriting large quantities of securities, or in trading in the securities of the industry of which the particular company is a part.

Unavailable prices or closely held corporation. If selling prices or bid and asked prices are not available, or if securities of a closely held corporation are involved, the fair market value is to be determined by taking into consideration the following factors:

For bonds, the soundness of the security, the interest yield, the date of maturity, and other relevant factors.

For shares of stock, the company's net worth, prospective earning power and dividend-paying capacity, and other relevant factors.

Other relevant factors include the goodwill of the business, the economic outlook in the particular industry, the company's position in the industry, and the value of securities of corporations engaged in the same or similar business. For preferred stock, the most important factors are its yield and dividend coverage, and protection of its liquidation preference.

You should keep complete financial and other information on which the valuation is based, including copies of reports of examinations of the company made by accountants, engineers, or any technical experts on or close to the valuation date.

Restricted securities. Some classes of stock cannot be traded publicly because of restrictions imposed by the Securities and Exchange Commission, or by the corporate charter or a trust agreement. These restricted securities usually are traded at a discount in relation to freely traded securities.

To arrive at the fair market value of restricted securities, factors that must be considered include the resale provisions found in the restriction agreements, the relative negotiating strengths of the buyer and seller, and the market experience of freely traded securities of the same class as the restricted securities.

Real Estate

Because each piece of real estate is unique and its valuation is complicated, a detailed appraisal by a professional appraiser is necessary.

The appraiser must be thoroughly trained in the application of appraisal principles and theory. In some instances the opinions of equally qualified appraisers may carry unequal weight, such as when one appraiser has a better knowledge of local conditions.

The appraisal report must contain a complete description of the property, such as street address, legal description, and lot and block number, as well as physical features, condition, and dimensions. The use to which the property is put, zoning and permitted uses, and its potential use for other higher and better uses are also relevant.

In general, there are three main approaches to the valuation of real estate. An appraisal may require the combined use of two or three methods rather than one method only.

1. Comparable Sales

The comparable sales method compares the donated property with several similar properties that have been sold. The selling prices, after adjustments for differences in date of sale, size, condition, and location, would then indicate the estimated fair market value of the donated property.

If the comparable sales method is used to determine the value of ***unimproved real property*** (land without significant buildings, structures, or any other improvements that add to its value), the appraiser should consider the following factors when comparing the potential comparable property and the donated property:

Location, size, and zoning or use restrictions,

Accessibility and road frontage, and available utilities and water rights,

Riparian rights (right of access to and use of the water by owners of land on the bank of a river) and existing easements, rights-of-way, leases, etc.,

Soil characteristics, vegetative cover, and status of mineral rights, and

Other factors affecting value.

For each comparable sale, the appraisal must include the names of the buyer and seller, the deed book and page number, the date of sale and selling price, a property description, the amount and terms of mortgages, property surveys, the assessed value, the tax rate, and the assessor's appraised fair market value.

The comparable selling prices must be adjusted to account for differences between the sale property and the donated property. Because differences of opinion may arise between appraisers as to the degree of comparability and the amount of the adjustment considered necessary for comparison purposes, an appraiser should document each item of adjustment.

Only comparable sales having the least adjustments in terms of items and/or total dollar adjustments should be considered as comparable to the donated property.

2. Capitalization of Income

This method capitalizes the net income from the property at a rate that represents a fair return on the particular investment at the particular time, considering the risks involved. The key elements are the determination of the income to be capitalized and the rate of capitalization.

3. Replacement Cost New or Reproduction Cost Minus Observed Depreciation

This method, used alone, usually does not result in a determination of fair market value. Instead, it generally tends to set the upper limit of value, particularly in periods of rising costs, because it is reasonable to assume that an informed buyer will not pay more for the real estate than it would cost to reproduce a similar property. Of course, this reasoning does not apply if a similar property cannot be created because of location, unusual construction, or some other reason. Generally, this method serves to support the value determined from other methods. When the replacement cost method is applied to ***improved realty,*** the land and improvements are valued separately.

The replacement cost of a building is figured by considering the materials, the quality of workmanship, and the number of square feet or cubic feet in the building. This cost represents the total cost of labor and material, overhead, and profit. After e replacement cost has been figured, considera- on must be given to the following factors:

Physical deterioration—the wear and tear on the building itself,

Functional obsolescence—usually in older buildings with, for example, inadequate lighting, plumbing, or heating, small rooms, or a poor floor plan, and

Economic obsolescence—outside forces causing the whole area to become less desirable.

nterest in a Business

he fair market value of any interest in a business, whether a sole proprietorship or a partnership, is he amount that a willing buyer would pay for the nterest of a willing seller after consideration of all elevant factors. The relevant factors to be considred in valuing the business are:

The fair market value of the assets of the business,

The prospective earning capacity of the business, based on a review of past and current earnings, and

The other factors used in evaluating corporate stock, if they apply.

The value of the goodwill of the business should also be taken into consideration. You should keep complete financial and other information on which he valuation is based. This includes copies of eports of examinations of the business made by accountants, engineers, or any technical experts on or close to the valuation date.

Annuities, Terms for Years, Remainders, and Reversions

The value of these kinds of property is their present value, except in the case of annuities under contracts issued by companies regularly engaged in their sale. The valuation of these commercial annuity contracts and of insurance policies is discussed later under *Certain Life Insurance and Annuity Contracts.*

Actuarial tables. It is usually necessary to refer to actuarial tables to determine your charitable deduction when annuities, income from trust property, or remainder interests are transferred to a charitable organization.

Transfers before May 1, 1989. The present value of an annuity, remainder (other than those specified), or reversion that is dependent on the continuation or termination of the life of one person is figured by the use of Table A in section 20.2031-7 of the Estate Tax Regulations. The present value of an annuity, term for years, remainder, or reversion that is dependent on a term certain (definite number of years) is figured by the use of Table B in the above regulations.

The value of a remainder interest in a charitable remainder annuity trust is determined under section 1.664-2 of the Income Tax Regulations. The value of a remainder interest in a charitable remainder unitrust is determined under section 1.664-4 of the Regulations. The value of a remainder interest in a pooled income fund is determined under section 1.642(c)-6 of the Regulations.

If the valuation of the interest depends on the continuation or termination of more than one life, or on a term certain concurrent with one or more lives, a special factor must be used. Many of these factors may be found in, or can be figured with the use of, IRS Publications 723C, 723D, and 723E.

Transfers after April 30, 1989. For gifts and certain other transfers after April 30, 1989, use the valuation tables set forth in IRS Publications 1457 (Alpha Volume), and 1458 (Beta Volume). Publications 1457 and 1458 provide tables containing actuarial factors to be used in determining the present value of an annuity, an interest for life or for a term of years, or a remainder or reversionary interest. Actuarial factors for computing the value of a remainder interest in a charitable remainder annuity trust, a charitable remainder unitrust, and a pooled income fund may be found in Publications 1457 and 1458. The publications containing the complete set of tables are available for purchase from the:

Superintendent of Documents
United States Government Printing Office
Washington, D.C. 20404.

Special factors. If a special factor is needed for an actual transaction, you may ask for it by writing to the:

Internal Revenue Service
Attention: E:EP:R
P.O. Box 14073, Ben Franklin Station
Washington, D.C. 20044.

Be sure to include the date of birth of each person, the duration of whose life may affect the value of the interest, and copies of the relevant instruments. IRS is required to charge a user fee for providing special factors.

For information on the circumstances under which a charitable deduction may be allowed for the donation of a partial interest in property, see *Partial Interest in Property,* later.

Certain Life Insurance and Annuity Contracts

The value of an annuity contract or a life insurance policy issued by a company regularly engaged in the sale of such contracts or policies is the amount that company would charge for a comparable contract.

But if the donee of a life insurance policy may reasonably be expected to cash the policy rather than hold it as an investment, then the fair market value is the cash surrender value rather than the replacement cost.

If an annuity is payable under a combination annuity contract and life insurance policy (for example, a retirement income policy with a death benefit) and there was no insurance element when it was transferred to the charity, the policy is treated as an annuity contract.

Personal Services

You may not deduct the value of the ***time*** or ***services*** that you contribute to a qualified organization. For example, if you are a carpenter, you may not deduct the value of the time or services you give to make repairs on a church. Lawyers, doctors, mechanics, artists, etc., may not deduct the value of their donated time or services.

However, you may deduct unreimbursed ***out-of-pocket expenses*** you pay in giving services to a charitable organization. These include amounts you pay for transportation from your home to the place where you serve. Also, if you use your car, expenses directly related to services you give to the charitable organization, such as gas and oil, are deductible. If you do not deduct the actual car expenses incurred, you may deduct a standard mileage rate of ***12 cents a mile.***

For more information on out-of-pocket expenses that qualify for a charitable contributions deduction, see Publication 526.

Partial Interest in Property

Generally, no deduction is allowed for a charitable contribution, not made in trust, of less than your entire interest in property. However, this does not apply to a transfer of less than your entire interest if it is a transfer of:

A remainder interest in your personal residence or farm,

An undivided part of your entire interest in property, or

A qualified conservation contribution.

Valuation of a remainder interest in real property, not transferred in trust. The amount of the deduction for a donation of a remainder interest in real property is the fair market value of the remainder interest at the time of the contribution. Depreciation (figured by the straight-line method) and depletion (figured by the cost-depletion method) must be considered in determining the fair market value. This value must be reduced at the rate of 10% a year, or at some other rate set by the government.

If the remainder interest includes both depreciable and nondepreciable property, for example a house and land, the fair market value must be allocated between each kind of property at the time of the contribution. This rule also applies to a gift of a remainder interest that includes a property that is part depletable and part not depletable. Depreciation or depletion will be taken into account only for the property that is subject to depreciation or depletion.

To figure the value of a remainder interest in real property, see section 1.170A-12 of the Income Tax Regulations.

Undivided part of your entire interest. A contribution of an undivided part of your entire interest in property must consist of a part of each and every substantial interest or right you own in the property and must extend over the entire term of your interest in the property. For example, if you are entitled to the income from certain property for your life (life estate) and you contribute 20% of that life estate to a qualified organization, you can claim a deduction for the contribution if you do not have any other interest in the property. To figure the value of a contribution involving a life estate, see section 20.2031-7 of the Estate Tax Regulations.

If the only interest you own in property is a remainder interest and you transfer part of that interest to a qualified organization, see section 1.170A-12 of the Income Tax Regulations for determining the value.

Qualified conservation contribution. A qualified conservation contribution is a contribution of a qualified real property interest to a qualified organization to be used only for a conservation purpose.

Qualified organization. For purposes of a qualified conservation contribution, a qualified organization is:

1) A governmental unit.
2) A publicly supported charitable, religious, scientific, literary, educational, etc., organization.
3) An organization that is controlled by, and operated for the exclusive benefit of, a governmental unit or a publicly supported charity.

Conservation purposes. Your contribution must be made only for one of the following conservation purposes:

1) Preservation of land areas for outdoor recreation by, or for the education of, the general public.
2) Protection of a natural fish, wildlife, or plant habitat.
3) Preservation of open space, including farmland and forest land. The preservation must

yield a significant public benefit and be either for the scenic enjoyment of the general public or under a clearly defined federal, state, or local governmental conservation policy.

4) Preservation of a historically important land area or a certified historic structure. A historically important land area includes independently significant land areas and historic sites and related land areas, the physical or environmental features of which contribute to the historic or cultural importance and continuing integrity of certified historic structures. A certified historic structure is any building, structure, or land area that is listed in the National Register, or is located in a registered historic district and is certified by the Secretary of the Interior as being of historic significance to the district.

A qualified real property interest is any of the following interests in real property:

1) Your entire interest in real estate other than a mineral interest (subsurface oil, gas, or other minerals, and the right of access to these minerals).
2) A remainder interest.
3) A restriction (granted in perpetuity, that is, granted forever) on how the property may be used.

Valuation. A qualified real property interest described in (1) should be valued in a manner that is consistent with the type of interest transferred. If you owned all the interest in the property, the fair market value of the entire property less the fair market value of any mineral interest you keep is the amount of the contribution. If you owned only a remainder interest or an income interest (life estate), or if you transferred a remainder interest (item (2)), the value should be determined as previously discussed in this section.

In determining the value of restrictions, you should take into account the selling price, in arm's-length transactions, of other properties that have comparable restrictions. If there are no qualified sales, the restrictions are valued indirectly as the difference between the fair market values of the property involved before and after the grant of the restriction.

The fair market value of the property before contribution of the restriction should take into account not only current use but the likelihood that the property, without the restriction, would be developed. You should also consider any zoning, conservation, or historical preservation laws that would restrict development. The granting of an easement may increase, rather than reduce, the value of property, and in such a situation no deduction would be allowed.

Example. You own 10 acres of farmland. Similar land in the area has a fair market value of $2,000 an acre. However, land in the general area that is restricted solely to farm use has a fair market value of $1,500 an acre. Your county wants to preserve open space and prevent further development in your area.

You grant to the county an enforceable open space easement in perpetuity on 8 of the 10 acres, restricting its use to farmland. The value of this easement is $4,000, determined as follows:

Fair market value of the property before granting easement:		
$2,000 × 10 acres		$20,000
Fair market value of the property after granting easement:		
$1,500 × 8 acres	$12,000	
$2,000 × 2 acres	4,000	16,000
Value of easement		$ 4,000

If you later transfer in fee your remaining interest in the 8 acres to another qualified organization, you must consider the easement in determining the fair market value of the remaining interest.

Note: Granting an easement on part of your property can affect the value of your remaining property.

Recordkeeping

If you make charitable contributions, you must keep certain records. Information from these records is needed to substantiate deductions claimed on your tax return. The information is also needed to complete Form 8283, *Noncash Charitable Contributions,* which must be attached to your tax return if the total claimed deduction for contributed property is more than $500. The following discusses the records that you must keep and certain other substantiation requirements for contributions of property other than money. For other information on recordkeeping, see Publication 526.

Receipts. If you claim a deduction of $5,000 or less for a charitable contribution of property other than money, you must maintain for each contribution a receipt from the donee organization showing the following information:

The name of the donee,

The date and location of the contribution, and

A description of the property in detail reasonably sufficient under the circumstances. One of the circumstances to be taken into account is the fair market value of the property. Therefore, the greater the value, the more detail that is needed.

A letter or other written communication from the donee organization acknowledging receipt of the contribution, showing the date of the contribution, and containing a sufficiently detailed description of the property contributed is considered a receipt. A receipt is not required if the contribution is made in circumstances where it is impractical to obtain a receipt, for example, if the property is deposited at a charity's unattended drop site.

Written Records

In all cases you must keep reliable written records covering each item of donated property. These records must include the following information:

1) The name and address of the donee organization to which the contribution was made.
2) The date and location of the contribution.
3) A description of the property in detail reasonably sufficient under the circumstances. One of the circumstances to be taken into account is the fair market value of the property. Therefore, the greater the value, the more detail that is needed. For securities, include the name of the issuer, the type of security, and whether the security is regularly traded on a stock exchange or in an over-the-counter market.
4) The fair market value of the property at the time the contribution was made, the method used in determining the fair market value and, if an appraisal was used, a copy of the signed report of the appraiser.
5) For contributions of appreciated property, the cost or adjusted basis of the property, the reduction for the ordinary income and long-term capital gain amounts, and the manner of determining the reductions.
6) For contributions of less than your entire interest in the property, the total amount claimed as a deduction for the tax year due to the contribution of the property, the amount claimed in prior years for contributions of other interests in the property, the name and address of each organization to which any such contribution was made, the place where any such tangible property is located or kept, and the name of any person, other than the donee organization, having actual possession of the property.
7) The terms of any agreement or understanding entered into by or on your behalf that relates to the use, sale, or other disposition of the property. This includes, for example, agreements that (a) restrict temporarily or permanently the right of the organization to use or dispose of the property, (b) reserve to, or confer upon, anyone other than the organization any right to the income from or possession of the property, including the right to vote donated securities, to acquire the property by purchase or otherwise, or to designate the person having such income, possession, or right to acquire, or (c) earmark donated property for a particular use.
8) For a qualified conservation contribution, the fair market value of the underlying property before and after the contribution and the conservation purpose furthered by the contribution.

Your written records must be reliable. Factors indicating that the written records are reliable include, but are not limited to:

- The contemporaneous nature of the writing evidencing the contribution.
- The regularity of your recordkeeping procedures. For example, if you regularly make contemporaneous diary entries stating the amount and date of the donation and the name of the donee organization, your diary would generally be considered a reliable written record.
- For a contribution of a small amount, the existence of any written or other evidence from the donee organization showing receipt of a donation, but not meeting the requirements of a receipt as discussed earlier. This evidence includes emblems, buttons, or other tokens traditionally associated with a charitable organization and regularly given by the organization to persons making cash donations.

Deductions of more than $500. If you make a charitable contribution of property other than money and claim a deduction of more than $500 for the contribution of that item, your written records must include the following information in addition to the eight items listed previously:

1) The manner of acquisition, such as by purchase, gift, bequest, inheritance, or exchange.
2) The approximate date you acquired the property or, if the property was created, produced, or manufactured by or for you, the approximate date the property was substantially completed.
3) The cost or adjusted basis of the property, other than publicly traded securities, held by you for a period of less than 12 months immediately preceding the date the contribution was made. When available, this information should also be shown for property held for a period of 12 months or more preceding the date the contribution was made.

Form 8283 must be completed and attached to your tax return if you claim a noncash charitable contribution deduction of more than $500.

eductions of More han $5,000

enerally, if the claimed deduction for an item or oup of similar items of donated property is more an $5,000, you must get a qualified appraisal ade by a qualified appraiser, and you must ach an appraisal summary (Section B of Form 83) to your tax return. See *Appraisals,* later. You ould keep the appraiser's report with your itten records, described earlier. For special rules at apply to publicly traded securities and non- blicly traded stock, see the discussions later in is section.

The phrase ***similar items*** means property of the me generic category or type (whether or not nated to the same donee), such as stamps, ins, lithographs, paintings, photographs, books, npublicly traded stock, nonpublicly traded curities other than nonpublicly traded stock, nd, buildings, clothing, jewelry, furniture, elec- onic equipment, household appliances, toys, eryday kitchenware, china, crystal, or silver. For ample, if you give books to three schools and u deduct $2,000, $2,500, and $900, respec- ely, your claimed deduction is more than $5,000 r these books. You must get a qualified praisal of the books and for each school you ust attach a fully completed appraisal summary ection B of Form 8283) to your tax return.

ublicly traded securities. Neither a qualified praisal nor an appraisal summary is required for blicly traded securities that are either:

- Listed on a stock exchange in which quotations are published on a daily basis, or
- Regularly traded in a national or regional over-the-counter market for which published quota-tions are available.

A partially completed appraisal summary (Parts I nd II of Section B, Form 8283), but not a qualified ppraisal, is required for publicly traded securities at do not meet either of those requirements, but at meet the following five requirements:

1) The issue is regularly traded during the com-putation period in a market for which there is an interdealer quotation system,
2) The issuer or agent computes the "average trading price" for the same issue for the com-putation period,
3) The average trading price and total volume of the issue during the computation period are published in a newspaper of general circulation not later than the last day of the month following the end of the calendar quar-ter in which the computation period ends,
4) The issuer or agent keeps books and records that list for each transaction the date of settlement of the transaction, the name and address of the broker or dealer making the market in which the transaction occurred, and the trading price and volume, and
5) The issuer or agent permits the Internal Reve-nue Service to review the books and records described in paragraph (4) with respect to transactions during the computation period upon receiving reasonable notice.

An ***interdealer quotation system*** is any system of general circulation to brokers and deal-ers that regularly disseminates quotations of obligations by two or more identified brokers or dealers who are not related to either the issuer or agent who computes the average trading price of the security. A quotation sheet prepared and dis-tributed by a broker or dealer in the regular course of business and containing only quotations of that broker or dealer is not an interdealer quotation system.

The ***average trading price*** is the mean price of all transactions (weighted by volume), other than original issue or redemption transactions, con-ducted through a United States office of a broker or dealer who maintains a market in the issue of the security during the computation period. Bid and asked quotations are not taken into account.

The ***computation period*** is weekly during October through December and monthly during January through September. The weekly computa-tion periods during October through December begin with the first Monday in October and end with the first Sunday following the last Monday in December.

Nonpublicly traded stock. If you contribute nonpublicly traded stock, for which you claim a deduction of more than $5,000 but not more than $10,000, a qualified appraisal is not required. However, you must attach a partially completed appraisal summary (Parts I and II of Section B, Form 8283) to your tax return.

Appraisals

Appraisals are not always necessary, particularly for items of property valued at $500 or less, or for which the value can easily be determined, such as securities whose prices are reported daily in the newspapers. However, you generally will need an appraisal for donated property with a value of more than $5,000. See *Qualified Appraisal,* next.

The weight given an appraisal depends on the completeness of the report, the qualifications of the appraiser, and the appraiser's demonstrated knowledge of the donated property. An appraisal must give all the facts on which to base an intelli-gent judgment of the value of the property.

The appraisal will not be given much weight if:

- All the factors that apply are not considered,
- The opinion is not supported with facts, such as purchase cost and comparable sales, or
- The opinion is not consistent with known facts.

The appraiser's opinion is never more valid than the facts on which it is based; without these facts it is simply a guess.

Membership in professional appraisal or dealer organizations does not automatically establish the appraiser's competency. Nor does the lack of cer-tificates, memberships, etc., automatically disprove the competency of the appraiser.

The opinion of a person claiming to be an expert is not binding on the Internal Revenue Service. All facts associated with the donation must be considered.

Cost of appraisals. You may not take a charita-ble contribution deduction for fees you pay for appraisals of your donated property. However, they may qualify as a miscellaneous deduction, subject to the 2% limit, on Schedule A (Form 1040) if they were paid to determine the amount allowable as a charitable contribution.

Qualified Appraisal

Generally, if the claimed deduction for an item of donated property is more than $5,000, you must get a qualified appraisal made by a qualified appraiser and you must attach an appraisal summary to your tax return. See *Deductions of More Than $5,000,* under *Recordkeeping,* earlier.

A qualified appraisal is an appraisal document that:

- Relates to an appraisal made not earlier than 60 days prior to the date of contribution of the appraised property,
- Does not involve a prohibited appraisal fee,
- Includes certain information (covered later), and
- Is prepared, signed, and dated by a qualified appraiser (defined later).

You must receive the qualified appraisal before the due date, including extensions, of the return on which a charitable contribution deduction is first claimed for the donated property. If the deduction is first claimed on an amended return, the qualified appraisal must be received before the date on which the return is filed.

An appraisal summary (discussed later) must be attached to your tax return. Generally, you do not need to attach the qualified appraisal itself, but you should keep a copy as long as it may be rele-vant under the tax law. If you donated art valued at $20,000 or more, however, you may have to attach the complete appraisal. See *Paintings, Antiques, and Other Objects of Art,* discussed ear-lier under *Valuation of Various Kinds of Property.*

Prohibited appraisal fee. No part of the fee arrangement for a qualified appraisal can be based on a percentage of the appraised value of the property. (If a fee arrangement is based on what is allowed as a deduction, after Internal Rev-enue Service examination or otherwise, it is treated as a fee based on a percentage of appraised value.) However, this rule does not apply to a fee paid to a generally recognized asso-ciation that regulates appraisers if:

- The association is not organized for profit and no part of the net earnings benefits any private shareholder or individual,
- The appraiser does not receive any compensation from the association or any other persons for making the appraisal, and
- The fee arrangement is not based in whole or in part on the amount of the appraised value that is allowed as a deduction after an Inter-nal Revenue Service examination or other-wise.

Information included in qualified appraisal. A qualified appraisal must include the following information:

1) A description of the property in sufficient detail for a person who is not generally famil-iar with the type of property to determine that the property appraised is the property that was (or will be) contributed,
2) The physical condition of any tangible property,
3) The date (or expected date) of contribution,
4) The terms of any agreement or understanding entered into (or expected to be entered into) by or on behalf of the donor (see item 7 of *Written Records,* earlier, under *Recordkeeping*),
5) The name, address, and taxpayer identifica-tion number of the qualified appraiser and, if the appraiser is a partner, an employee, or an independent contractor engaged by a person other than the donor, the name, address, and taxpayer identification number of the partner-ship or the person who employs or engages the appraiser,
6) The qualifications of the qualified appraiser who signs the appraisal, including the appraiser's background, experience, educa-tion, and any membership in professional appraisal associations,
7) A statement that the appraisal was prepared for income tax purposes,
8) The date (or dates) on which the property was valued,
9) The appraised fair market value on the date (or expected date) of contribution,
10) The method of valuation used to determine fair market value, such as the income approach, the comparable sales or market data approach, or the replacement cost less depreciation approach,
11) The specific basis for the valuation, such as any specific comparable sales transaction, and
12) A description of the fee arrangement between the donor and appraiser.

Examples of information that should be included in a description of donated property follow. These examples are for art objects, but the same kind of detailed information may be given for other property. Appraisals of art objects—paintings in particular—should include:

1) A complete description of the object, indicating the size, the subject matter, the medium, the name of the artist, and the approximate date created.
2) A history of the ownership and public exhibitions of the item, including such proof of authenticity as a certificate of authenticity and citations in literature.
3) A photograph of a size and quality fully showing the object, preferably an 8 inch × 10 inch color print, or a color transparency no smaller than 4 inches × 5 inches.
4) The facts on which the appraisal was based, such as:

   Sales or analyses of similar works by the artist, particularly on or around the valuation date,

   For a living artist, prices in dealers' catalogs of the artist's works, and

   The state of the art market at the time of valuation, particularly with respect to the specific artist, school, or price range.

A separate qualified appraisal is required for each item of property that is not included in a group of similar items of property. You need only one qualified appraisal for a group of similar items of property contributed in the same tax year, but you may get separate appraisals for each item. A qualified appraisal for a group of similar items must provide all of the required information for each item of similar property. The appraiser, however, may provide a group description for selected items whose total value is not more than $100.

Qualified appraiser. A qualified appraiser is an individual who declares on the appraisal summary that he or she:

Holds himself or herself out to the public as an appraiser or performs appraisals on a regular basis,

Is qualified to make appraisals of the type of property being valued,

Is not an excluded individual, and

Understands the penalty for aiding and abetting an understatement of tax liability.

An appraiser must complete Part IV of Section B (Form 8283) to be considered a qualified appraiser. More than one appraiser may appraise the property, provided that each complies with the requirements, including signing the qualified appraisal and appraisal summary.

Excluded individuals. The following persons cannot be qualified appraisers with respect to particular property:

1) The donor of the property.
2) The donee of the property.
3) A party to the transaction in which the donor acquired the property being appraised, unless the property is donated within 2 months of the date of acquisition and its appraised value does not exceed its acquisition price. This applies to the person who sold, exchanged, or gave the property to the donor, or any person who acted as an agent for the transferor or donor in the transaction.
4) Any person employed by, or related (or, for appraisals made after June 6, 1988, married to a person who is related) under section 267(b) of the Internal Revenue Code, to any of the above persons. For example, if the donor acquired a painting from an art dealer, neither the dealer nor persons employed by the dealer can be qualified appraisers for that painting.
5) An appraiser who is regularly used by a person in (1), (2), or (3), and who does not perform a majority of his or her appraisals made during his or her tax year for other persons.

In addition, a person is not a qualified appraiser for a particular donation if the donor had knowledge of facts that would cause a reasonable person to expect the appraiser to falsely overstate the value of the donated property. For example, if a donor makes an agreement with the appraiser that the property will be valued at more than its fair market value, the appraiser is not a qualified appraiser for the donation.

Penalties. Any appraiser who falsely or fraudulently overstates the value of property described in a qualified appraisal or an appraisal summary that the appraiser has signed may be subject to a civil penalty for aiding and abetting an understatement of tax liability, and may have his or her appraisals disregarded.

Appraisal Summary

Generally, if the claimed deduction for an item of donated property is more than $5,000, you must attach an appraisal summary to your tax return. Only a partially completed appraisal summary is required in some situations. See *Deductions of More Than $5,000* under *Recordkeeping,* earlier.

Note: If you deduct $20,000 or more for donated art, you may have to attach the complete appraisal. See *Paintings, Antiques, and Other Objects of Art,* discussed earlier under *Valuation of Various Kinds of Property.*

Form 8283. Section B of Form 8283 is the appraisal summary. You must complete and attach the form to your return. If you fail to attach the form, the deduction will not be allowed unless your failure was due to a good faith omission. If the IRS requests that you submit the form because you did not attach it to your return, you must comply within 90 days of the request or the deduction will be disallowed.

A separate Form 8283 for each item of contributed property must be attached to the return. If you contribute similar items of property to the same donee organization, you need attach only one Form 8283 for those items. If you contribute similar items of property to more than one donee organization, you must attach a separate form for each donee.

The following is a brief description of the appraisal summary. See the Form 8283 instructions for more information.

Part I, Donee Acknowledgement, is completed by the charitable organization. This part must be signed by an official authorized to sign the tax or information returns of the donee organization, or by a person authorized by such an official to sign Form 8283. The signature does not indicate agreement with the appraised value of the property. It represents acknowledgement of receipt of the property on the date specified on the form. It also acknowledges that the organization understands its information reporting requirements if it disposes of the property in any way within 2 years after the date of receipt. In this situation, the organization usually must file Form 8282, *Donee Information Return,* and send you a copy of that form.

However, the donee is not required to report the disposition of a charitable deduction property if the appraisal summary signed by the donee contains, at the time of the donee's signature, a statement signed by the donor that the appraised value of an item does not exceed $500. If the appraisal summary includes more than one item, the reporting exception applies only to the item clearly identified as having a value of $500 or less.

The donee is also not required to report the disposition of a charitable deduction property if the donee consumes or distributes the item without payment for a purpose or function which is a basis for its charitable exemption. For example, no reporting is required for medical supplies consumed or distributed by a tax-exempt relief organization in aiding disaster victims.

After completing Part I of Section B (Form 8283), the donee organization will return the form to you.

Part II, Information on Donated Property, is completed by you or the appraiser. The information needed for this part should come from the qualified appraisal and your written records.

Part III, Taxpayer (Donor) Statement. If you complete Part III, the donee is relieved of filing Form 8282, *Donee Information Return,* for items having a value of $500 or less.

Part IV, Certification of Appraiser, is completed by the appraiser of the property. This section must be completed for the appraiser to be considered a qualified appraiser.

Internal Revenue Service Review of Appraisals

In reviewing an income tax return, the Service may accept the claimed value of the donated property, based on information or appraisals sent with the return, or may make its own determination of fair market value. In either case, the Service may:

Contact the taxpayer to get more information,

Refer the valuation problem to a Service appraiser or valuation specialist,

Refer the issue to the Commissioner's Art Advisory Panel (a 12-member group of dealers and museum directors who review and recommend acceptance or adjustment of taxpayers' claimed values for major paintings, sculptures, or antiques), or

Contract with an independent dealer, scholar, or appraiser to appraise the property when the objects require appraisers of highly specialized experience and knowledge.

The Service is responsible for reviewing appraisals, but it is not responsible for making them. Supporting the fair market value listed on your return is your responsibility.

The Service does not give recognition to any appraiser or organization of appraisers and does not accept their appraisals without question.

The Service does not approve valuations or appraisals before the actual filing of the tax return to which the appraisal applies. In addition, the Service does not issue advance rulings approving or disapproving such appraisals.

Form **6251**

Department of the Treasury
Internal Revenue Service

Alternative Minimum Tax—Individuals

► See separate Instructions.

► Attach to Form 1040 or Form 1040NR. Estates and trusts, use Form 8656.

OMB No. 1545-0227

1990

Attachment Sequence No. **32**

Name(s) shown on Form 1040 | Your social security number

1	Taxable income from Form 1040, line 37. (If Form 1040, line 37 is zero, see Instructions.)		1	
2	Net operating loss deduction, if any, from Form 1040, line 22. (Enter as a positive amount.)		2	
3	Combine lines 1 and 2		3	
4	**Adjustments:** (See Instructions before completing.)			
a	Standard deduction, if any, from Form 1040, line 34	4a		
b	Personal exemption amount from Form 1040, line 36	4b		
c	Medical and dental expenses	4c		
d	Miscellaneous itemized deductions from Schedule A (Form 1040), line 25	4d		
e	Taxes from Schedule A (Form 1040), line 8	4e		
f	Refund of taxes	4f ( )		
g	Personal interest from Schedule A (Form 1040), line 12b	4g		
h	Other interest adjustments	4h		
i	Reserved	4i		
j	Depreciation of tangible property placed in service after 1986	4j		
k	Circulation and research and experimental expenditures paid or incurred after 1986	4k		
l	Mining exploration and development costs paid or incurred after 1986	4l		
m	Long-term contracts entered into after 2/28/86	4m		
n	Pollution control facilities placed in service after 1986	4n		
o	Installment sales of certain property	4o		
p	Adjusted gain or loss	4p		
q	Certain loss limitations	4q		
r	Tax shelter farm loss	4r		
s	Passive activity loss	4s		
t	Beneficiaries of estates and trusts	4t		
u	Combine lines 4a through 4t		4u	
5	**Tax preference items:** (See Instructions before completing.)			
a	Appreciated property charitable deduction	5a		
b	Tax-exempt interest from private activity bonds issued after 8/7/86	5b		
c	Depletion	5c		
d	Accelerated depreciation of real property placed in service before 1987	5d		
e	Accelerated depreciation of leased personal property placed in service before 1987	5e		
f	Amortization of certified pollution control facilities placed in service before 1987	5f		
g	Intangible drilling costs	5g		
h	Add lines 5a through 5g		5h	
6	Combine lines 3, 4u, and 5h		6	
7	Alternative tax net operating loss deduction. (Do not enter more than 90% of line 6.) See Instructions		7	
8	Alternative minimum taxable income. Subtract line 7 from line 6. If married filing a separate return, see Instructions		8	
9	Enter: $40,000 ($20,000 if married filing separately; $30,000 if single or head of household)		9	
10	Enter: $150,000 ($75,000 if married filing separately; $112,500 if single or head of household)		10	
11	Subtract line 10 from line 8. If zero or less, enter -0- here and on line 12 and go to line 13		11	
12	Multiply line 11 by 25% (.25)		12	
13	Subtract line 12 from line 9. If zero or less, enter -0-. If completing this form for a child under age 14, see Instructions for amount to enter		13	
14	Subtract line 13 from line 8. If zero or less, enter -0- here and on line 19 and skip lines 15 through 18		14	
15	Multiply line 14 by 21% (.21)		15	
16	Alternative minimum tax foreign tax credit. See Instructions		16	
17	Tentative minimum tax. Subtract line 16 from line 15		17	
18	Enter your tax from Form 1040, line 38, minus any foreign tax credit on Form 1040, line 43. If an amount is entered on line 39 of Form 1040, see Instructions		18	
19	**Alternative minimum tax.** Subtract line 18 from line 17. If zero or less, enter -0-. Enter this amount on Form 1040, line 49. If completing this form for a child under age 14, see Instructions for amount to enter		19	

For Paperwork Reduction Act Notice, see separate Instructions.

★U.S.GPO:1990-0-265-372

1990

Department of the Treasury
Internal Revenue Service

Instructions for Form 6251

Alternative Minimum Tax—Individuals

(Section references are to the Internal Revenue Code.)

Paperwork Reduction Act Notice.—We ask for the information on this form to carry out the Internal Revenue laws of the United States. You are required to give us this information. We need it to ensure that you are complying with these laws and to allow us to figure and collect the right amount of tax.

The time needed to complete and file this form will vary depending on individual circumstances. The estimated average time is:

Recordkeeping	2 hrs., 17 min.
Learning about the law or the form	1 hr., 10 min.
Preparing the form	1 hr., 20 min.
Copying, assembling, and sending the form to IRS	20 min.

If you have comments concerning the accuracy of these time estimates or suggestions for making this form more simple, we would be happy to hear from you. You can write to both the IRS and the Office of Management and Budget at the addresses listed in the instructions of the tax return with which this form is filed.

General Instructions

Who Must File.—Complete Form 6251 to see if the alternative minimum tax (AMT) applies to you. Attach it to your return only if:

- You are liable for the AMT; or
- Line 6 (computed without regard to any negative adjustments on line 4) is more than line 9, and

(a) you have one or more adjustments on line 4h and lines 4j through 4t; or

(b) you have tax preference items on line 5.

Also, certain credits are limited by the amount shown on line 15, or in some cases, line 17. If this applies to you, Form 6251 must be attached to your return. The forms used to figure these credits have information on the tentative minimum tax limit.

Additional Information.—For more details, get **Pub. 909,** Alternative Minimum Tax for Individuals.

Recordkeeping.—For AMT purposes, certain items of income, deductions, etc., receive different tax treatment than for regular tax purposes. Therefore, for the AMT you need to recompute items that you figured for the regular tax. In some cases, you may wish to do this by completing the applicable tax form a second time. If you do complete another form, do not attach it to your tax return.

For the regular tax, some deductions and credits may result in carrybacks or carryforwards to other tax years. Examples are investment interest expense, a net operating loss, a capital loss, and the foreign tax credit. Because you may have to refigure these items for the AMT, the carryback or carryforward amount may be different for the AMT than for the regular tax. Therefore, you should keep records of these different amounts for the AMT and the regular tax. An AMT carryforward amount will be important in completing Form 6251 for the following year.

Partners, Shareholders, etc.—If you are a member of a partnership or a shareholder in an S corporation, the partnership or S corporation will give you information on any adjustments or tax preference items relating to it that you have to take into account for Form 6251.

Nonresident Alien Individuals.—If you disposed of U.S. real property interests at a gain, see the instructions for line 45 of **Form 1040NR**, U.S. Nonresident Alien Income Tax Return. You may have to enter a different figure on line 15 of Form 6251 if the amount figured in the worksheet in the instructions for line 45 of Form 1040NR is more than the tentative amount you figured on line 15 of Form 6251.

Credit For Prior Year Minimum Tax.—Get **Form 8801,** Credit for Prior Year Minimum Tax, if you paid AMT for 1989, or if you had a minimum tax credit carryforward on line 28 of your 1989 Form 8801.

Earned Income Credit.—If you have an earned income credit, you must reduce the credit by any AMT.

Optional Write-off for Certain Adjustments and Tax Preference Items (section 59(e)).—For the regular tax, you may elect to deduct certain adjustment and preference items ratably over a period of time, instead of treating them as adjustments or tax preference items on Form 6251. These items are: circulation expenditures under section 173, research and experimental expenditures under section 174(a), intangible drilling and developmental expenditures under section 263(c), development expenditures under section 616(a), and mining exploration expenditures under section 617(a). You may elect to deduct circulation expenditures over 3 years, intangible drilling and development expenditures over 60 months, and the other items over 10 years.

The election is made in the year of the expenditure. You can revoke it only with the consent of IRS. If you made the election for one of the above items, do not make an adjustment for that item on Form 6251. See section 59(e) for more details.

Specific Instructions

Line 1—Taxable income.—Enter the amount from Form 1040, line 37. If line 37 is zero, subtract line 36 from line 35 and enter the result as a negative amount.

If your taxable income includes an amount from the alcohol fuel credit under section 87, reduce your taxable income by the amount of the credit included in income.

Lines 4a through 4t—Adjustments.—Enter all adjustments on lines 4a through 4t as positive amounts, unless otherwise indicated.

Line 4c—Medical and dental expenses.—If you have an entry on line 4 of Schedule A (Form 1040), figure this adjustment as follows:

Step 1.—Multiply your adjusted gross income (line 32 of Form 1040) by 2½% (.025).

Step 2.—Compare the amount from Step 1 to the amount on line 4 of Schedule A (Form 1040), and enter the smaller amount.

Line 4f—Refund of taxes.—Include any refund from line 10 of Form 1040 that is attributable to state or local income taxes deducted in a tax year after 1986.

Also include on this line any refunds received in 1990 attributable to state or local personal property taxes, or foreign income or real property taxes, deducted in a tax year after 1986. If you include such amounts, you **must** write a description of the amount on the dotted line to the left of line 4f. For example, if you include a refund of real property taxes, write "real property" to the left of the entry space.

Line 4h—Other interest adjustments.—Include on this line home mortgage interest from line 9a, 9b, or 10 of Schedule A (Form 1040) that:

- is for a mortgage whose proceeds were not used to buy, build, or substantially rehabilitate your main home or qualified dwelling; **AND**
- if the mortgage was taken out before 7/1/82, the mortgage was not secured by property that was your main home or a qualified dwelling used by you or a member of your family at the time the mortgage was taken out. (A qualified dwelling is any house, apartment, condominium, or mobile home not used on a transient basis. See section 163(h)(4).)

See Regulations section 1.56A.

Investment Interest Expense.—If you completed **Form 4952,** Investment Interest Expense Deduction, you may have an adjustment on this line. Refigure your investment interest expense on another Form 4952 as follows:

Step 1.—Complete lines 1 and 2 of Form 4952. Follow the Form 4952 instructions for lines 1 and 2, but add to line 1 any interest expense that is included on line 4h of Form 6251 as a mortgage interest adjustment that is paid or accrued on indebtedness properly attributable to property held for investment within the meaning of section 163(d)(5). An example is interest on a home equity loan whose proceeds were invested in preferred stock, which is deductible as home mortgage interest expense for regular tax purposes, but not for alternative minimum tax purposes. Add to this amount any interest expense that would have been deductible if interest earned on specified private activity bonds issued after 8/7/86 had been includible in gross income.

When completing line 2, recompute your gross investment income, any net gain attributable to the disposition of property held for investment, and any investment expenses taking into account all AMT adjustments and tax preference items that apply. Include any interest income and investment expenses from private activity bonds issued after 8/7/86.

Step 2.—Enter -0- on line 3 and complete lines 4 and 5.

Step 3.—Skip lines 6 through 12 and enter the amount from line 5 on line 13.

Step 4.—Complete lines 14 through 24. When entering your disallowed investment interest expense from 1989 on line 17, use your AMT disallowed investment interest expense from 1989.

To figure your adjustment, find the difference between line 24 of your AMT Form 4952 and line 24 of the Form 4952 completed for regular tax purposes. If your investment interest expense allowed for the AMT is more than that allowed for the regular tax, enter the difference as a negative amount on line 4h.

Note: *If you took the standard deduction instead of itemizing your deductions, and you had investment interest expense, do not enter an amount on line 4h unless you reported investment interest expense on Schedule E. If you did, follow the instructions on page 1 for completing Form 4952. Allocate the investment interest expense allowed on line 24 of the AMT Form 4952 in the same way you did for the regular tax. Enter on line 4h the difference between the amount allowed on Schedule E for the regular tax and the amount allowed on Schedule E for the AMT.*

Line 4i—Reserved.—This line is reserved for future use.

Line 4j—Depreciation of tangible property placed in service after 1986 (or after 7/31/86 if election was made under the transitional provision of section 203(a)(1) of the Tax Reform Act of 1986).—

Caution: *Do not include on this line any depreciation adjustment from: (1) an activity for which you are not at risk; (2) amounts received from a partnership or an S corporation if the basis limitations under section 704(d) or 1366(d) apply; (3) a passive activity; or (4) a tax shelter farm activity. Instead, take these depreciation adjustments into account when figuring the amount to enter on line 4q, 4r, or 4s, whichever applies.*

For the AMT, the depreciation deduction must be recomputed using the alternative depreciation system (ADS) described in section 168(g) for tangible property as follows:

(1) For any real property described in section 1250(c) (generally nonresidential real and residential rental), use the straight line method over 40 years.

(2) For any tangible property (other than the property described in (1) above) which is depreciated using the straight line method for regular tax purposes, recompute your depreciation using the straight line method over the property's class life (explained below).

(3) For all other tangible property, use the 150% declining balance method over the property's class life, switching to the straight line method in the first tax year it yields a larger deduction.

In applying the above rules:

(1) Use the same convention you used for regular tax purposes;

(2) The "class life" to be used for AMT purposes has a different meaning than the recovery period used for regular tax purposes (although these periods could be the same in some instances). The class lives you need to use for AMT purposes can be found in Rev. Proc. 87-56, 1987-2 C.B. 674 or in **Pub. 534,** Depreciation. Use 12 years for any tangible personal property that does not have an assigned class life;

(3) See Rev. Proc. 87-57, 1987-2 C.B. 687 for optional tables (14 through 18) that can be used in computing depreciation for AMT purposes. (These optional tables have been reproduced in Pub. 534.); and

(4) Do not make an adjustment for property depreciated under the unit-of-production method, or any other method not expressed in terms of years. See section 168(f)(1), (2), (3), or (4).

Subtract the recomputed depreciation for AMT purposes from the depreciation deducted for regular tax purposes. If the depreciation figured for the AMT is more than the depreciation deducted for the regular tax, enter the difference as a negative amount on line 4j.

If depreciation is capitalized to inventory under the uniform capitalization rules, refigure the inventory using the rules discussed above.

Line 4k—Circulation expenditures and research and experimental expenditures paid or incurred after 12/31/86.—

Caution: *Skip this line, if for regular tax purposes, you elected to take the optional 3-year write-off period for circulation expenditures, or the optional 10-year write-off period for research and experimental expenditures under section 59(e).*

Circulation expenditures incurred after 1986.—For regular tax purposes, section 173 allows circulation expenditures to be deducted in full in the tax year they were paid or incurred. However, for the AMT these expenditures must be amortized over 3 years beginning with the year the expenditures were paid or incurred. Refigure these circulation expenditures for the AMT. Subtract your recomputed AMT expense from the expense claimed for regular tax purposes and enter the result on line 4k. If the current year deduction for the AMT is more than that figured for the regular tax, enter the difference as a negative amount.

Research and experimental expenditures incurred after 1986.—Research and experimental expenditures deducted during the current year for the regular tax under section 174(a) must be amortized over 10 years for the AMT. Refigure these expenditures for the AMT and enter the adjustment on line 4k. Figure the adjustment in the same manner as described above for circulation expenditures.

If you had a loss on property for which a deduction for circulation or research and experimental expenditures was allowed for regular tax purposes, see section 56(b)(2)(B).

Line 4l—Mining exploration and development costs paid or incurred after 12/31/86.—

Caution: *Skip this line if, for the regular tax, you elected to take the optional 10-year write-off under section 59(e).*

The deduction you claimed for regular tax purposes under sections 616(a) and 617(a) is not allowed for AMT purposes. Instead, you must capitalize such costs and amortize them ratably over a 10-year period beginning with the tax year in which they were paid or incurred.

Subtract your recomputed AMT expense from the expense you claimed for regular tax purposes and enter the result on line 4l. If your recomputed AMT expense is greater than the expense you claimed for regular tax purposes, enter the difference as a negative amount.

If you had a loss on property for which a deduction for mining exploration and development costs was allowed for regular tax purposes, see section 56(a)(2)(B).

Line 4m—Long-term contracts entered into after 2/28/86.—For AMT purposes, you must use the percentage of completion method rules described in section 460(b) to determine your taxable income from any "long-term contract" (defined in section 460(f)) you entered.into after 2/28/86. However, this rule does not apply to any "home construction contract" (as defined in section 460(e)(6)) you entered into after 6/20/88 if you meet the 2-year estimated completion requirement of section 460(e)(1)(B)(i) and the $10 million ceiling on average annual gross receipts requirement of section 460(e)(1)(B)(ii).

Note: *In the case of a contract described in section 460(e)(1), use the simplified procedures for allocating costs outlined in section 460(b)(4) to determine the percentage of completion.*

Subtract the income you reported for regular tax purposes from the income you recomputed for AMT purposes and enter the result on line 4m. If the amount reportable for the AMT is less than that reported for the regular tax, enter the difference as a negative amount on line 4m.

Line 4n—Pollution control facilities placed in service after 12/31/86.—The election under section 169 to amortize the basis of a certified pollution control facility over a 60-month period is not available for AMT purposes.

Instead, the deduction is determined using the ADS and the class life asset depreciation range for the facility under the straight line method.

Subtract your recomputed AMT deduction from the deduction you claimed under section 169 for regular tax purposes. If the amount allowed for AMT is more than the amount allowed for regular tax, enter the difference as a negative amount on line 4n.

Line 4o—Installment sales of certain property.—For any disposition of inventory (as defined in section 1221(1)) after 3/1/86, the installment method of accounting cannot be used in determining income for AMT purposes (except for certain dispositions of timeshares or residential lots if you made an election to pay interest under section 453(l)(2)(B)).

Application of rules in computing adjustment:

Dealer dispositions.— For dealer dispositions occurring after 3/1/86 but before 1/1/88, you will have adjustments for those dispositions if you used the installment method for regular tax purposes but were required for AMT purposes to report the entire gain in the year of disposition. Enter the income you reported for regular tax purposes for the current year for those dispositions on line 4o as a negative amount.

For dealer dispositions occurring after 1987, generally no adjustments are necessary because the installment method of accounting generally cannot be used for either regular tax purposes or for AMT purposes.

Nondealer dispositions.—For nondealer dispositions occurring after 3/1/86, but before the first day of your tax year that began in 1987, you will have adjustments for those dispositions if you used the installment method for regular tax purposes but were required for AMT purposes to report the entire gain in the year of disposition. Enter the income you reported for regular tax purposes for the current year for those dispositions on line 4o as a negative amount.

For nondealer dispositions occurring on or after the first day of your tax year that began in 1987, generally no adjustments are necessary since you are allowed to use the installment method of accounting for both regular tax purposes and AMT purposes.

Line 4p—Adjusted gain or loss.—Use this line to report:

(a) Any AMT adjustment resulting from the recomputation of a gain or loss from the sale or exchange of property during the year, or from the recomputation of a casualty gain or loss to business or income-producing property; and

(b) Any AMT adjustment from the exercise of incentive stock options after 12/31/87.

Recomputed gain or loss.—For item **(a)** above, this line can apply only if you reported gain or loss on **Form 4797,** Sale of Business Property, Schedule D (Form 1040), or Section B of **Form 4684,** Casualties and Thefts. Recompute your gain or loss for those forms. When figuring your adjusted basis, take into account any AMT adjustment you made this year or in previous years for items related to lines 4j, 4k, 4l, and 4n, of Form 6251. On line 4p, enter the difference between the gain or loss reported for the regular tax, and that figured for the AMT.

If the gain recomputed for AMT purposes is less than the gain computed for regular tax purposes, **OR** if the loss recomputed for AMT purposes is more than the loss computed for regular tax purposes, **OR** if you recomputed a loss for AMT purposes and computed a gain for regular tax purposes, enter the difference as a negative amount.

Incentive stock options.—The rules of section 421 that give favorable tax treatment to incentive stock options do not apply for AMT purposes to stock received from options exercised after 12/31/87. Instead, the rules of section 83 apply. Include as an adjustment on line 4p the difference between the amount reported as income for regular tax purposes, if any, from the exercise of these options, and that reportable as income under section 83.

If you acquired stock by exercising an incentive stock option and you disposed of that stock in the same year, the regular tax and AMT treatments are the same.

Line 4q—Certain loss limitations.— **Caution:** *If the loss is from a passive activity, use line 4s instead. If the loss is from a tax shelter farm activity (that is not passive), use line 4r.*

Refigure your gains and losses from activities for which you are not at risk and basis limitations applicable to partnerships and S corporations by taking into account your AMT adjustments and tax preference items. See sections 59(h), 465, 704(d), and 1366(d).

Enter on line 4q the difference between the amount that would be reported for the activity on Schedule C, E, F, or **Form 4835,** Farm Rental Income and Expenses, for AMT purposes and the amount that was reported for the activity on that form or schedule for regular tax purposes.

Enter any adjustment for amounts reported on Schedule D, Form 4684 or Form 4797 for the activity on line 4p instead of line 4q. See Instructions for line 4p.

Line 4r—Tax shelter farm loss.—Complete line 4r only if you have a gain or loss from a tax shelter farm activity (as defined in section 58(a)(2)) that is **not** a passive activity. If the tax shelter farm activity **is** a passive activity, you must include the gain or loss with your other passive activities on line 4s below.

Recompute all gains and losses you reported for regular tax purposes from tax shelter farm activities by taking into account your AMT adjustments and tax preference items. **Caution:** *To avoid duplication, any AMT adjustment or tax preference item taken into account on line 4r should not be taken into account in figuring the amount to enter on any other line of this form.*

Determine your tax shelter farm activity gain or loss for AMT purposes using the same rules you used for regular tax purposes with the following modifications. No recomputed loss is allowed, except to the extent you are insolvent (see section 58(c)(1)). A recomputed loss may not be used in the current tax year to offset gains from other tax shelter farm activities. Instead, any recomputed loss must be suspended and carried forward indefinitely until: **(1)** you have a gain in a subsequent tax year from that same tax shelter farm activity, **or (2)** the activity is disposed of.

Note: *The amount of any tax shelter farm activity loss that is not deductible (and is therefore carried forward) for AMT purposes is likely to differ from the amount (if any) that is carried forward for regular tax purposes. Therefore, it is essential that you keep adequate records for both AMT purposes and regular tax purposes.*

Enter on line 4r the difference between the amount that would be reported for the activity on Schedule E, F, or Form 4835 for AMT purposes and the amount that was reported for the activity on that form or schedule for regular tax purposes.

Enter any adjustment for amounts reported on Schedule D, Form 4684, or Form 4797 for the activity on line 4p instead of line 4r. See Instructions for line 4p.

Line 4s—Passive activity loss.—Your passive activity gains and losses must be refigured for the AMT by taking into account all AMT adjustments, tax preference items, and AMT prior year unallowed losses that apply to that activity. You may wish to fill out a second **Form 8582,** Passive Activity Loss Limitations, to determine your passive activity loss allowed for AMT purposes, but do not file the second Form 8582. When refiguring your passive activity loss, no phase-in under section 469(m) is allowed. Skip lines 10 through 15 of Form 8582 when filling out an AMT Form 8582.

Example. Assume you are a partner in a partnership and the Schedule K-1 (Form 1065) you received shows the following:

- A passive activity loss of ($4,125),
- A depreciation adjustment of $500 on property placed in service after 12/31/86, and
- A tax preference item of $225 for accelerated depreciation on property placed in service before 1/1/87.

Because the depreciation adjustment and the depreciation tax preference item are deductions that are not allowed for the AMT, you must first reduce the passive activity loss by those amounts. The result is a passive activity loss for the AMT of ($3,400). You would then enter this amount on Worksheet 2 of the AMT Form 8582 and refigure the allowable passive activity loss for AMT purposes.

Note: *The amount of any passive activity loss that is not deductible (and is therefore carried forward) for AMT purposes is likely to differ from the amount (if any) that is carried forward for regular tax purposes. Therefore, it is essential that you keep adequate records for both AMT purposes and regular tax purposes.*

Enter on line 4s the difference between the amount that would be reported for the activity on Schedule C, E, F, or Form 4835 for AMT purposes and the amount that was reported for the activity on that form or schedule for regular tax purposes.

Enter any adjustment for amounts reported on Schedule D, Form 4684, or Form 4797 for the activity on line 4p instead of line 4s. See Instructions for line 4p.

Caution: *To avoid duplication, any AMT adjustment or tax preference item taken into account on this line should not be taken into account in figuring the amounts to enter on any other line of this form.*

Publicly Traded Partnership (PTP).—If you had losses from a PTP, you will have to refigure the loss using any AMT adjustments, tax preference items, and any AMT prior year unallowed loss. Any phase-in amount allowed on pre-enactment activities for regular tax purposes is not allowed for AMT purposes.

Tax shelter passive farm activities.—Refigure any gain or loss from a tax shelter passive farm activity taking into account all AMT adjustments, tax preference items, and AMT prior year unallowed losses. If the amount is a gain, it can be included on the AMT Form 8582, but if it is a loss, the adjustment for the tax shelter passive farm activity is the loss you reported for regular tax purposes. The AMT loss to carry forward is the refigured AMT loss.

Insolvency.—If at the end of the tax year, your liabilities exceed the fair market value of your assets, increase your passive activity loss allowed by that excess (but not more than your total loss). See section 58(c)(1).

Line 4t—Beneficiaries of estates and trusts.—Enter on this line the amount from line 7 of your Schedule K-1 (Form 1041). This is your share of the distributable alternative minimum taxable income from the estate or trust.

Lines 5a through 5g—Tax preference items.—Enter all tax preference items on lines 5a through 5g as positive amounts. When you refigure an item for AMT, and the AMT amount is more than that figured for the regular tax, do not enter an amount on the line.

Line 5a—Appreciated property charitable deduction.—Enter the amount by which your contribution deduction would be reduced if all capital gain and section 1231 property was taken into account at its cost or other basis (rather than its fair market value).

Do not make an adjustment for carryforwards of charitable contributions made before 8/16/86. Also, do not include property for which you elected under section 170(b)(1)(C)(iii) to figure the contribution deduction using the property's adjusted basis rather than its fair market value.

Line 5b—Tax-exempt interest from private activity bonds issued after 8/7/86.—Enter interest you earned on "specified private activity bonds" reduced by any deduction that would have been allowable if the interest were includible in gross income for regular tax purposes. Generally, the term "specified private activity bonds" means any private activity bond (as defined in section 141) issued after 8/7/86. See section 57(a)(5) for exceptions and more details.

Exempt-interest dividends paid by a regulated investment company are treated as interest on a specified private activity bond to the extent the company received interest on the bond.

If you are filing **Form 8814,** Parent's Election To Report Child's Interest and Dividends, any tax-exempt interest from line 1b of that form that is a tax preference item must be included on line 5b.

Line 5c—Depletion.—In the case of mines, wells, and other natural deposits, enter the amount by which your depletion deduction under section 611 exceeds the adjusted basis of the property at the end of your tax year. In computing your year-end adjusted basis, use the rules of section 1016. However, do not reduce the adjusted basis by the current year's depletion.

Figure the excess amount separately for each property. If the depletion deduction for any property does not exceed the adjusted basis at year end, do not include a tax preference amount for that property.

Line 5d—Accelerated depreciation of real property placed in service before 1987.—For AMT purposes, you must use the straight line method to figure depreciation on this property. Enter on line 5d the excess of the depreciation taken on this property for the regular tax over the depreciation as refigured for the AMT (using the straight line method). Figure this amount separately for each property and include only positive amounts on line 5d. For 15-year, 18-year, or 19-year real property, use the straight line method over 15, 18, or 19 years. For low-income housing property, use the straight line method over 15 years.

Line 5e—Accelerated depreciation of leased personal property placed in service before 1987.—For AMT purposes, you must use the straight line method to figure depreciation on this leased property. Enter on line 5e the excess of the depreciation taken for the regular tax over the depreciation as refigured for the AMT (using the straight line method). Figure this amount separately for each property and include only positive amounts on line 5e.

For leased recovery property, other than 15-year, 18-year, or 19-year real property, or low-income housing, enter the amount by which your depreciation deduction figured for the regular tax exceeds the deduction allowable using the straight line method with a half-year convention, no salvage value, and the following recovery period:

3-year property	5 years
5-year property	8 years
10-year property	15 years
15-year public utility property	22 years

Line 5f—Amortization of certified pollution control facilities placed in service before 1987.—The election under section 169 to amortize the basis of a certified pollution control facility over a 60-month period is not available for AMT purposes. If the election was made for regular tax purposes, compute the adjustment by subtracting the depreciation deduction you would have been allowed under section 167 from the current year amortization deduction.

Line 5g—Intangible drilling costs.—*If, for regular tax purposes, you elected the optional 60-month write-off under section 59(e) for all property in this category, skip this line. No adjustment is necessary.*

Intangible drilling costs (IDCs) from oil, gas, and geothermal wells are a tax preference item to the extent that the "excess IDCs" exceed 65% of the "net income" from the wells. The tax preference item is computed separately for oil and gas properties and geothermal properties.

Excess IDCs are computed as follows: Figure the amount of your IDCs allowed for regular tax purposes under section 263(c), but do not include any section 263(c) deduction for nonproductive wells. Then, subtract the amount that would have been allowed had you amortized that amount over a 120-month period starting with the month the well was placed in production.

Note: *If you prefer not to use the 120-month period, you can elect to use any method that is permissible in determining cost depletion.*

Net income is determined by taking the gross income that you received or accrued during the tax year from all oil, gas, and geothermal wells and reducing it by the deductions allocable to these properties (reduced by the excess IDCs).

Note: *When refiguring net income, use only income and deductions allowed for AMT purposes.*

Line 7—Alternative tax net operating loss deduction (ATNOLD).—The ATNOLD is the aggregate of the alternative minimum tax net operating loss (ATNOL) carryovers and carrybacks to the tax year limited to 90% of alternative minimum taxable income (AMTI) determined without regard to the ATNOLD. Your ATNOLD is figured as follows:

For loss years beginning after 1986, your ATNOL is the excess of the deductions allowed for computing AMTI (excluding the ATNOLD) over the income included in computing the AMTI. This excess is computed with the modifications contained in section 172(d), taking into account the adjustments in sections 56 and 58 and the preferences in section 57 (i.e., the section 172(d) modifications should be separately computed in figuring the ATNOL). For example, the limitation of nonbusiness deductions to the amount of nonbusiness income must be separately computed in figuring the ATNOL, using only nonbusiness income and deductions that are included in computing AMTI.

For loss years beginning before 1987, see section 56(d)(2)(B) to refigure your ATNOLD.

Enter on line 7 the smaller of the ATNOLD or 90% of the amount shown on line 6 of Form 6251. If the 90% amount is smaller, the unused NOL can be carried back or forward according to section 172(b). The treatment of NOLs for AMT purposes does not affect the amount of your NOL for regular tax purposes.

Note: *If you elected under section 172(b)(3)(C) to forego the carryback period for regular tax purposes, the election will also apply for the AMT.*

Line 8—Alternative minimum taxable income.— If you are married filing a separate return and the amount on line 8 is more than $155,000, you must enter the amount from line F below on line 8 instead.

A. Enter amount from line 8	
B. Maximum amount	$155,000
C. Subtract line B from line A	
D. Multiply line C by 25% (.25)	
E. Enter the **smaller** of line D or $20,000	
F. Add lines A and E. Enter here and replace the amount on line 8 of Form 6251 with this amount	

Line 13.—If you are completing this form for a child who was under age 14 on January 1, 1991, and at least one of the child's parents was alive on December 31, 1990, use the worksheet below to figure the amount to enter on line 13. To the left of the entry space on line 13, write "Exemption Worksheet."

Line 13 Worksheet For Computing Minor Child's Alternative Minimum Tax Exemption

A. Enter amount from line 9	
B. Enter amount from line 12	
C. Subtract line B from line A. If zero or less, enter -0-	
D. Enter the child's earned income. See below	
E. Enter the greater of $1,000 or the child's share of the unused parental minimum tax exemption, if any. See below	
F. Add lines D and E	
G. Enter the **smaller** of line C or line F here and on line 13	

Line D.—Earned income includes wages, tips, and other payments received for personal services performed. Generally, earned income is the amount reported on Form 1040, line 7; Form 1040A, line 7; or Form 1040NR, lines 8, 13, and 20. Earned income also includes the amount from line 29 of Schedule C for statutory employees. See the Instructions for Schedule C (Form 1040).

Note: *If the child is self-employed, earned income also includes the amount from Schedule SE, Part I, line 3, or Part II, lines 3 and 4b, minus any amount reported on Form 1040, line 25.*

Line E.—The unused parental minimum tax exemption is the excess, if any, of the parent's minimum tax exemption over the parent's AMTI. The child's share is determined by dividing the child's AMTI by the sum of the AMTI of all of the parent's children under age 14 and multiplying the result by the unused parental minimum tax exemption. See section 59(j).

If the child's parents are married and file separate returns, the above rule applies to the parent with the greater AMTI. If the child's parents are not married, the above rule applies to the custodial parent.

Line 16—Alternative minimum tax foreign tax credit.—Your AMT foreign tax credit is your foreign tax credit refigured as follows:

(1) Complete and attach a separate **Form 1116,** Foreign Tax Credit, for each separate limitation specified at the top of Form 1116 to help you determine your AMT foreign tax credit. Write across the top of each Form 1116–"Alt. Min. Tax."

(2) Complete Part I using only income and deductions allowed for AMT purposes attributable to sources outside the U.S.

(3) Complete Part III, but do not enter on line 9 any taxes taken into account in a tax year beginning after 12/31/86 that are treated under section 904(c) as paid or accrued in a tax year beginning before 1987. Enter on line 10 of Form 1116 your alternative minimum foreign tax credit carryover, and on line 17 of Form 1116, enter the alternative minimum taxable income from line 8 of Form 6251. On line 19 of Form 1116, enter the amount from line 15 of Form 6251.

(4) Complete Part IV of Form 1116. The foreign tax credit from line 32 of Form 1116 used for AMT purposes is limited to the tax on line 15 of Form 6251 minus 10% of what the tax on line 15 would have been if line 7 of Form 6251 had been zero. If you have no entry on line 7 of Form 6251, enter on line 16 of Form 6251 the smaller of 90% of line 15 of Form 6251 or the amount from line 32 of Form 1116. If line 7 of Form 6251 has an amount, for purposes of this line, recompute what your tax on line 15 would have been if line 7 were zero. Multiply that amount by 10% and subtract the result from the tax on line 15. Enter the smaller of that amount or the amount from line 32 of Form 1116 on line 16 of Form 6251.

If your foreign tax credit is limited for AMT purposes, the unused amount can be carried back or forward according to section 904(c).

Line 18—Tax.—Enter the amount from Form 1040, line 38 plus any tax from Form 4970 entered on line 39 of Form 1040. Subtract from that amount any foreign tax credit entered on line 43 of Form 1040. Enter the result on line 18.

Line 19.—If you are completing this form for a child who was under age 14 on January 1, 1991, (the line 13 worksheet was completed) and line 17 is more than line 18, get **Form 8803,** Limit on Alternative Minimum Tax for Children Under Age 14. Using Form 8803 may reduce or eliminate the child's AMT if:

- the child's parent has regular tax that is more than the parent's tentative minimum tax (line 18 is more than line 17 if the parent completed Form 6251); **or**
- another child of the parent who was under age 14 on January 1, 1991, has regular tax that is more than that child's tentative AMT.

★U.S.GPO:1990-0-265-373

General Instructions

For Privacy Act notice, see the Form 1040 instructions.

Paperwork Reduction Act Notice.—We ask for the information on this form to carry out the Internal Revenue laws of the United States. You are required to give us this information. We need it to ensure that you are complying with these laws and to allow us to figure and collect the right amount of tax.

The time needed to complete and file this form will vary depending on individual circumstances. The estimated average time is:

Recordkeeping	13 mins.
Learning about the law or the form	11 mins.
Preparing the form	14 mins.
Copying, assembling, and sending the form to IRS	20 mins.

If you have comments concerning the accuracy of these time estimates or suggestions for making this form more simple, we would be happy to hear from you. You can write to both the Internal Revenue Service, Washington, DC 20224, Attention: IRS Reports Clearance Officer, T:FP; and the Office of Management and Budget, Paperwork Reduction Project (1545-0021), Washington, DC 20503. DO NOT send the tax form to either of these offices. Instead, see the instructions below for information on where to file.

Introduction

Form 709-A is an annual short form gift tax return that certain married couples may use instead of Form 709, United States Gift (and Generation-Skipping Transfer) Tax Return, to report nontaxable gifts that they consent to split.

A. Who May File

Gifts to your spouse.—For gifts to your spouse who is a U.S. citizen, you must only file a gift tax return to report certain gifts of terminable interests. For details on this and for filing rules for gifts to a spouse who is not a U.S. citizen, see the Instructions for Form 709.

Gifts to donee other than your spouse.—You must file a gift tax return if you gave either of the following gifts to someone other than your spouse:

(1) gifts of future interests of any amount; or

(2) gifts of present interests of more than $10,000 to any one donee.

Exceptions.—You do not have to file a gift tax return for any year in which the only gifts you made were for either of the following:

(1) gifts that were paid on behalf of an individual as tuition to an educational organization; or

(2) gifts that were paid on behalf of an individual as payment for medical care to a provider of medical care.

You may use Form 709-A if all of the following requirements are met:

(1) You are a citizen or resident of the U.S., and were married during the entire calendar year to one individual who is also a citizen or resident of the U.S. Both you and your spouse must have been alive at the end of the calendar year.

(2) Your only gifts (other than gifts for tuition or medical care) to a third party consisted entirely of present interests in tangible personal property, cash, U.S. Savings Bonds, or stocks and bonds listed on a stock exchange. A "third-party donee" is any donee other than your spouse.

(3) Your gifts to any one third-party donee (other than gifts for tuition or medical care) during the calendar year did not total more than $20,000. If the donee is a charity, no part of that gift may be given to a noncharitable donee.

(4) During the calendar year you did not make any gifts of terminable interests to your spouse.

(5) During the calendar year your spouse did not make any gifts to any of the donees listed on this form, did not make gifts of terminable interests to you, did not make gifts (other than gifts for tuition or medical care) of over $10,000 to any other donee, and did not make any gifts of future interests to any other donee.

(6) You and your spouse agree to split all of the gifts either of you made during the calendar year.

(7) You did not file a Form 709 for this calendar year.

If all seven requirements above are met, you may also use Form 709-A to report gifts made under the "Uniform Gifts to Minors Act."

Note: *Gifts include transfers of property when no money changes hands and also transfers when some payment was made, but the payment made was less than the value of the item transferred.*

B. When To File

Form 709-A is a calendar-year return to be filed on or after January 1 but not later than April 15 of the calendar year following the year when the non-taxable split gifts were made.

Any extension of time granted to file your calendar year income tax return will also extend the time to file Form 709-A. Income tax extensions are made using Forms 4868, 2688, or 2350. If you received an extension, attach a copy of it to Form 709-A.

Note: *At the time this form went to print, IRS was considering eliminating Forms 4868 and 2688 beginning with returns due in 1992. If this occurs, IRS will issue guidance on how to extend the filing date for Form 709-A.*

You may not file Form 709-A later than April 15 (or the extension due date). Instead, you must file Form 709.

C. Where To File

File Form 709-A with the Internal Revenue Service Center where you would file your Federal income tax return. See the Form 1040 instructions for a list of filing locations.

D. Additional Help

Pub. 448, Federal Estate and Gift Taxes, contains further information on the gift tax, including information about the following matters:

(1) Annual exclusion.

(2) Present and future interest.

(3) Fair market value.

(4) Adjusted basis. See **Pub. 551,** Basis of Assets, and the instructions for Schedule D (Form 1040).

(5) Extension of time to file.

(6) Terminable interest.

(7) Gifts for tuition or medical care.

Specific Instructions

Column (a).—Donee's Name and Address and Description of Gift

List the names and addresses of all third party donees to whom you made gifts (other than gifts for tuition or medical care) totaling more than $10,000 during the calendar year. Do not list the names of donees to whom you gave only gifts for tuition or medical care or to whom you gave gifts (other than tuition or medical care) of present interests of $10,000 or less.

Describe the gifts in enough detail so they may be easily identified.

If you list **bonds,** include in your description:

- The number of bonds transferred;
- The principal amount of the bonds;
- The name of the obligor;
- The date of maturity of the bonds;
- The rate of interest;
- The date or dates on which interest is payable;
- The series number (if there is more than one issue);
- The exchange where the bond is listed; and
- The CUSIP number, if available. The CUSIP number is a nine digit number assigned by the American Banking Association to traded securities.

If you list **stocks,** you should include:

- The number of shares transferred;
- Whether the stocks are common or preferred. (If the stocks are preferred, list the issue and par value.);
- Exact name of corporation;
- Principal exchange where the stocks are sold; and
- The CUSIP number, if available (see "bonds" above).

If you list **tangible personal property** (such as a car), describe the property in enough detail so that its fair market value can be accurately figured.

Column (b).—Donor's Adjusted Basis of Gift

Show the basis you would use for income tax purposes if you sold or exchanged the property.

Column (d).—Value at Date of Gift

If you make the gift in property other than money, determine the fair market value as of the date the gift was made.

Consent

Your spouse must consent to split all gifts made by either of you. Your spouse gives this consent by signing in the space provided. You give your consent by signing in the space for the donor's signature. The guardian of a legally incompetent spouse may sign the consent. The executor for a deceased spouse may sign the consent if the spouse died after the close of the calendar year. Although a properly filed Form 709-A will not result in any gift tax liability, you should know that if you and your spouse consent to split gifts, either or both of you will be liable in the event any gift tax is later determined to be due.

Signature

You, as a donor, must sign the return. If you pay another person, firm, or corporation to prepare your return, that person must also sign the return as preparer unless he or she is your regular full-time employee.

★U.S. GPO:1990-518-673/20326

Form **709-A**
(Rev. November 1990)
Department of the Treasury
Internal Revenue Service

United States Short Form Gift Tax Return

(For "Privacy Act" notice, see the Form 1040 instructions)

Calendar year 19 ....

OMB No. 1545-0021

Expires 10-31-93

1 Donor's first name and middle initial	2 Donor's last name	**3 Donor's social security number**
4 Address (number, street, and apartment number)		5 Legal residence (domicile)
6 City, state, and ZIP code		7 Citizenship

8 Did you file any gift tax returns for prior periods? . . . ☐ **Yes** ☐ **No**

If "Yes," state when and where earlier returns were filed ▶ ....

9 Name of consenting spouse	**10 Consenting spouse's social security number**

Note: Do not use this form to report gifts of closely held stock. Instead, use Form 709.

List of Gifts

Donee's name and address and description of gift **(a)**	Donor's adjusted basis of gift **(b)**	Date of gift **(c)**	Value at date of gift **(d)**

Consent

I consent to have the gifts made by my spouse to third parties during the calendar year considered as made one-half by each of us.

Consenting spouse's signature ▶ **Date ▶**

Under penalties of perjury, I declare that I have examined this return, and to the best of my knowledge and belief it is true, correct, and complete. Declaration of preparer (other than donor) is based on all information of which preparer has any knowledge.

Donor's signature ▶ .... **Date ▶** ....

Preparer's signature (other than donor's) ▶ .... **Date ▶** ....

Preparer's address (other than donor's) ▶

Form **709** (Rev. October 1990)
Department of the Treasury
Internal Revenue Service

United States Gift (and Generation-Skipping Transfer) Tax Return

(Section 6019 of the Internal Revenue Code) (For gifts made after December 31, 1989, and before January 1, 1993)

Calendar year 19 _____

▶ **See separate instructions. For Privacy Act Notice, see the Instructions for Form 1040.**

OMB No. 1545-0020
Expires 8-31-93

Part 1.—General Information

1 Donor's first name and middle initial	2 Donor's last name	3 **Social security number**
4 Address (number, street, and apartment number)		5 Domicile
6 City, state, and ZIP code		7 Citizenship

	Yes	No
8 If the donor died during the year, check here ▶ ☐ and enter date of death ____________, 19 ____.		
9 If you received an extension of time to file this Form 709, check here ▶ ☐ and attach the Form 4868, 2688, 2350, or extension letter.		
10 Enter the total number of separate donees listed on Schedule A—count each person only once . . . ☐		
11 If you (the donor) filed a previous Form 709 (or 709-A), has your address changed since the last Form 709 (or 709-A) was filed?		
12 Gifts by husband or wife to third parties.—Do you consent to have the gifts (including generation-skipping transfers) made by you and by your spouse to third parties during the calendar year considered as made one-half by each of you? (See instructions.) (If the answer is "Yes," the following information must be furnished and your spouse is to sign the consent shown below. If the answer is "No," skip lines 13–18 and go to Schedule A.) . . .		
13 Name of consenting spouse — 14 SSN		
15 Were you married to one another during the entire calendar year? (See instructions.) . . .		
16 If the answer to 15 is "No," check whether ☐ married ☐ divorced or ☐ widowed, and give date (see instructions) ▶		
17 Will a gift tax return for this calendar year be filed by your spouse? . . .		

18 **Consent of Spouse**—I consent to have the gifts (and generation-skipping transfers) made by me and by my spouse to third parties during the calendar year considered as made one-half by each of us. We are both aware of the joint and several liability for tax created by the execution of this consent.

Consenting spouse's signature ▶ **Date** ▶

Part 2.—Tax Computation

1	Enter the amount from Schedule A, Part 3, line 15 . . .	1		
2	Enter the amount from Schedule B, line 3 . . .	2		
3	Total taxable gifts (add lines 1 and 2) . . .	3		
4	Tax computed on amount on line 3 (see Table for Computing Tax in separate instructions)	4		
5	Tax computed on amount on line 2 (see Table for Computing Tax in separate instructions)	5		
6	Balance (subtract line 5 from line 4) . . .	6		
7	Maximum unified credit (nonresident aliens, see instructions) . . .	7	192,800	00
8	Enter the unified credit against tax allowable for all prior periods (from Sch. B, line 1, col. C) .	8		
9	Balance (subtract line 8 from line 7) . . .	9		
10	Enter 20% (.20) of the amount allowed as a specific exemption for gifts made after September 8, 1976, and before January 1, 1977 (see instructions) . . .	10		
11	Balance (subtract line 10 from line 9) . . .	11		
12	Unified credit (enter the smaller of line 6 or line 11) . . .	12		
13	Credit for foreign gift taxes (see instructions) . . .	13		
14	Total credits (add lines 12 and 13) . . .	14		
15	Balance (subtract line 14 from line 6) (do not enter less than zero) . . .	15		
16	Generation-skipping transfer taxes (from Schedule C, Part 3, col. H, total) . . .	16		
17	Total tax (add lines 15 and 16) . . .	17		
18	Gift and generation-skipping transfer taxes prepaid with extension of time to file . . .	18		
19	If line 18 is less than line 17, enter BALANCE DUE (see instructions) . . .	19		
20	If line 18 is greater than line 17, enter AMOUNT TO BE REFUNDED . . .	20		

Please attach check or money order here

Under penalties of perjury, I declare that I have examined this return, including any accompanying schedules and statements, and to the best of my knowledge and belief it is true, correct, and complete. Declaration of preparer (other than donor) is based on all information of which preparer has any knowledge.

Donor's signature ▶ Date ▶

Preparer's signature (other than donor) ▶ Date ▶

Preparer's address (other than donor) ▶

For Paperwork Reduction Act Notice, see page 1 of the separate instructions for this form.

SCHEDULE A Computation of Taxable Gifts

Part 1.—Gifts Subject Only to Gift Tax. *Gifts less political organization, medical, and educational exclusions—see instructions*

A Item number	B Donee's name, relationship to donor (if any), and address and description of gift. If the gift was made by means of a trust, enter trust's identifying number below and attach a copy of the trust instrument. If the gift was securities, enter the CUSIP number(s), if available.	C Donor's adjusted basis of gift	D Date of gift	E Value at date of gift
1				

Part 2.—Gifts Which are Direct Skips and are Subject to Both Gift Tax and Generation-Skipping Transfer Tax. You must list the gifts in chronological order. *Gifts less political organization, medical, and educational exclusions—see instructions. (Also list here direct skips that are subject only to the GST tax at this time as the result of the termination of an "estate tax inclusion period." See instructions.)*

A Item number	B Donee's name, relationship to donor (if any), and address and description of gift. If the gift was made by means of a trust, enter trust's identifying number below and attach a copy of the trust instrument. If the gift was securities, enter the CUSIP number(s), if available.	C Donor's adjusted basis of gift	D Date of gift	E Value at date of gift
1				

Part 3.—Gift Tax Reconciliation

1	Total value of gifts of donor (add column E of Parts 1 and 2)	1	
2	One-half of items ______ attributable to spouse (see instructions)	2	
3	Balance (subtract line 2 from line 1)	3	
4	Gifts of spouse to be included (from Schedule A, Part 3, line 2 of spouse's return—see instructions)	4	
	If any of the gifts included on this line are also subject to the generation-skipping transfer tax, check here ▶ ☐ and enter those gifts also on Schedule C, Part 1.		
5	Total gifts (add lines 3 and 4)	5	
6	Total annual exclusions for gifts listed on Schedule A (including line 4, above) (see instructions)	6	
7	Total included amount of gifts (subtract line 6 from line 5)	7	

Deductions (see instructions)

8	Gifts of interests to spouse for which a marital deduction will be claimed, based on items ______ of Schedule A	8			
9	Exclusions attributable to gifts on line 8	9			
10	Marital deduction—subtract line 9 from line 8	10			
11	Charitable deduction, based on items ______ to ______ less exclusions	11			
12	Total deductions—add lines 10 and 11			12	
13	Subtract line 12 from line 7			13	
14	Generation-skipping transfer taxes payable with this Form 709 (from Schedule C, Part 3, col. H, Total)			14	
15	Taxable gifts (add lines 13 and 14). Enter here and on line 1 of the Tax Computation on page 1			15	

(If more space is needed, attach additional sheets of same size.)

SCHEDULE A Computation of Taxable Gifts (continued)

16 Terminable Interest (QTIP) Marital Deduction. (See instructions.)

☐ ◀ Check here if you elected, under the rules of section 2523(f), to include gifts of qualified terminable interest property on line 8, on page 2. Enter the item numbers (from Schedule A) of the gifts for which you made this election ▶ ____________

17 Election out of QTIP Treatment of Annuities

☐ ◀ Check here if you elect under section 2523(f)(6) to **NOT** treat as qualified terminable interest property any joint and survivor annuities that are reported on Schedule A and would otherwise be treated as qualified terminable interest property under section 2523(f). (See instructions.) Enter the item numbers (from Schedule A) for the annuities for which you are making this election ▶

SCHEDULE B Gifts From Prior Periods

Did you (the donor) file gift tax returns for prior periods? (If "Yes," see instructions for completing Schedule B below.) . . . . ☐ **Yes** ☐ **No**

A Calendar year or calendar quarter (see instructions)	B Internal Revenue office where prior return was filed	C Amount of unified credit against gift tax for periods after December 31, 1976	D Amount of specific exemption for prior periods ending before January 1, 1977	E Amount of taxable gifts
1 Totals for prior periods (without adjustment for reduced specific exemption)	1			

2 Amount, if any, by which total specific exemption, line 1, column D, is more than $30,000	2	
3 Total amount of taxable gifts for prior periods (add amount, column E, line 1, and amount, if any, on line 2) (Enter here and on line 2 of the Tax Computation on page 1.)	3	

SCHEDULE C Computation of Generation-Skipping Transfer Tax

Note: *Inter vivos direct skips which are completely excluded by the GST exemption must still be fully reported (including value and exemptions claimed) on Schedule C.*

Part 1.—Generation-Skipping Transfers

A Item No. (from Schedule A, Part 2, col. A)	B Value (from Schedule A, Part 2, col. E)	C Split Gifts (enter ½ of col. B) (see instructions)	D Subtract col. C from col. B	E Nontaxable portion of transfer	F Net Transfer (subtract col. E from col. D)
1					
2					
3					
4					
5					
6					

If you elected gift splitting and your spouse was required to file a separate Form 709 (see the instructions for "Split Gifts"), you must enter all of the gifts shown on Schedule A, Part 2, of your spouse's Form 709 here. In column C, enter the item number of each gift in the order it appears in column A of your spouse's Schedule A, Part 2. We have preprinted the prefix "S-" to distinguish your spouse's item numbers from your own when you complete column A of Schedule C, Part 3. In column D, for each gift, enter the amount reported in column C, Schedule C, Part 1, of your spouse's Form 709.	Split gifts from spouse's Form 709 (enter item number)	Value included from spouse's Form 709		
	S-			
	S-			
	S-			
	S-			
	S-			
	S-			
	S-			
	S-			

(If more space is needed, attach additional sheets of same size.)

Part 2.—GST Exemption Reconciliation (Code section 2631) and Section 2652(a)(3) Election

Check box ▶ ☐ if you are making a section 2652(a)(3) (special QTIP) election (see instructions)

Enter the item numbers (from Schedule A) of the gifts for which you are making this election ▶ ....

1	Maximum allowable exemption	1	$1,000,000
2	Total exemption used for periods before filing this return	2	
3	Exemption available for this return (subtract line 2 from line 1)	3	
4	Exemption claimed on this return (from Part 3, col. C total, below)	4	
5	Exemption allocated to transfers not shown on Part 3, below. You must attach a Notice of Allocation. (See instructions.)	5	
6	Add lines 4 and 5	6	
7	Exemption available for future transfers (subtract line 6 from line 3)	7	

Part 3.—Tax Computation

A Item No. (from Schedule C, Part 1)	B Net transfer (from Schedule C, Part 1, col. F)	C GST Exemption Allocated	D Divide col. C by col. B	E Inclusion Ratio (subtract col. D from 1.000)	F Maximum Estate Tax Rate	G Applicable Rate (multiply col. E by col. F)	H Generation-Skipping Transfer Tax (multiply col. B by col. G)
1					55% (.55)		
2					55% (.55)		
3					55% (.55)		
4					55% (.55)		
5					55% (.55)		
6					55% (.55)		
7					55% (.55)		
8					55% (.55)		
					55% (.55)		
					55% (.55)		
					55% (.55)		
					55% (.55)		
					55% (.55)		
					55% (.55)		
					55% (.55)		
					55% (.55)		
Total exemption claimed. Enter here and on line 4, Part 2, above. May not exceed line 3, Part 2, above			**Total generation-skipping transfer tax.** Enter here, on line 14 of Schedule A, Part 3, and on line 16 of the Tax Computation on page 1				

(If more space is needed, attach additional sheets of same size.)

★U.S. GPO:1991-518-940/20362

Department of the Treasury
Internal Revenue Service

Instructions for Form 709

(Revised October 1990)

United States Gift (and Generation-Skipping Transfer) Tax Return

(For gifts made after December 31, 1989, and before January 1, 1993)

For Privacy Act Notice, see the Instructions for Form 1040

(Section references are to the Internal Revenue Code unless otherwise noted.)

If you are filing this form solely to elect gift-splitting for gifts of not more than $20,000 per donee, you may be able to use Form 709-A, United States Short Form Gift Tax Return, instead of this form. See the instructions for "Who Must File" on page 2.

If you made gifts before January 1, 1982, do not use this Form 709 to report these gifts. Instead, use the November 1981 revision of Form 709. For gifts made after December 31, 1981, and before January 1, 1987, use the January 1987 revision of Form 709. For gifts made after December 31, 1986, and before January 1, 1989, use the December 1988 revision of Form 709. For gifts made after December 31, 1988, and before January 1, 1990, use the December 1989 revision of Form 709.

Paperwork Reduction Act Notice.—We ask for the information on this form to carry out the Internal Revenue laws of the United States. You are required to give us this information. We need it to ensure that taxpayers are complying with these laws and to allow us to figure and collect the right amount of tax.

The time needed to complete and file this form will vary depending on individual circumstances. The estimated average time is:

Recordkeeping	40 min.
Learning about the law or the form	51 min.
Preparing the form	1 hr., 41 min.
Copying, assembling, and sending the form to IRS	1 hr., 3 min.

If you have comments concerning the accuracy of these time estimates or suggestions for making this form more simple, we would be happy to hear from you. You can write to both the **Internal Revenue Service,** Washington, DC 20224, Attention: IRS Reports Clearance Officer, T:FP; and the **Office of Management and Budget,** Paperwork Reduction Project (1545-0020), Washington, DC 20503. DO NOT send the tax form to either of these offices. Instead, see the instructions below for information on where to file.

Change You Should Note

Use Form 709 also to report certain generation-skipping transfers that you are reporting due to the close of an "estate tax inclusion period" (ETIP), provided the ETIP closed as the result of something other than the death of the transferor. See "Transfers Subject to an 'Estate Tax Inclusion Period'" on page 2 for a discussion of such transfers.

Note: *New Code section 2701, added by section 11601 of the Omnibus Budget Reconciliation Act of 1990 (OBRA), provides for two elections regarding certain transfers of interests in corporations or partnerships. While section 2701 is applicable to transfers made after October 8, 1990, these elections will **not** have to be made on the Form 709 otherwise due on April 15, 1991, with respect to these transfers. The IRS will issue regulations in the future specifying when these elections must be made.*

Taxpayers should be aware that section 11601 of OBRA also amended Code section 6501(c) (relating to limitations on assessment and collection of the gift tax) to provide that the limitations do not apply to transfers valued under Code sections 2701 and 2702 (relating to transfers in trust), until the transfer is disclosed in a gift tax return, or in a statement attached to a gift tax return, in a manner that is adequate to apprise the IRS of the nature of the transaction.

General Instructions

Note: *If you meet all of the following requirements, you are **not** required to file Form 709:*

1. You made no gifts during the year to your spouse;

2. You gave no more than $10,000 during the year to any one donee; and,

3. All of the gifts you made were of present interests.

For additional information, see "Who Must File" on page 2.

Purpose of Form.—Form 709 is used to report transfers subject to the Federal gift and certain generation-skipping (GST) taxes and to figure the tax, if any, due on those transfers.

All gift and GST taxes are computed and filed on a calendar year basis regardless of your income tax accounting period.

Transfers Subject to the Gift Tax.—Generally, the Federal gift tax applies to any transfer by gift of real or personal property, whether tangible or intangible, that you made directly or indirectly, in trust, or by any other means to a donee.

The gift tax applies not only to the gratuitous transfer of any kind of property, but also to sales or exchanges, not made in the ordinary course of business, where money or money's worth is exchanged but the value of the money received is less than the value of what is sold or exchanged. The gift tax is in addition to any other tax, such as Federal income tax, paid or due on the transfer.

The exercise or release of a power of appointment may be a gift by the individual possessing the power.

The gift tax may also apply to the forgiveness of a debt, to interest-free (or below market interest rate) loans, to the assignment of the benefits of an insurance policy, to certain property settlements in divorce cases, and to certain survivorship annuities.

Bonds that are exempt from Federal income taxes are not exempt from Federal gift taxes.

Pub. 448, Federal Estate and Gift Taxes, contains further information on the gift tax.

Transfers Not Subject to the Gift Tax.—Three types of transfers are not subject to the gift tax. These are transfers to political organizations and payments that qualify for the educational and medical exclusions. These transfers are not "gifts" as that term is used on Form 709 and its instructions. You need not file a Form 709 to report these transfers and should not list them on Schedule A of Form 709.

Political organizations.—The gift tax does not apply to a transfer to a political organization (defined in section 527(e)(1)) for the use of the organization.

Educational exclusion.—The gift tax does not apply to an amount you paid on behalf of an individual to a qualifying domestic or foreign educational organization as tuition for the education or training of the individual. A *qualifying educational organization* is one that normally maintains a regular faculty and curriculum and normally has a regularly enrolled body of pupils or students in attendance at the place where its educational activities are regularly carried on. See section 170(b)(1)(A)(ii) and its regulations.

The payment must be made directly to the qualifying educational organization and it must be for tuition. No educational exclusion is allowed for amounts paid for books, supplies, dormitory fees, board or other similar expenses that do not constitute direct tuition costs. To the extent that the payment to the educational institution was for something other than tuition, it is a gift to the individual for whose benefit it was made, and may be offset by the annual exclusion if it is otherwise available.

Medical exclusion.—The gift tax does not apply to an amount you paid on behalf of an individual to a person or institution that provided medical care for the individual. The payment must be to the care provider. The medical care must meet the requirements of section 213(d) (definition of medical care for income tax deduction purposes). Medical care includes expenses incurred for the diagnosis, cure, mitigation, treatment, or prevention of disease, or for the purpose of affecting any structure or function of the body, or for transportation primarily for and essential to medical care. Medical care also includes amounts paid for medical insurance on behalf of any individual.

The medical exclusion does not apply to amounts paid for medical care that are reimbursed by the donee's insurance. If payment for a medical expense is reimbursed by the donee's insurance company, your payment for that expense, to the extent of the reimbursed amount, is not eligible for the medical exclusion and you have made a gift to the donee.

To the extent that the payment was for something other than medical care, it is a gift to the individual on whose behalf the payment was made, and may be offset by the annual exclusion if it is otherwise available.

The medical and educational exclusions are allowed without regard to the relationship between you and the donee. For examples illustrating these exclusions, see Regulations section 25.2503-6.

Disclaimers.—For the rules governing when a disclaimer is a qualified disclaimer and not subject to the gift tax, see Pub. 448.

Transfers Subject to the Generation-Skipping Transfer Tax.—The GST tax to report on Form 709 is that imposed on inter vivos direct skips made after September 25, 1985. (See Temp. Regs. section 26.2662-1(b), for instructions on how to report other generation-skipping transfers.) An *inter vivos direct skip* is a transfer of an interest in property that is: (1) subject to the gift tax; and (2) made to a skip person. (See page 4.)

A transfer is *subject to the gift tax* if it is required to be reported on Schedule A of Form 709 under the rules contained in the gift tax portions of these instructions, including the split gift rules. Therefore, transfers made to political organizations, transfers that qualify for the medical or educational exclusions, transfers that are fully excluded under the annual exclusion, and most transfers made to your spouse are not subject to the GST tax.

Transfers subject to the GST tax are described in further detail in the instructions for Schedule A, on page 4.

Transfers Subject to an "Estate Tax Inclusion Period".—If property that is transferred by gift in a GST direct skip would have been includible in the donor's estate if the donor had died immediately after the transfer (other than by reason of the donor having died within 3 years of making the gift), the direct skip will be treated as having been made at the end of the "estate tax inclusion period" (ETIP) rather than at the time it was actually made. For details, see section 2642(f).

Report the gift portion of such a transfer on Schedule A, Part 1, at the time of the actual transfer. Report the GST portion on Schedule A, Part 2, but only at the close of the ETIP. Use Form 709 only to report those transfers where the ETIP closed due to something other than the death of the transferor. If the ETIP closed as the result of the death of the transferor, report the transfer on Form 706.

If you are filing this Form 709 solely to report transfers subject to an ETIP, complete the form as you normally would with the following exceptions:

1. Write "ETIP" at the top of page 1;

2. Complete only lines 1-4, 6, 8, and 9 of Part 1, General Information;

3. Complete Schedule A, Part 2, as explained in the instructions for that schedule on page 5;

4. Complete Column B of Schedule C, Part 1, as explained in the instructions for that schedule on page 6;

5. Complete only lines 14 and 15 of Schedule A, Part 3. (Also list here direct skips that are subject only to the GST tax as the result of the termination of an "estate tax inclusion period." See instructions.)

Who Must File

Only individuals are required to file gift tax returns. If a trust, estate, partnership, or corporation makes a gift, the individual beneficiaries, partners, or stockholders are considered donors and may be liable for the gift and GST taxes.

If a donor dies before filing a return, the donor's executor must file the return.

A married couple may not file a joint gift tax return. However, see "Split Gifts" on page 3.

If a gift is of community property, it is considered made one-half by each spouse. For example, a gift of $100,000 of community property is considered a gift of $50,000 made by each spouse, and each spouse must file a gift tax return.

Likewise, each spouse must file a gift tax return if they have made a gift of property held by them as joint tenants or tenants by the entirety.

Citizens or Residents of the United States.—If you are a citizen or resident of the United States, you must file a gift tax return (whether or not any tax is ultimately due) in the following situations:

Gifts to your spouse.—**Except as described below, you do not have to file a gift tax return to report gifts to your spouse regardless of the amount of these gifts and regardless of whether the gifts are present or future interests.**

However, you must file a gift tax return if your spouse is not a U.S. citizen and the total gifts you made to your spouse during the year exceed $100,000, or if you made any gift of a terminable interest that does not meet the "Life Estate With Power of Appointment" exception described on page 6. You must also file a gift tax return to make a QTIP (Qualified Terminable Interest Property) election described on page 6.

Gifts to donees other than your spouse (including charitable donees).—You must file a gift tax return if you gave gifts to any such donee that are not fully excluded under the $10,000 annual exclusion (as described below). Thus, you must file a gift tax return to report any gift of a future interest (regardless of amount) or to report gifts to any donee that total more than $10,000 for the year.

Gift splitting.—You must file a gift tax return to split gifts (regardless of their amount) with your spouse as described in the Specific Instructions for Part 1 on page 3.

The term *citizen of the United States* includes a person who, at the time of making the gift:

- was domiciled in a possession of the United States;
- was a U.S. citizen; and
- became a U.S. citizen for a reason other than being a citizen of a U.S. possession or being born or residing in a possession.

Annual Exclusion.—The first $10,000 of gifts of present interests to each donee during the calendar year is subtracted from total gifts in figuring the amount of taxable gifts.

All of the gifts made during the calendar year to a donee are **fully excluded under the annual exclusion** if they are all gifts of *present interests* and if they total $10,000 or less.

Note: *For gifts made to spouses who are* **not** *U.S.* **citizens,** *the annual exclusion has been increased from $10,000 to $100,000, provided the additional $90,000 gift would otherwise qualify for the gift tax marital deduction.*

A gift of a *future interest* cannot be excluded under the annual exclusion.

A gift is considered a *present interest* if the donee has all immediate rights to the use, possession, and enjoyment of the property and income from the property. A gift is considered a *future interest* if the donee's rights to the use, possession, and enjoyment of the property and income from the property will not begin until some future date. Future interests include reversions, remainders, and other similar interests or estates.

The gift of a present interest to more than one donee as joint tenants qualifies for the annual exclusion for each donee.

In the case of transfers for the benefit of a minor and for the transitional rules for certain trusts with a power of appointment referenced to the annual exclusion, see Pub. 448.

Nonresident Aliens.—Nonresident aliens are subject to gift and GST taxes for gifts of tangible property situated in the United States. Under certain circumstances they are also subject to gift and GST taxes for gifts of intangible property. (See section 2501(a).)

If you are a nonresident alien who made a gift subject to gift tax, you must file a gift tax return if: (1) you gave *any* gifts of future interests; or (2) your gifts of present interests to *any donee* other than your spouse total more than $10,000; or (3) your outright gifts to your spouse who is not a U.S. citizen total more than $100,000.

When To File

Form 709 is an annual return.

Generally, you must file Form 709 on or after January 1 but not later than April 15 of the year following the calendar year when the gifts were made.

If the donor of the gifts died during the year in which the gifts were made, the executor must file the donor's Form 709 not later than the earlier of: (1) the due date (with extensions) for filing the donor's estate tax return; or (2) April 15 of the year following the calendar year when the gifts were made. Under this rule, Form 709 may be due before April 15 if the donor died before July 15 of the year in which the gifts were made. If the donor died after July 14, the due date for Form 709 (without extensions) will always be April 15 of the following year. If no estate tax return is required to be filed, the due date for Form 709 (without extensions) is April 15. For more information, see Regulations section 25.6075-1.

Extension of Time To File.— There are two methods of extending the time to file the gift tax return. *Neither method extends the time to pay the gift or GST taxes.* If you want an extension of time to pay the gift or GST taxes, you must request that separately. (See Regulations section 25.6161-1.)

(1) By letter.—You can request an extension of time to file your gift tax return by writing to the district director or service center for your area. You must explain the reasons for the delay.

(2) By form.—Any extension of time granted for filing your calendar year Federal income tax return will also extend the time to file any gift tax return. Income tax extensions are made by using Form 4868, 2688, or 2350, which have check boxes for Form 709.

Note: *At the time this form went to print, IRS was considering eliminating Forms 4868 and 2688 beginning with returns due in 1992. If this occurs, IRS will issue guidance on how to extend the filing date for Form 709.*

Where To File

File Form 709 with the Internal Revenue Service center where you would file your Federal income tax return. See the Form 1040 instructions for a list of filing locations.

Penalties

The law provides for penalties for both late filing of returns and late payment of tax unless you have reasonable cause. There are also penalties for valuation understatements that cause an underpayment of the tax, willful failure to file a return on time, and for willful attempt to evade or defeat payment of tax.

Joint Tenancy

If you buy property with your own funds and the title to such property is held by yourself and the donee as joint tenants with right of survivorship and if either you or the donee may give up those rights by severing your interest, you have made a gift to the donee in the amount of half the value of the property. If you create a joint bank account for yourself and the donee (or a similar kind of ownership by which you can get back the entire fund without the donee's consent), you have made a gift to the donee when the donee draws on the account for his or her own benefit. The amount of the gift is the amount that the donee took out without any obligation to repay you. If you buy a U.S. savings bond registered as payable to yourself or the donee, there is a gift to the donee when he or she cashes the bond without any obligation to account to you.

Transfer of Certain Life Estates

If you received a qualifying terminable interest (see page 6) from your spouse for which a marital deduction was elected on your spouse's estate or gift tax return, you will be subject to the gift (and GST, if applicable) tax if you dispose of (by gift, sale, or otherwise) all or part of your life income interest.

The entire value of the property involved less: (1) the amount you received on the disposition, and (2) the amount (if any) of the life income interest you retained after the transfer will be treated as a taxable gift. That portion of the property's value that is attributable to the remainder interest is a gift of a future interest for which no annual exclusion is allowed. To the extent you made a gift of the life income interest, you may claim an annual exclusion, treating the person to whom you transferred the interest as the donee for purposes of computing the annual exclusion.

Specific Instructions

Part I.—General Information

Split Gifts—Gifts by Husband or Wife to Third Parties

A married couple may not file a joint gift tax return.

If you and your spouse agree, all gifts (including gifts of property held with your spouse as joint tenants or tenants by the entirety) either of you make to third parties during the calendar year may be considered as made one-half by each of you if:

- you and your spouse were married to one another at the time of the gift;
- you did not remarry during the rest of the calendar year;
- neither of you was a nonresident alien at the time of the gift; and
- you did not give your spouse a general power of appointment over the property interest transferred.

If you transferred property partly to your spouse and partly to third parties, you can only split the gifts if the interest transferred to the third parties is ascertainable at the time of the gift.

If you meet these requirements and want your gifts to be considered made one-half by you and one-half by your spouse, check the "Yes" box on line 12, page 1; complete lines 13 through 17; and have your spouse sign the consent on line 18. If you are not married or do not wish to split gifts, skip to Schedule A.

Line 15.—If you were married to one another for the entire calendar year, check the "Yes" box and skip to line 17. If you were married for only part of the year, check the "No" box and go to line 16.

Line 16.—Check the box that explains the change in your marital status during the year and give the date you were married, divorced, or widowed.

Consent of Spouse

To have your gifts (and generation-skipping transfers) considered as made one-half by each of you, your spouse must sign the consent. The consent may generally be signed at any time after the end of the calendar year. However, there are two exceptions. They are:

1. The consent may not be signed after April 15 following the end of the year in which the gift was made. (But, if neither you nor your spouse has filed a gift tax return for the year on or before that date, the consent must be made on the first gift tax return for the year filed by either of you.)
2. The consent may not be signed after a notice of deficiency for the gift or GST tax for the year has been sent to either you or your spouse.

The executor for a deceased spouse or the guardian for a legally incompetent spouse may sign the consent.

The consent is effective for the entire calendar year; therefore, all gifts made by both you and your spouse to third parties during the calendar year (while you were married) must be split.

If the consent is effective, the liability for the entire gift and GST taxes of each spouse is joint and several.

When the Consenting Spouse Must Also File a Gift Tax Return.—If the spouses elect gift splitting (described under "Split Gifts," above), then both the donor spouse and the consenting spouse must each file separate gift tax returns unless all the requirements of either Exception 1 or 2 below are met.

Exception 1.—During the calendar year:

- Only one spouse made any gifts;
- The total value of these gifts to each third-party donee does not exceed $20,000; and
- All of these gifts constitute present interests.

Exception 2.—During the calendar year:

- Only one spouse (the donor spouse) made gifts of more than $10,000 but not more than $20,000 to any third-party donee;
- The only gifts made by the other spouse (the consenting spouse) were gifts of not more than $10,000 to third-party donees other than those to whom the donor spouse made gifts; and
- All of the gifts by both spouses constitute present interests.

If either Exception 1 or 2 is met, only the donor spouse needs to file a return and the consenting spouse signifies consent on that return. This return may be made on **Form 709-A**, United States Short Form Gift Tax Return. This form is much easier to complete than Form 709, and you should consider filing it whenever your gifts to each third-party donee are not more than $20,000 for the year and consist entirely of tangible personal property.

Schedule A.—Computation of Taxable Gifts

Do not enter on Schedule A any gift or part of a gift that qualifies for the political organization, educational, or medical exclusions. In the instructions below, "gifts" means gifts (or parts of gifts) that do not qualify for the political organization, educational, or medical exclusions.

Gifts to Donees Other Than Your Spouse.—You must always enter all gifts of *future interests* that you made during the calendar year regardless of their value.

If you do not elect gift splitting.—If the total gifts of *present interests* to any donee are more than $10,000 in the calendar year, then you must enter *all such gifts* that you made during the year to or on behalf of that donee, including those gifts that will be excluded under the annual exclusion. If the total is $10,000 or less, you need not enter on Schedule A any gifts (except gifts of future interests) that you made to that donee.

If you elect gift splitting.—Enter on Schedule A the entire value of every gift you made during the calendar year while you were married, even if the gift's value will be less than $10,000 after it is split on line 2 of Part 3.

Gifts to Your Spouse.—You do not need to enter any of your gifts to your spouse on Schedule A unless you gave a gift of a terminable interest to your spouse, you gave a gift of a future interest to your spouse as described below, or your spouse was not a citizen of the U.S. at the time of the gift.

Terminable interest.—Terminable interests are defined on page 6 in the instructions to line 8. If all the terminable interests you gave to your spouse qualify as life estates with power of appointment (defined below) you do not need to enter any of them on Schedule A. However, if you gave your spouse *any* terminable interest that does not qualify as a life estate with power of appointment, you must report on Schedule A *all* gifts of terminable interests you made to your spouse during the year. You should not report any gifts you made to your spouse who is a U.S. citizen that are not terminable interests (except as described under *Future interest* on page 4); however, you must report all terminable interests, whether or not they can be deducted.

Charitable remainder trusts.—If you make a gift to a charitable remainder trust and your spouse is the only noncharitable beneficiary (other than yourself), the interest you gave to your spouse is not considered a terminable interest and, therefore, should not be shown on Schedule A. For definitions and rules concerning these trusts, see section 2056(b)(8)(B) and Regulations section 20.2055-2.

Future interest.—Generally, you should not report gifts of future interests to your spouse unless the future interest is also a terminable interest that is required to be reported as described above. However, if you gave a gift of a future interest to your spouse and you are required to report the gift on Form 709 because you gave the present interest to a donee other than your spouse, then you should enter the entire gift, including the future interest given to your spouse, on Schedule A. You should use the rules under "Gifts Subject to Both Gift and GST Taxes," below, to determine where to enter the gift on Schedule A.

Non-U.S. Citizen Spouse Donee.—If your spouse is not a U.S. citizen and you gave him or her a gift of a future interest, you must report on Schedule A all gifts to your spouse for the year. If all gifts to your spouse were present interests, do not report on Schedule A any gifts to your spouse if the total of such gifts for the year does not exceed $100,000 and all gifts in excess of $10,000 would otherwise qualify for a marital deduction. If the gifts exceed $100,000, you must report all of the gifts even though some may be excluded.

How To Complete Schedule A.—After you determine which gifts you made are subject to the gift tax and therefore should be listed on Schedule A, you must divide these gifts between those subject only to the gift tax (gifts made to non-skip persons—see below) and those subject to both the gift and GST taxes (gifts made to skip persons—see below). Gifts made to non-skip persons are entered on Part 1. Gifts made to skip persons are entered on Part 2.

If you need more space than that provided, attach a separate sheet, using the same format as Schedule A.

Gifts Subject to Both Gift and GST Taxes.—

Direct Skip.—The GST tax to be reported on Form 709 is imposed only on inter vivos direct skips. An "inter vivos direct skip" is a gift that: (1) is subject to the gift tax; (2) is an interest in property; and (3) is made to a skip person. All three requirements must be met before the gift is subject to the GST tax.

A gift is "subject to the gift tax" if you are required to list it on Schedule A of Form 709 (as described above). However, if you make a nontaxable gift (which is a direct skip) to a trust for the benefit of an individual, this transfer is subject to the GST tax unless:

(1) During the lifetime of the beneficiary, no corpus or income may be distributed to anyone other than the beneficiary; and

(2) If the beneficiary dies before the termination of the trust, the assets of the trust will be included in the gross estate of the beneficiary.

Note: *If the property transferred in the direct skip would have been includible in the donor's estate if the donor had died immediately after the transfer, see "Transfers Subject to an 'Estate Tax Inclusion Period'" on page 2.*

To determine if a gift "is of an interest in property" and "is made to a skip person," you must first determine if the donee is a "natural person" or a "trust" as defined below.

Trust.—For purposes of the GST tax, "trust" includes not only an explicit trust, but also any other arrangement (other than an estate) which although not explicitly a trust, has substantially the same effect as a trust. For example, "trust" includes life estates with remainders, terms for years, and insurance and annuity contracts.

Interest in Property.—If a gift is made to a "natural person," it is always considered a gift of an interest in property for purposes of the GST tax.

If a gift is made to a "trust," a natural person will have an interest in the property transferred to the trust if that person either has a present right to receive income or corpus from the trust (such as an income interest for life) or is a permissible current recipient of income or corpus from the trust (e.g., possesses a general power of appointment).

Skip Person.—A donee who is a "natural person" is a "skip person" if that donee is assigned to a generation which is two or more generations below the generation assignment of the donor. See "Determining the Generation of a Donee," below.

A donee who is a "trust" is a "skip person" if all the interests in the property transferred to the trust (as defined above) are held by skip persons.

A trust will also be a "skip person" if there are no interests in the property transferred to the trust held by any person, and future distributions or terminations from the trust can be made only to skip persons.

Non-Skip Person.—A non-skip person is any donee who is not a skip person.

Determining the Generation of a Donee.—Generally, a generation is determined along family lines as follows:

(1) A lineal descendant of a grandparent of the donor is assigned to the generation that results from comparing the number of generations between the grandparent and the descendant with the number of generations between the grandparent and the donor.

(2) A lineal descendant of a grandparent of a spouse (or former spouse) of the donor (other than the spouse; see (3), below) is assigned to the generation that results from comparing the number of generations between the grandparent and the descendant with the number of generations between the spouse (or former spouse) and the grandparent.

(3) A person who at any time was married to a person described in (1) or (2) above is assigned to the generation of that person. A person who at any time was married to the donor is assigned to the donor's generation.

(4) A relationship by adoption or half-blood is treated as a relationship by whole-blood.

(5) A person who is not assigned to a generation according to (1), (2), (3), or (4) above is assigned to a generation based on his or her birth date as follows:

(a) A person who was born not more than 12½ years after the donor is in the donor's generation.

(b) A person born more than 12½ years, but not more than 37½ years, after the donor is in the first generation younger than the donor.

(c) Similar rules apply for a new generation every 25 years.

If more than one of the rules for assigning generations applies to a donee, that donee is generally assigned to the youngest of the generations that would apply.

If an estate or trust, partnership, corporation, or other entity (other than certain charitable organizations and trusts described in sections 511(a)(2) and 511(b)(2) and governmental entities) is a donee, then each person who indirectly receives the gift through the entity is treated as a donee and is assigned to a generation as explained in the above rules.

Generation Assignment Where Intervening Parent Is Dead.—If you made a gift to your grandchild and at the time you made the gift, the grandchild's parent (who is your or your spouse's or your former spouse's child) is dead, then for purposes of generation assignment, your grandchild will be considered to be your child rather than your grandchild. Your grandchild's children will be treated as your grandchildren rather than your greatgrandchildren.

This rule is also applied to your lineal descendants below the level of grandchild. For example, if your grandchild is dead, your greatgrandchildren who are lineal descendants of the dead grandchild are considered your grandchildren for purposes of the GST tax.

Charitable organizations and trusts described in sections 511(a)(2) and 511(b)(2) and governmental entities are assigned to the donor's generation. Transfers to such organizations are therefore not subject to the GST tax. These gifts should always be listed in Part 1 of Schedule A.

Charitable Remainder Trusts.—Gifts in the form of charitable remainder annuity trusts, charitable remainder unitrusts, and pooled income funds are not transfers to skip persons and therefore are not direct skips. You should always list these gifts on Part 1 of Schedule A even if all of the life beneficiaries are skip persons.

The rules above can be illustrated by the following examples:

Example 1.—You give your house to your daughter for her life with the remainder then passing to her children. This gift is made to a "trust" even though there is no explicit trust instrument. The interest in the property transferred (the present right to use the house) is transferred to a non-skip person (your daughter). Therefore, the trust is not a skip person because there is an interest in the transferred property that is held by a non-skip person. The gift is not a direct skip and you should list it on Part 1 of Schedule A. (Note, however, that upon the death of the daughter, a termination of her interest in the "trust" will occur which may be subject to the generation-skipping transfer tax. See the instructions for line 5, Part 2, Schedule C (on page 7) for a discussion of how to allocate GST exemption to such a trust.)

Example 2.—You give $100,000 to your grandchild. This gift is a direct skip that is not made in trust. You should list it on Part 2 of Schedule A.

Example 3.—You establish a trust that is required to accumulate income for 10 years and then pay its income to your grandchildren for their lives and upon their deaths distribute the corpus to their children. Since the trust has no current beneficiaries, there are no present interests in the property transferred to the trust. All of the persons to whom the trust can make future distributions (including distributions upon the termination of interests in property held in trust) are skip persons (i.e., your grandchildren and greatgrandchildren). Therefore, the trust itself is a skip person and you should list the gift on Part 2 of Schedule A.

Example 4.—You establish a trust which pays all of its income to your grandchildren for 10 years. At the end of 10 years, the corpus is to be distributed to your children. Since for this purpose "interests" in trusts are defined only as present interests, all of the interests in this trust are held by skip persons (the children's "interests" are future interests). Therefore, the trust is a skip person and you should list the entire amount you transferred to the trust on Part 2 of Schedule A even though some of the trust's ultimate beneficiaries are non-skip persons.

Part 1.—List gifts subject only to the gift tax on Part 1. Generally, all of the gifts you made to your spouse (that are required to be listed, as described earlier), to your children, and to charitable organizations are not subject to the GST tax and should, therefore, be listed only on Part 1.

Group the gifts in four categories: gifts made to your spouse; gifts made to third parties that are to be split with your spouse; charitable gifts (if you are not splitting gifts with your spouse); and other gifts. If a transfer results in gifts to two or more individuals (such as a life estate to one with remainder to the other), list the gift to each separately.

Number and describe all gifts (including charitable, public, and similar gifts) in the columns provided in Schedule A. Describe each gift in enough detail so that the property can be easily identified, as explained below.

For real estate provide:

- a legal description of each parcel;
- the street number, name, and area if the property is located in a city; and
- a short statement of any improvements made to the property.

For bonds, give:

- the number of bonds transferred;
- the principal amount of each bond;
- name of obligor;
- date of maturity;
- rate of interest;
- date or dates when interest is payable;
- series number if there is more than one issue;
- exchanges where listed or, if unlisted, give the location of the principal business office of corporation; and
- CUSIP number, if available. The CUSIP number is a nine-digit number assigned by the American Banking Association to traded securities.

For stocks:

- give number of shares;
- state whether common or preferred;
- if preferred, give the issue, par value, quotation at which returned, and exact name of corporation;
- if unlisted on a principal exchange, give location of principal business office of corporation, state in which incorporated, and date of incorporation;
- if listed, give principal exchange; and
- give CUSIP number, if available. The CUSIP number is a nine-digit number assigned by the American Banking Association to traded securities.

For interests in property based on the length of a person's life, give the date of birth of the person.

For life insurance policies, give the name of the insurer and the policy number.

Clearly identify in the description column which gifts are subject to an "estate tax inclusion period" (ETIP) as described under **Transfers Subject to an "Estate Tax Inclusion Period"** on page 2.

Donor's Adjusted Basis of Gifts.—Show the basis you would use for income tax purposes if the gift were sold or exchanged. Generally, this means cost plus improvements, less applicable depreciation, amortization, and depletion.

For more information on adjusted basis, please see **Pub. 551**, Basis of Assets.

Date and Value of Gift.—The value of a gift is the fair market value of the property on the date the gift is made. The fair market value is the price at which the property would change hands between a willing buyer and a willing seller, when neither is forced to buy or to sell, and when both have reasonable knowledge of all relevant facts. Fair market value may not be determined by a forced sale price, nor by the sale price of the item in a market other than that in which the item is most commonly sold to the public. The location of the item must be taken into account wherever appropriate.

Stock of close corporations or inactive stock must be valued on the basis of net worth, earnings, earning and dividend capacity, and other relevant factors.

Note: *IRS has issued revised valuation tables to be used in determining the present value of an annuity, an interest for life or for a term of years, or a remainder or reversionary interest. The revised tables* ***must*** *be used for gifts made after* ***April 30, 1989.*** *For details, see Notice 89-60, 1989-1 C.B. 700.*

Supplemental Documents.—To support the value of your gifts, you must provide information showing how it was determined.

For stock of close corporations or inactive stock, attach balance sheets, particularly the one nearest the date of the gift, and statements of net earnings or operating results and dividends paid for each of the five preceding years.

For each life insurance policy, attach **Form 712,** Life Insurance Statement.

Note for single premium or paid-up policies: *In certain situations, for example, where the surrender value of the policy exceeds its replacement cost, the true economic value of the policy will be greater than the amount shown on line 56 of Form 712. In these situations, you should report the full economic value of the policy on Schedule A. See Rev. Rul. 78-137, 1978-1 C.B. 280 for details.*

If the gift was made by means of a trust, attach a certified or verified copy of the trust instrument.

Also attach any appraisal used to determine the value of real estate or other property.

If you do not attach this information, you must include in Schedule A full information to explain how the value was determined.

Part 2.—List on Part 2 only those gifts that are subject to both the gift and GST taxes. **You must list the gifts on Part 2 in the chronological order that you made them.** Number, describe, and value the gifts as described in the instructions for Part 1, above.

If you made a gift in "trust," list the entire gift as one line entry in Part 2. Enter the entire value of the property transferred to the "trust" even if the "trust" has non-skip person future beneficiaries.

How To Report Transfers Subject to an ETIP.—If you are reporting a generation-skipping transfer that was subject to an "estate tax inclusion period" (ETIP) (provided the ETIP closed as a result of something other than the death of the transferor), and you are also reporting gifts made during the year, complete Schedule A as you normally would with the following changes:

Sch. A, Part 2. Report the transfer subject to an ETIP on Schedule A, Part 2.

a. Column B.—In addition to the information already requested, describe the interest that is closing the ETIP; explain what caused the interest to terminate; and, list the year the gift portion of the transfer was reported and its item number on the Schedule A.

b. Column D.—give the date the ETIP closed rather than the date of the initial gift.

c. Column E.—Enter "N/A" in Column E.

Part 3.—Gift Tax Reconciliation

If you have made no gifts yourself and are filing this return only to report gifts made by your spouse but which are being split with you, skip lines 1–3 and enter your share of the split gifts on line 4.

Line 1.—Add the value of all your gifts shown in column E, Parts 1 and 2. Enter the total on line 1.

Line 2.—If you are not splitting gifts with your spouse, skip this line and enter the amount from line 1 on line 3. If you are splitting gifts with your spouse, show half of the gifts you made to third parties on line 2. On the dotted line indicate which numbered items from Parts 1 and 2 of Schedule A you treated this way.

Line 4.—If you are not splitting gifts, skip this line and go to line 5. If you gave all of the gifts, and your spouse is only filing to show his or her half of those gifts, you need not enter any gifts on line 4 of your return, or include your spouse's half anywhere else on your return. Your spouse should enter the amount from Schedule A, line 2, of your return on Schedule A, line 4, of his or her return. If both you and your spouse make gifts for which a return is required, the amount each of you shows on Schedule A, line 2, of his or her return must be shown on Schedule A, line 4, of the other's return.

Line 6.—Enter the total annual exclusions you are claiming for the gifts listed on Schedule A (including gifts listed on line 4). See "Annual Exclusion" on page 2. If you split a gift with your spouse, the annual exclusion you claim against that gift may not be more than your half of the gift.

Deductions

Line 8.—Enter on line 8 all of the gifts to your spouse which you listed on Schedule A and for which you are claiming a marital deduction. **Do not enter any gift that you did not include on Schedule A**. On the dotted line on line 8, indicate which numbered items from Schedule A are gifts to your spouse for which you are claiming the marital deduction.

You may deduct all gifts of nonterminable interests made during this time that you entered on Schedule A regardless of amount, and certain gifts of terminable interests as outlined below. **Do not enter on line 8 any gifts to your spouse who was not a U.S. citizen at the time of the gift.**

Terminable Interests.—Generally, you cannot take the marital deduction if the gift to your spouse is a terminable interest. In most instances, a terminable interest is nondeductible if someone other than the donee spouse will have an interest in the property following the termination of the donee spouse's interest. Some examples of terminable interests are:

- a life estate;
- an estate for a specified number of years; or
- any other property interest that after a period of time will terminate or fail.

If you transfer an interest to your spouse as sole joint tenant with yourself or as a tenant by the entirety, the interest is not considered a terminable interest just because the tenancy may be severed.

Life Estate With Power of Appointment.—You may deduct, without an election, a gift of a terminable interest if all four requirements below are met:

1. your spouse is entitled for life to all of the income from the entire interest;
2. the income is paid yearly or more often;
3. your spouse has the unlimited power, while he or she is alive or by will, to appoint the entire interest in all circumstances; and
4. no part of the entire interest is subject to another person's power of appointment (except to appoint it to your spouse).

If only part of the property interest meets the above requirements, see Pub. 448 for the part that qualifies for the marital deduction.

Election To Deduct Qualified Terminable Interest Property (QTIP).—You may *elect* to deduct a gift of a terminable interest if it meets requirements 1, 2, and 4 above, even though it does not meet requirement 3.

Make the election by checking the box on line 16 of Schedule A and entering the appropriate item numbers from Schedule A. You may not make the election on a late filed Form 709.

Line 9.—Enter the amount of the annual exclusions that were claimed for the gifts you listed on line 8.

Line 11.—You may deduct from the total gifts made during the calendar year all gifts you gave to or for the use of:

- The United States, a state or political subdivision of a state or the District of Columbia, for exclusively public purposes;
- Any corporation, trust, community chest, fund, or foundation organized and operated only for religious, charitable, scientific, literary, or educational purposes, or to prevent cruelty to children or animals, or to foster national or international amateur sports competition (if none of its activities involve providing athletic equipment (unless it is a qualified amateur sports organization)), as long as no part of the earnings benefits any one person, no substantial propaganda is produced, and no lobbying or campaigning for any candidate for public office is done;
- A fraternal society, order, or association operating under a lodge system, if the transferred property is to be used only for religious, charitable, scientific, literary, or educational purposes, including the encouragement of art and the prevention of cruelty to children or animals;
- Any war veterans organization organized in the United States (or any of its possessions), or any of its auxiliary departments or local chapters or posts, as long as no part of any of the earnings benefits any one person.

On line 11, show your total charitable, public, or similar gifts (minus exclusions allowed). On the dotted line indicate which numbered items from the top of Schedule A are charitable gifts.

See Pub. 448 for more information.

Line 14.—If you did not list any gifts on Part 2, enter "-0-" on line 14. If you entered gifts on Part 2, or if you and your spouse elected gift splitting and your spouse made gifts subject to the GST tax that you are required to show on your Form 709, complete Schedule C, and enter on line 14 the total of Schedule C, Part 3, column H.

Line 16.—If you make the election under section 2523(f) (see instructions for line 8 of Schedule A), the terminable interest property involved will be included in your spouse's gross estate upon his or her death (section 2044). If your spouse disposes (by gift or otherwise) of all or part of the qualifying life income interest, he or she will be considered to have made a transfer of the entire property that is subject to the gift tax (see "Transfer of Certain Life Estates" on page 3).

Line 17.—Section 2523(f)(6) creates an automatic QTIP election for gifts of joint and survivor annuities where the spouses are the only possible recipients of the annuity prior to the death of the last surviving spouse.

The donor spouse can elect out of QTIP treatment, however, by checking the box on line 17 and entering the item number from Schedule A for the annuities for which you are making the election. Any annuities entered on line 17 cannot also be entered on line 8 of Schedule A, Part 3. Any such annuities that are not listed on line 17 must be entered on line 8 of Part 3, Schedule A. If there is more than one such joint and survivor annuity, you are not required to make the election for all of them. Once made, the election is irrevocable.

Schedule B.—Gifts From Prior Periods

If you did not file gift tax returns for previous periods, check the "No" box at the top of Schedule B and skip to the Tax Computation on page 1. (However, be sure to complete Schedule C, if applicable.) If you filed gift tax returns for previous periods, check the "Yes" box and complete Schedule B by listing the years or quarters in chronological order as described below. If you need more space than that provided, attach a separate sheet, using the same format as Schedule B.

If you filed returns for gifts made before 1971 or after 1981, show the calendar years in column A. If you filed returns for gifts made after 1970 and before 1982, show the calendar quarters.

In column B, identify the Internal Revenue Service office where you filed the returns. If you have changed your name, be sure to list any other names under which the returns were filed. If there was any other variation in the names under which you filed, such as the use of full given names instead of initials, please explain.

In column E, show the correct amount (the amount finally determined) of the taxable gifts for each earlier period.

Schedule C.—Computation of Generation-Skipping Transfer Tax

Part 1.—Generation-Skipping Transfers

You must enter on Part 1 all of the gifts you listed on Part 2 of Schedule A in that order and using those same values.

Column B.—*Transfers Subject to an ETIP.*—If you are reporting a generation-skipping transfer that was subject to an "estate tax inclusion period" (ETIP), complete column B for such transfer as follows:

a. Provided the GST exemption is being allocated on a timely filed gift tax return, enter the value as of the close of the ETIP;

b. Otherwise, enter the value as of the time the exemption allocation was made.

Column C.—If you elected gift splitting, enter half the value of each gift entered in column B. If you did not elect gift splitting, enter "-0-" in column C.

Column E.—You are allowed to claim the gift tax annual exclusion currently allowable with respect to your reported direct skips (other than certain direct skips to trusts), using the rules and limits discussed earlier for the gift tax annual exclusion. However, you must allocate the exclusion on a gift by gift basis for GST computation purposes. You must allocate the exclusion to each gift to the maximum allowable amount and in chronological order, beginning with the earliest gift that qualifies for the exclusion. Be sure that you do not claim a total exclusion of more than $10,000 per donee.

Note: *You may not claim any annual exclusion for a direct skip made to a trust unless the trust meets the requirements discussed under "Direct Skip" on page 4.*

Part 2.—GST Exemption Reconciliation

Special QTIP Election.—If you have elected QTIP treatment on line 16, Schedule A, Part 3, for any gifts in trust listed on Schedule A, Part 1, then you may make an election on Schedule C to treat the entire trust as non-QTIP for purposes of the GST tax. The election must be made for the entire trust which contains the particular gift involved on this return. Be sure to identify by item number the specific gift for which you are making this special QTIP election.

Line 5.—You may wish to allocate your exemption to transfers made in "trust" that are not direct skips. For example, if you transferred property to a trust that has your children as its present beneficiaries and your grandchildren and greatgrandchildren as future beneficiaries, the transfer was not a direct skip because the present interests in the trust are held by non-skip persons. However, future terminations and distributions made from this trust would be subject to the GST tax. You may elect to reduce the trust's inclusion ratio by allocating part or all of your exemption to the transfer. Since this transfer would be entered on Schedule A, Part 1, it will not be shown on Schedule C. In other cases you may wish to allocate your exemption to a trust which is not involved in a transfer listed on Schedule A or C.

To allocate your exemption to such transfers, you should attach a statement to this Form 709 and entitle it "Notice of Allocation." You may file one Notice of Allocation and consolidate on it all of your Schedule A, Part 1, transfers, plus all transfers not appearing on Form 709, to which you wish to allocate your exemption. The notice should contain the following for each "trust":

- The trust's EIN, if known;
- The item number(s) from column A, Schedule A, Part 1, of the gifts to that trust;
- The values shown in column E, Schedule A, Part 1 for the gifts (adjusted to account for split gifts, if any, reported on Schedule A, Part 3, line 2);
- The annual exclusion claimed against each gift;
- The net value of each gift after the reduction for the annual exclusion, if applicable; and
- The amount of your GST exemption allocated to each gift.

Total the exemption allocations and enter this total on line 5.

Note: *Where the property involved in such a transfer would be includible in the donor's estate if the donor died immediately after the transfer (other than by reason of the donor having died within 3 years of making the gift), you cannot allocate the GST exemption at the time of the transfer but must wait until the end of the "estate tax inclusion period." For details, see "Transfers Subject to an 'Estate Tax Inclusion Period'" on page 2, and section 2642(f).*

Part 3.—Tax Computation

You must enter on Part 3 every gift you listed on Part 1 of Schedule C.

Column C.— You are not required to allocate your available exemption. You may allocate some, all, or none of your available exemption, as you wish, among the gifts listed in Part 3 of Schedule C. However, the total exemption claimed in column C may not exceed the amount you entered on line 3 of Part 2 of Schedule C.

You may enter an amount in column C that is greater than the amount you entered in column B.

Column D.—Carry your computation to three decimal places (e.g., "1.000").

Part 2.—Tax Computation (Page 1)

Line 7.—If you are a citizen or resident of the United States, you must take any available unified credit against gift tax. Nonresident aliens may not claim the unified credit. If you are a nonresident alien, delete the 192,800 entry and write in "-0-" on line 11.

Line 10.—Enter 20% of the amount allowed as a specific exemption for gifts made after September 8, 1976, and before January 1, 1977. (These amounts will be among those listed in column D of Schedule B, for gifts made in the third and fourth quarters of 1976.)

Line 13.—Gift tax conventions are in effect with France, the United Kingdom, Australia, West Germany, and Japan. If you are claiming a credit for payment of foreign gift tax, figure the credit on an attached sheet and attach evidence that the foreign taxes were paid. See the applicable convention for details of computing the credit.

Line 19.—Make your check or money order payable to "Internal Revenue Service" and write the donor's social security number on it. You may not use an overpayment on Form 1040 to offset the gift and GST taxes owed on Form 709.

Signature.—You, as a donor, must sign the return. If you pay another person, firm, or corporation to prepare your return, that person must also sign the return as preparer unless he or she is your regular full-time employee.

Table for Computing Tax

Column A Taxable amount over—	Column B Taxable amount not over—	Column C Tax on amount in Column A	Column D Rate of tax on excess over amount in Column A
--------	$10,000	--------	18%
$10,000	20,000	$1,800	20%
20,000	40,000	3,800	22%
40,000	60,000	8,200	24%
60,000	80,000	13,000	26%
80,000	100,000	18,200	28%
100,000	150,000	23,800	30%
150,000	250,000	38,800	32%
250,000	500,000	70,800	34%
500,000	750,000	155,800	37%
750,000	1,000,000	248,300	39%
1,000,000	1,250,000	345.800	41%
1,250,000	1,500,000	448,300	43%
1,500,000	2,000,000	555,800	45%
2,000,000	2,500,000	780,800	49%
2,500,000	3,000,000	1,025,800	53%
3,000,000	10,000,000	1,290,800	55%
10,000,000	21,040,000	5,140,800	60%
21,040,000	----------	11,764,800	55%

☆U.S. GOVERNMENT PRINTING OFFICE: 1991 518-939/21076

Department of the Treasury
Internal Revenue Service
Catalog Number 15056O

Publication 529

Miscellaneous Deductions

For use in preparing

1990 Returns

Important Change for 1990

Cellular telephones. Beginning in 1990, you must use special rules to figure your depreciation deduction for a cellular telephone you used in a trade or business or in your work as an employee.

Introduction

What this publication includes. This publication explains what expenses are deductible as miscellaneous itemized deductions on Schedule A (Form 1040). It discusses:

- Deductions subject to the 2% limit, namely:
  - Unreimbursed employee business expenses, and
  - Other expenses,
- Deductions not subject to the 2% limit,
- How to report these deductions, and
- Expenses that are not deductible.

These expenses are first presented in convenient lists. They are followed by detailed information on the various expenses and an explanation of how, if deductible, they should be reported on your return.

What is not in this publication. This publication does not discuss itemized deductions you may claim for:

- Medical and dental expenses
- Interest you paid
- Contributions you made
- Casualty and theft losses
- Moving expenses

These deductions are discussed in the following publications:

Medical and Dental Expenses	Publication 502
Interest Expense	Publication 545
Charitable Contributions	Publication 526
Nonbusiness Disasters, Casualties, and Thefts	Publication 547
Moving Expenses	Publication 521

Free Publications and Forms

If you need information on a subject not covered in this publication, you may check our other free publications. To order publications and forms, call our toll-free telephone number 1–800–TAX–FORM (1–800–829–3676) or write the IRS Forms Distribution Center for your area as shown in the income tax package.

List of Miscellaneous Deductions Subject To the 2% Limit

You can claim the following expenses only to the extent that the total you claim is more than 2% of your adjusted gross income. Some of the more common expenses listed are discussed later.

Unreimbursed employee business expenses:

- Deductible employment-related education
- Depreciation on a home computer or cellular telephone your employer requires you to use in your work
- Dues to professional societies
- Job search expenses in your present occupation
- Laboratory breakage fees
- Liquidated damages paid to former employer for breach of employment contract
- Malpractice insurance premiums
- Medical examinations required by employer
- Occupational taxes paid by an employee
- Part of home used regularly and exclusively in work
- Passport for business trip
- Research expenses of a college professor
- Small tools and supplies used in your work
- Subscriptions to professional journals and trade magazines related to your work
- Travel, transportation, entertainment, and gift expenses that are unreimbursed and related to your work
- Union dues and expenses
- Work clothes and uniforms if required and not suitable for everyday use

Other expenses:

- Appraisal fees for a casualty loss or charitable contribution
- Clerical help and office rent in caring for investments
- Custodial and trust administration fees in connection with property held for producing income
- Depreciation on home computers to the extent used for investments
- Fees to collect interest and dividends
- Hobby expenses, but generally not more than hobby income
- Indirect miscellaneous deductions passed through grantor trusts, partnerships, and S corporations
- Investment fees and expenses
- Legal fees related to producing or collecting taxable income, doing or keeping your job, or for tax advice
- Repayments of social security benefits
- Safe deposit box rental
- Tax advice and preparation fees
- Trustee's fees for your IRA, if separately billed and paid

List of Miscellaneous Deductions Not Subject To the 2% Limit

- Gambling losses to the extent of gambling winnings
- Federal estate tax on income in respect of a decedent
- Amortizable premium on taxable bonds purchased before October 23, 1986
- Deduction for repayment of substantial amounts under a claim of right
- Unrecovered investment in pension
- Impairment-related work expenses of persons with disabilities

List of Nondeductible Expenses

- Adoption expenses
- Base rate of first residential telephone line
- Burial or funeral expenses
- Campaign expenses
- Capital expenses
- Certain fees and licenses, such as car licenses, marriage licenses, and dog tags
- Check-writing fees
- Commuting expenses
- Fines and penalties, such as parking tickets
- Gifts to influence legislation
- Health spa expenses
- Hobby losses
- Home repairs, insurance, and rent

Illegal bribes and kickbacks—See *Bribes and kickbacks* in Chapter 13 of Publication 535, *Business Expenses*

Life insurance premiums

Losses from the sale of your home, furniture, personal car, etc.

Lost or misplaced cash or property—See Publication 547

Lunches and meals while working late

Personal legal expenses

Personal, living, or family expenses

Political contributions

Professional accreditation fees

Relief fund contributions for fellow employee

Self-improvement expenses

Stockholders' meeting, expenses of attending

Tax-exempt income expenses

Voluntary unemployment benefit fund contributions

Wristwatches

Deductions Subject To the 2% Limit

Most miscellaneous itemized deductions are deductible only to the extent the total of all these deductions is more than 2% of your adjusted gross income. Miscellaneous deductions that are not subject to the limit are discussed later under *Deductions Not Subject To the 2% Limit.*

Deductions subject to the 2% limit are discussed in the two general categories that are shown on Schedule A (Form 1040): unreimbursed employee expenses, and other expenses. Your deduction is the excess of the total of the allowable deductions in these two categories over 2% of your adjusted gross income. The 2% limit is applied after any other deduction limit (such as the 80% limit on meals and entertainment) is applied. See *How To Report,* later, for more information on applying the limit.

Exception for performing artists. Although most unreimbursed employee expenses are subject to the 2% limit, there is an exception for unreimbursed business expenses of certain performing artists. See *Performing Artists,* later.

For information on deductible employee business expenses such as travel, transportation, entertainment, and gift expenses, get Publication 463, *Travel, Entertainment, and Gift Expenses,* and Publication 917, *Business Use of a Car.*

Unreimbursed Employee Business Expenses

If you are an employee and have business expenses that are not reimbursed or that are more than the amount reimbursed by your employer, you can generally deduct them only as a miscellaneous deduction (subject to the 2% limit) on Schedule A (Form 1040). If you received a Form W-2 with the box on line 6 checked to indicate "Statutory employee," do not use Schedule A to deduct your expenses. See *Statutory employees,* later.

Your "reimbursed" employee business expenses are treated as not reimbursed if your employer's reimbursement or other expense allowance arrangement either:

- Does not require you to adequately account for your expenses to the person providing the reimbursement, or
- Allows you to keep any reimbursement or allowance in excess of the expenses adequately accounted for.

Form 2106. File Form 2106, *Employee Business Expenses,* if you are an employee and are deducting expenses attributable to your job.

Exceptions. Do not complete Form 2106 if any of the following apply:

- You account to your employer by means of an account book, diary, or similar statement, your business expenses equal your reimbursement, and the reimbursement is not included on your Form W-2 as if it were wages. If this exception applies, do not deduct the expenses or report the reimbursement as income.
- You are not claiming job expenses for travel, transportation, meals or entertainment, and you were not reimbursed for any of the expenses you do claim. (Examples are educational expenses, uniforms, home office, and union dues.) If this exception applies, list the expenses directly on line 20 of Schedule A (Form 1040).
- You are a statutory employee.

Statutory employees. If you are a statutory employee, deduct your employee business expenses on Schedule C (Form 1040) instead of Schedule A (Form 1040).

You may be a statutory employee if:

1) You are a driver who distributes meat, vegetable, fruit, or bakery products; distributes beverages (other than milk); or picks up and delivers laundry or dry cleaning, if you are an agent of your employer or you are paid on commission.
2) You are a full-time life insurance sales agent whose principal business activity is selling life insurance or annuity contracts, or both, primarily for one life insurance company.
3) You work at home on materials or goods furnished by your employer. Your employer must furnish specifications for the work to be done and the work must be returned to your employer or a person named by your employer.
4) As a full-time traveling or city salesperson, you turn in orders to your employer from wholesalers, retailers, contractors, or operators of hotels, restaurants, or other similar establishments. The goods sold must be merchandise for resale or supplies for use in the buyer's business operation. This work must be your principal business activity.

If you are a statutory employee, you will receive a Form W-2 from your employer with the box on line 6 checked to indicate "Statutory employee."

Travel, Transportation, Meals, Entertainment, and Gift Expenses

If you are an employee and have ordinary and necessary travel, transportation, meals, entertainment, and gift expenses related to your work, you may be able to deduct these expenses on your income tax return.

Travel expenses are those incurred while traveling away from home for your employer. They include the cost of getting to and from your business destination (air, rail, bus, etc.), meals and lodging while away from home, and other expenses, such as taxi fares, baggage charges, and cleaning and laundry expenses.

Transportation expenses are the expenses of getting from one work place to another, or going between your residence and a temporary work place within your metropolitan area, provided you have a regular workplace within that same area, when you are not traveling away from home. They include the cost of transportation by air, rail, bus, taxi, and the cost of using your car. Within your metropolitan area, a temporary work place is any location you perform services on a short-term basis (generally a matter of days or weeks).

Meals and entertainment expenses generally must be directly related to the active conduct of your trade or business. However, the expense only needs to be associated with the active conduct of your trade or business if it directly precedes or follows a substantial and bona fide business related discussion.

You can deduct only 80% of your business-related meal and entertainment expenses unless the expenses meet certain exceptions. This limit applied before the 2% limit.

You can generally deduct up to $25 of business gifts you give to any one individual during the year. Certain awards and generally distributed items costing $4 or less which display your name are excluded from this limit.

Reimbursement for meals and entertainment. If you pay for work-related meal or entertainment, and it is not clear that a reimbursement excludes these expenses or it is not clear what amount of them the reimbursement covers, see the worksheet in the Form 2106 instructions.

For more information on travel, meals, entertainment, and gift expenses and reimbursements, get Publication 463. For transportation expenses, get Publication 917.

Work Clothes and Uniforms

You can deduct the cost and upkeep of work clothes only if they are required as a condition of your employment and are not suitable for everyday wear. To qualify for the deduction, both conditions must be met. It is not enough that you wear distinctive clothing; it must be specifically required by your employer. Nor is it enough that you do not in fact wear your work clothes away from work; the clothing must not be suitable for taking the place of your regular clothing.

Examples of occupations in which you may be required to wear uniforms which qualify are: delivery workers, firefighters, health care workers, law enforcement officers, letter carriers, professional athletes, and transportation workers (air, rail, bus, etc.).

Musicians and entertainers can deduct the cost of theatrical clothing and accessories if they are not suitable for ordinary use.

However, work clothing consisting of white cap, white shirt or white jacket, white bib overalls, and standard work shoes, which a painter is required by his union to wear on the job, is not distinctive in character or in the nature of a uniform. Similarly, the cost and maintenance of blue work clothes worn by a welder at the request of a foreman are not deductible.

Protective clothing. You can deduct the cost of protective clothing required in your work, such as safety shoes or boots, safety glasses, hard hats, and work gloves.

Examples of occupations in which you may be required to wear safety items are: carpenters, cement workers, chemical workers, electricians, fishers, linemen, machinists, oil field workers, pipe fitters, steamfitters, and truck drivers.

Military uniforms. You generally cannot deduct the cost of your uniforms if you are on full-time active duty in the armed forces. However, if you are an armed forces reservist, you can deduct the unreimbursed cost of your uniform if military regulations restrict you from wearing it except while on duty as a reservist. In figuring the deduction, you must reduce the cost by any nontaxable allowance you receive for these expenses.

If local military rules do not allow you to wear fatigue uniforms when you are off duty, you can deduct the amount by which the cost of buying and keeping up these uniforms is more than the uniform allowance you receive.

If you are a student at an armed forces academy, you cannot deduct the cost of your uniforms if they replace regular clothing. You can deduct the cost of insignia, shoulder boards, and related items.

You can deduct the cost of your uniforms if you are a civilian faculty or staff member of a military school.

Home Computers and Cellular Telephones

If you purchased a home computer or cellular telephone, you can claim a depreciation deduction and a section 179 deduction (these deductions did not apply to a cellular telephone before 1990) if you meet the tests explained below.

Employee use of a computer or cellular telephone. If you are an employee and you use your computer or cellular telephone in connection with your work, you must meet the following tests to claim a deduction. Your use of a computer in your home or your use of a cellular telephone must be:

For the convenience of your employer, and

Required as a condition of your employment.

"Required as a condition of your employment" means that you are not able to properly perform your duties without it. Whether or not you are able to properly perform your duties without the computer or cellular telephone depends on all the facts and circumstances. It is not necessary that your employer explicitly requires you to use your computer or cellular telephone. Also, it is not sufficient that your employer merely states that your use of these items is a condition of your employment.

If you use your home computer or cellular telephone in your work as an employee, but do not meet the above tests, you cannot deduct the costs for these items as business expenses.

Example. You are employed as an engineer with an engineering firm. You occasionally take work home at night rather than working late at the office. You own and use a computer that is similar to the one you use at the office to complete your work at home. Since your use of the computer is not for the convenience of your employer, and is not required as a condition of your employment, no deduction is allowed.

More than 50% test. If you meet the two tests above, and also use your home computer or cellular telephone more than 50% of the time during the year in your work, you can claim an accelerated depreciation deduction and a section 179 deduction.

If you meet the above two tests, but do not use your home computer or cellular telephone more than 50% of the time during the year in your work, you must depreciate these items using the straight line method, as explained in Publication 534, *Depreciation.*

The more-than-50% test does not apply if part of your home is treated as a regular business establishment and you use the computer exclusively in that part. To be treated as a regular business establishment, that part of your home must meet the use tests described under *Using Your Home in Your Work,* later.

Nonemployee use of a computer. If you use your computer to produce income other than from a business, such as from investments, see *Home Computer,* under *Other Expenses,* later.

The time you use your computer for investments does not count as business-use time for the more-than-50% test. However, if you meet the more-than-50% test, you can combine the business/investment time to figure your section 179 deduction and accelerated depreciation deduction. If you do not meet the more-than-50% test, you can use the combined time to figure the depreciation deduction under the straight line method.

Reporting and substantiation requirements. The unreimbursed depreciation expense (including the section 179 deduction) for your home computer or cellular telephone is claimed as a miscellaneous deduction, subject to the 2% limit, on Schedule A (Form 1040). To claim the deduction for these items, you must complete Part V of Form 4562, *Depreciation and Amortization,* and attach it to your tax return.

You must maintain records to prove your percentage of business use.

Note. The rules relating to cellular telephones applies to property placed in service or leased in tax years beginning after December 31, 1989.

For more information about depreciation (including the section 179 deduction) and recordkeeping requirements, get Publication 534.

Union Dues and Expenses

You can deduct dues and initiation fees you pay for union membership.

Assessments for benefit payments to unemployed union members are deductible. However, you cannot deduct the part of the assessments or contributions that provides funds for the payment of sick, accident, or death benefits. Also, you cannot deduct contributions to a pension fund even if the union requires you to make such contributions.

Educational Expenses

You can deduct expenses you have for education, even though the education may lead to a degree, if the education:

- Is required by your employer, or the law, to keep your salary, status, or job, and serves a business purpose of your employer, or
- Maintains or improves skills required in your present work.

You cannot deduct expenses you have for education, even though the preceding requirements are met, if the education:

- Is needed to meet the minimum educational requirements to qualify you in your work or business, or
- Will lead to qualifying you in a new trade or business.

If the education qualifies you in a new trade or business, you cannot deduct the educational expenses even if you do not intend to enter that trade or business.

If your education meets the requirements, you can deduct expenses for tuition, books, supplies, laboratory fees, and similar items, and certain transportation costs. You can also deduct the cost of a correspondence course if it meets the requirements.

You cannot deduct the cost of travel that in itself constitutes a form of education. For example, a French teacher who travels to France in order to maintain general familiarity with the French language and culture cannot deduct such expenses.

Get Publication 508, *Educational Expenses,* for a complete discussion of education expenses.

Job Search Expenses

You may be able to deduct certain expenses you have in looking for a new job in your present occupation, even if you do not get a new job. You cannot deduct these expenses if you are looking for a job in a new occupation, even if you get the job.

If you are unemployed, the kind of work you did for your past employer is your occupation. If there is a substantial break between the time of your past job and your looking for a new one, you cannot deduct your expenses.

You cannot deduct your expenses if you are seeking employment for the first time, even if you get the job.

Employment agency fees. If you pay employment agency fees in looking for a new job in your same occupation, you can deduct these expenses as an itemized deduction. If, in a later year, your employer pays you back for employment agency fees, you must include the amount you receive in gross income to the extent of your tax benefit in the earlier year (as explained under *Recoveries* in Publication 525, *Taxable and Nontaxable Income*). If your employer pays the fees directly to the employment agency and you were not responsible for them, you do not include them in your gross income.

Résumé. Amounts you spend for typing, printing, and mailing copies of a résumé to prospective employers are deductible as a miscellaneous deduction if you spent the amounts in looking for a new job in your present occupation.

Travel and transportation expenses. If you travel to an area and, while there, you look for a new job in your present occupation and also engage in personal activities, travel expenses to and from this area may be deductible as a miscellaneous itemized deduction. To be deductible, the trip must be primarily to look for a new job. The amount of time you spend on personal activity compared to the amount of time you spend in looking for work is important in determining whether the trip is primarily personal.

Even if the travel expenses to and from an area are not deductible, the expenses of looking for a new job in your present occupation, while in the area, are deductible.

Two Places of Work

If you work at two places in a day, whether or not for the same employer, you may be able to deduct the expenses of getting from one place to the other. For more information, get Publication 917.

Research Expenses of a College Professor

If you are a college professor, you can deduct research expenses, including travel expenses, for teaching, lecturing, or writing and publishing on subjects that relate directly to the field of your teaching duties.

Repayment of Income Aid Payment

If you repay a lump-sum income aid payment that you received and included in income in an earlier year, you can deduct the repayment on Schedule A (Form 1040). An "income aid payment" is one that is received under an employer's plan to aid employees who lose their jobs due to lack of work.

Using Your Home in Your Work

If you are not self-employed and you use a part of your home ***regularly and exclusively*** for business purposes, you may be able to deduct a part of the operating and depreciation expenses on your home. You cannot deduct any part of personal expenses that are for family household purposes.

Use tests. You may deduct certain expenses for operating a part of your home only if that part of your home is used ***regularly and exclusively*** as:

- Your principal place of business for any trade or business in which you engage,
- A place to meet or deal with your patients, clients, or customers in the normal course of your trade or business, or
- A separate structure that is used in your trade or business and is not attached to your house or residence.

In addition, if the regular and exclusive business use is for your work as an employee, the use must be ***for the convenience of your employer*** and not just appropriate and helpful in your job.

If you claim a home office deduction based on meeting with patients, clients, or customers, you must physically meet with them on your premises, and your meetings with them must be substantial and integral to the conduct of your business.

Occasional meetings and telephone calls are insufficient.

You may have a principal place of business for ***each*** trade or business in which you engage. For example, as a teacher, your principal place of business for teaching is the school. If you also engage in a retail sales business and use part of your home as your principal place of business for retail selling, expenses for this business use of your home may be deductible.

The business use of your home. You cannot deduct any operating or depreciation expenses for the use of your home if the use is for a profit-seeking activity that is not a trade or business. For example, you cannot deduct these expenses if you use a part of your home, even though regularly and exclusively, to read financial periodicals and reports, clip bond coupons, and perform similar investment activities on your own behalf, because these activities are not a trade or business.

The use of a part of your home for ***both personal and business purposes*** does not meet the exclusive use test and you cannot deduct expenses for business use. If, for example, you use the den of your home to write legal briefs, prepare tax returns, or perform similar activities, as well as for personal purposes, you cannot deduct any expenses for the business use of that part of your home. There is an exception for the use of your home as a day-care center.

Use of your home as a day-care center. The exclusive use requirement does not apply when you regularly use your home, or any part of your home, in your business of providing day-care services to children, persons with disabilities, or the elderly.

Storage use. You can deduct certain business expenses for the part of your home you regularly use to store goods you sell at retail or wholesale in your trade or business. Your home must be the only fixed location of that business. This storage space can have other uses, but the space must be a specific area.

Percentage of business use. To figure the percentage of your home used for business, compare the square feet of space used for business to the total square feet in your home. Or, if the rooms in your home are approximately the same size, you may compare the number of rooms used for business to the total number of rooms in your home. If neither of these methods applies to your situation, use any other reasonable method. Generally, you figure the business part of your expenses by applying the percentage to the total of each expense.

If you use part of your home as a day-care center and you make any use of that part for personal purposes, you must also figure what percentage of available time you actually use it for business. You then apply the business percentage of time to the business part of your expenses.

Limit on deduction for business use. The deduction for the business use of your home is limited to the gross income from that business use minus the sum of:

1) The business percentage of the otherwise deductible mortgage interest, real estate taxes, and casualty and theft losses, and
2) The expenses for your business that are not attributable to the use of your home (for example, salaries or supplies).

This limit is discussed under *Deduction Limit* in Publication 587, *Business Use of Your Home.*

The cost of repairs. You can deduct the cost of painting and repairing rooms that are used only for business purposes. You cannot deduct the costs of painting and repairing rooms used for other purposes.

You can deduct part of the cost of painting the outside of your home or repairing the roof based on the percentage of business use. However, you cannot deduct expenses for lawn care and landscaping.

Depreciation. You can deduct depreciation on the part of your home used for business.

Home leased to employer. If you lease any part of your home to your employer, you cannot claim home office expenses for any period you use any part of your home to perform services for your employer.

How to report. If you are an employee, you generally report your expenses for the business use of your home (insurance, maintenance, utilities, depreciation) on Form 2106. If the business use of the home expenses were your only employee business expenses in 1990 and your employer did not pay you for any of them, do not fill out Form 2106. Instead, enter your total expenses directly on line 20, Schedule A.

Fill out Form 2106 if either:

- You claim any travel, transportation, meal, or entertainment expenses for your job, or
- Your employer paid you for any of your job expenses reportable on line 20, Schedule A.

If either applies, enter the amount from line 11 of Form 2106 on line 20 of Schedule A.

If you do not receive any reimbursement for the business use of your home expenses or if your expenses exceed reimbursement, you can deduct the expenses only if you itemize deductions on Schedule A. Include the office-in-home expenses for mortgage interest under *Interest You Paid,* real estate taxes under *Taxes You Paid,* and casualty and theft losses under *Casualty and Theft Losses* on Schedule A. You enter the rest of your office-in-the-home expenses, as well as any other employee business expenses, as miscellaneous itemized deductions on line 20 of Schedule A, subject to the 2% of adjusted gross income limit.

You can include the remaining real estate taxes, mortgage interest, or casualty losses on the appropriate lines on Schedule A (Form 1040).

Records. You should keep records that will give the information needed to figure the deduction according to these rules. Also keep canceled checks and receipts of the expenses paid to prove the deductions you claim.

For more information on using your home in your work and how to compute your allowable deduction, get Publication 587.

Other Expenses

You can deduct certain other expenses as miscellaneous itemized deductions subject to the 2% of adjusted gross income limit. They are listed on line 21 of Schedule A (Form 1040). These are expenses you pay:

1) To produce or collect income,
2) To manage, conserve, or maintain property held for producing income, or
3) To determine, contest, pay, or claim a refund of any tax.

The expenses must be directly related to the income or income-producing property, and the income must be taxable to you.

Indirect deductions of pass-through entities (partnerships and S corporations). Deductions of pass-through entities are passed through to the partners or shareholders. If the deductions are miscellaneous itemized deductions, they are generally subject to the 2% limit.

Information returns. You should receive information returns from these entities. Partnerships and S corporations issue Schedule K–1, which lists the items and amounts you must report, and identifies the tax return schedules and lines to use.

Example. If you are a member of an investment club partnership that is formed solely to invest in securities, and its income is solely from taxable dividends, interest, and gains from sales of securities, you can deduct your share o the partnership's operating expenses as miscell neous itemized deductions subject to the 2% lin However, if the investment club partnership has investments that also produce nontaxable incor you cannot deduct your share of the partnershir expenses that produce the nontaxable income. You should receive a copy of Schedule K–1 (Fo 1065), *Partner's Share of Income, Credits, Dedu tions, etc.*

Allocated expenses of mutual funds. The allocable investment expenses of nonpublicly-offered mutual funds are subject to the 2% limit Those of publicly-offered mutual funds are not subject to the 2% limit.

Nonpublicly-offered mutual funds report to y your share of gross income and investment expenses. You can only claim the expenses as miscellaneous itemized deduction subject to the 2% limit.

Publicly-offered mutual funds will send you a Form 1099–DIV, or substitute form, showing the net amount of dividend income (gross dividends minus investment expenses). This net figure is t amount you report on your return.

"Publicly-offered" mutual funds are funds tha are usually traded on an established securities market. Contact your mutual fund if you are not sure if your fund is publicly-offered.

Clerical help and office rent. You can deduc office expenses, such as rent and clerical help, that you incur in connection with your investmer and collecting the taxable income on them.

Custodian fees and service charges to subscribers in a dividend reinvestment plan are deductible. These services include:

- Holding shares acquired through a plan,
- Collecting and reinvesting cash dividends, an
- Keeping individual records and providing detailed statements of accounts.

Service fees. You can deduct fees you pay to broker, bank, trustee, or similar agent to collect your taxable bond interest or dividends on shar of stock. But you cannot deduct a fee you pay t broker to buy investment property, such as stoc or bonds. You must add the fee to the cost of th property.

You must offset against the selling price a fe you pay to a broker to sell securities. You cann deduct the fee unless you are a dealer in securities.

Hobby expenses generally are deductible on up to the amount of hobby income. A hobby is a business, because it is not carried on to make profit. See *Not-for-Profit Activities* in Chapter 1 Publication 535, *Business Expenses.*

Home computer. You can deduct depreciatio on your home computer to the extent you use i for the production of income (for example, man ing your investments that produce taxable income). However, certain limits may apply, as explained under *Partial Business Use of Listed Property* in Publication 534. If you work as an employee and use the computer in that work, s *Home Computers and Cellular Telephones* und *Unreimbursed Employee Business Expenses,* earlier.

Investment fees and expenses paid for man ing your investments are deductible if they relat to investments that produce taxable income.

IRA trustee's administrative fees that are bi separately and that you paid in connection with your individual retirement arrangement (IRA) ar deductible, if they are ordinary and necessary. These fees do not include capital expenditures (such as brokers' commissions that you must a to the cost of securities you buy through broke These fees also do not include disguised IRA c tributions. These trustee's fees are not subject e annual dollar limit on contributions you can ake to an IRA. Deduct them on line 21, Schedule A (Form 1040), not with your IRA deduction. or more information about IRAs, get Publication 90, *Individual Retirement Arrangements (IRAs).*

gal expenses that you have to produce taxable income are usually deductible. You may have gal expenses that are related to either doing or eping your job.

You can deduct legal fees you paid to defend urself against criminal charges arising out of ur trade or business.

You can deduct legal expenses for tax advice lated to a divorce if the bill specifies how much for tax advice and it is determined in a reasonable way. You also may have legal expenses to llect taxable alimony. Because you pay tax on s income, you can deduct your legal costs as an pense necessary to produce taxable income. You can also deduct legal fees you pay in nnection with the determination, collection, or fund of any tax.

payments of social security benefits. If the m of the amount shown in Box 5 of all of your rms SSA–1099 and Forms RRB–1099 is a negative figure and all or part of this negative figure presents benefits you included in gross income 1984, or later, you can take an itemized deduction for the amount of the negative figure that represents those benefits. However, if the deduction more than $3,000, you will have to use a special mputation to figure your tax. Get Publication 5, *Social Security Benefits and Equivalent Railroad Retirement Benefits,* for additional ormation.

fe deposit box rent is deductible if you use box to store taxable income-producing stocks, nds, or investment-related papers and documents. You cannot deduct the rent if you use the x only for jewelry or other personal items or for x-exempt securities.

praisal fees are deductible if you pay them to termine the amount of a casualty loss or the fair arket value of donated property.

x preparation fees usually are deductible in year you pay them. Thus, you can deduct on ur 1990 return fees paid in 1990 for preparing ur 1989 return.

ss on deposits in an insolvent or bankrupt ancial institution. If you have a loss on your posit in a qualified financial institution because the bankruptcy or insolvency of the institution, d you can reasonably estimate your loss, you n choose to treat the amount as a current:

Casualty/theft loss on Form 4684, or an

Ordinary loss (miscellaneous itemized deduction n Schedule A (Form 1040)).

the alternative, you can wait until the year of al determination of the actual loss and treat that ount as a nonbusiness bad debt (short-term pital loss on Schedule D (Form 1040)).

f you choose to report your loss as an ordinary s, report it as a miscellaneous itemized deduction. The maximum amount you can claim is 0,000 ($10,000 if you are married filing separately). Your deduction is reduced by any pected state insurance proceeds, and is subject the 2% limit.

You cannot choose to claim the loss as a miscellaneous itemized deduction if:

Any part of the deposit related to the loss is federally insured,

You own at least 1% of the financial institution,

You are an officer of the financial institution, or

You are related to an owner or officer of the financial institution.

You should, on an appropriate line or space, early indicate the name of the financial titution, write "Insolvent Financial Institution Election," and include the calculation of the reasonably estimated loss claimed.

Deductions Not Subject To the 2% Limit

The following expenses are deductible as miscellaneous itemized deductions. However, they are not subject to the 2% limit. Report these expenses on line 26, Schedule A (Form 1040).

Federal estate tax on income in respect of a decedent. You can deduct the federal estate tax attributable to income in respect of a decedent that is ordinary income and that you as a beneficiary include in your gross income. Income in respect of the decedent is gross income that the decedent had a right to receive, could have received had death not occurred, and that was not properly includable in the decedent's final income tax return. Get Publication 559, *Tax Information for Survivors, Executors, and Administrators,* for information about figuring the amount of this deduction.

Amortizable premium on taxable bonds. Bond premium is the amount you pay for bonds that is greater than the face value of the bonds. You can choose to amortize the premium on taxable bonds.

For a bond purchased before October 23, 1986, the amortization of the premium is a miscellaneous itemized deduction not subject to the 2% limit.

For a bond purchased after October 22, 1986, and before January 1, 1988, the amortization of the premium is investment interest expense subject to the investment interest limit, unless you choose to treat it as an offset to interest income on the bond.

For a bond acquired after December 31, 1987, the amortization of the premium is an offset to interest income on the bond rather than a separate interest deduction item.

For more information, see *Bond Premium Amortization* in Publication 550, *Investment Income and Expenses.*

Gambling losses to the extent of gambling winnings. You cannot deduct more than the gambling winnings you report on line 22, Form 1040. You must keep an accurate diary or similar record of your losses and winnings, and you must be able to prove the amounts of your winnings and losses by receipt, ticket, or statement.

Unrecovered investment in pension. If a retiree had contributed to the cost of a pension or annuity, a part of each payment received can be excluded from income as a tax-free return of the retiree's investment. If the retiree dies before the entire investment is returned, any unrecovered investment is allowed as a deduction on the retiree's final return. Get Publication 575, *Pension and Annuity Income (Including Simplified General Rule),* for more information.

Repayments under claim of right. If you had to repay more than $3,000 that you included in income in an earlier year because at the time you thought you had an unrestricted right to it, you may be able to deduct the amount you repaid. See *Repayments* in Publication 525, *Taxable and Nontaxable Income,* for more information.

Impairment-related work expenses. If you have a physical or mental disability that limits your being employed, or substantially limits one or more of your major life activities, such as performing manual tasks, walking, speaking, breathing, learning, and working, your impairment-related work expenses are deductible.

Impairment-related work expenses are expenses for attendant care services at your place of work and other expenses in connection with your place of work that are necessary for you to be able to work and that are ordinary and necessary in your kind of work.

If you are an employee, you enter impairment-related work expenses on Form 2106. You enter the amount from line 11 of Form 2106 on Schedule A (Form 1040), line 26, instead of Schedule A, line 20. Also, get *Instructions for Form 2106,* for more information.

If you are self-employed, you deduct impairment-related work expenses on Schedule C (Form 1040).

Performing Artists

If you are a performing artist, you may qualify to deduct your employee business expenses as an adjustment to gross income rather than as a miscellaneous itemized deduction. To qualify, you must meet ***all*** of the following requirements.

1) During the tax year, you perform services in the performing arts for at least two employers and receive at least $200 each from any two of these employers.
2) Your related performing arts business expenses exceed 10% of your gross income from the performance of such services.
3) Your adjusted gross income is not more than $16,000 before deducting these business expenses.
4) If you are married, you must file a joint return unless you lived apart from your spouse at all times during the tax year.
5) If you file a joint return, figure requirements (1) and (2) separately for each spouse, but requirement (3) applies to you and your spouse's combined adjusted gross income.

If you meet all of the above requirements, you should complete Form 2106. Include your performing-arts related expenses shown on Form 2106, line 11, in the total on Form 1040, line 30. Write "Form 2106" and the amount in the space to the left of line 30.

If you do not meet all of the above requirements, you can deduct your expenses only in the way described under *How To Report,* next.

How To Report

You must itemize deductions to be able to claim miscellaneous deductions on Schedule A (Form 1040).

If you have unreimbursed employee business expenses, generally you must first complete Form 2106. You should carry over the amount on line 11 of Form 2106 to Schedule A (Form 1040), line 20. Attach the completed Form 2106 to Form 1040.

However, if none of your employee business expenses are reimbursed by your employer and you are not claiming any meal, entertainment, travel, or transportation expenses, you do not have to complete Form 2106. Instead, list your employee business expenses on line 20, Schedule A (Form 1040).

Any other miscellaneous deductions subject to the 2% limit should be claimed on line 21 of Schedule A (Form 1040).

If you have miscellaneous deductions ***not*** subject to the 2% limit, you should claim these amounts on line 26 of Schedule A (Form 1040).

Example. Debra Smith is employed as a salesperson. She has adjusted gross income of $40,000 and has the following qualifying miscellaneous deductions:

Entertainment expenses (unreimbursed)	$ 500
Local transportation expenses (unreimbursed)	$ 500
Professional association dues (unreimbursed)	$ 100
Home office expenses	$1,000
Tax return preparation	$ 200
Investment counseling/safety deposit box	$ 300
Gambling losses (reported $200 as income)	$ 200

The following discussions explain how Debra will report her miscellaneous itemized deductions on the illustrated page 1 of Form 2106 and miscellaneous deductions section of Schedule A (Form 1040) shown at the end of this publication.

Of Debra's deductions, only gambling losses are not subject to the 2% of adjusted gross income limit. The gambling losses are shown on line 26 of Schedule A (Form 1040). The other items are subject to the 2% limit and are shown on lines 20 or 21 of Schedule A (Form 1040).

Since Debra is claiming entertainment and transportation expenses, she must complete Part I of Form 2106. She enters the local transportation expenses of $500 on line 2. The expenses for professional association dues ($100) and home office ($1,000) are entered on line 4. The entertainment expenses ($500) are subject to the 80% limit and are entered on line 5. She then completes the rest of the form. The total expenses on line 11 ($2,000) are entered on line 20 of Schedule A (Form 1040).

Debra's expenses for tax return preparation and investment counseling are entered directly on line 21, Schedule A (Form 1040). She then totals the amounts on lines 20 and 21 and enters this total on line 22. She enters $40,000, her adjusted gross income, on line 23. She multiplies this amount by 2% (.02) and enters the result ($800) on line 24. She subtracts the amount on line 24 from the amount on line 22 and enters $1,700, her allowable deduction, on line 25.

Nondeductible Expenses

The following expenses are not deductible.

Adoption expenses you paid for the adoption of a child are not deductible.

Campaign expenses of a candidate for any office, even if the candidate is running for reelection to the office, are not deductible. These include qualification and registration fees for primary elections.

Legal fees paid to defend charges that arise from participation in a political campaign are not deductible.

Capital expenses. You cannot currently deduct amounts paid to buy property that has a useful life of more than 1 year or amounts paid to increase the value or prolong the life of property. If you use such property in your work, you may be able to take a depreciation deduction. Get Publication 534. If the property is a car used in your work, also get Publication 917.

Check-writing fees. If you have a personal checking account, you cannot deduct fees charged by the bank for the privilege of writing checks, even if the account pays interest.

Commuting expenses to and from your main or regular place of work are not deductible. If you haul tools, instruments, etc., in your car to and from work, you can only deduct additional costs, such as renting a trailer that is towed by your vehicle.

Fees and licenses. You cannot deduct amounts paid for car licenses, marriage licenses, dog tags, etc.

Fines or penalties you pay to a governmental unit for violating a law are not deductible. These include parking tickets, tax penalties, and penalties deducted from teachers' paychecks after an illegal strike.

Gifts or amounts spent to influence the general public on legislative matters, elections, or referenda are not deductible.

Health spa expenses are not deductible, even if there is a job requirement to stay in excellent physical condition, such as might be required of a law enforcement officer.

Insurance premiums that you pay or that are placed in escrow for your home, such as fire and liability or mortgage insurance, are not deductible. Premiums you pay on your life insurance or personal disability insurance are not deductible. Premiums you pay on life insurance policies assigned as alimony may be deductible as alimony.

Lunches or meals while working late, except while traveling away from home, are not deductible.

Personal legal expenses, such as the following, are not deductible:

- Defense of a breach of promise (to marry) suit,
- Defense of civil or criminal charges resulting from a personal relationship,
- Defense of property claims in a divorce,
- Preparation of a will, and
- Property settlement in a divorce.

This is true even though a result of the legal proceeding is the loss of income-producing property.

Personal, living, or family expenses are not deductible. These include burial expenses and the cost of a cemetery lot; losses from the sale of your home, furniture, personal car, etc.; and repairs, insurance, and rent on your home.

Political contributions. You cannot deduct contributions made to a political candidate, a campaign committee, or a newsletter fund.

Professional accreditation fees, such as the following, are not deductible:

- Accounting certificate fees paid for the initial right to practice accounting,
- Bar exam fees and incidental expenses in sec ing admission to the bar, and
- Medical and dental license fees paid to get initial licensing.

Relief fund contributions withheld from your salary are not deductible if the fund pays benefi to any covered employee who cannot work because of any injury or illness not related to th job.

Residential telephone service. You cannot deduct any charge (including taxes) for basic lo telephone service for the first telephone line to your residence.

Self-improvement. You cannot deduct expenses for increasing your personal prestige establishing your professional reputation.

Stockholders' meetings. You cannot deduct transportation and other expenses you pay to attend stockholders' meetings of companies in which you own stock but have no other interest You cannot deduct these expenses even if you are attending the meeting to get information tha would be useful in making further investments.

You cannot deduct any expenses for attendi a convention, seminar, or similar meeting for investment purposes.

Tax-exempt income. You cannot deduct expenses to produce tax-exempt income. You cannot deduct interest on a debt incurred or co tinued to buy or carry tax-exempt securities.

If you have expenses to produce both taxabl and tax-exempt income, but you cannot identify the expenses that produce each type of incom you must divide them to determine the amount that you can deduct.

Example. During the year you received tax interest of $4,800 and tax-exempt interest of $1,200. In earning this income, you had expens of $500 during the year. If you cannot identify t amount of each expense item for each income item, you must allocate 80% ($4,800/$6,000) the expense to taxable interest and 20% ($1,200/$6,000) to tax-exempt interest. You ca deduct, subject to the 2% limit, expenses of $4

Voluntary unemployment benefit fund contributions you make to a union fund or a private fund are not deductible. However, contributions are deductible as taxes if you make them to a state unemployment fund that covers you for th loss of wages from unemployment caused by b iness conditions.

Form **2106**

Department of the Treasury
Internal Revenue Service

Employee Business Expenses

► See separate Instructions.

► Attach to Form 1040.

OMB No. 1545-0139

1990

Attachment Sequence No. 54

Your name	Social security number	Occupation in which expenses were incurred
Debra Smith	000 : 00 : 0000	Salesperson

Part I **Employee Business Expenses and Reimbursements**

STEP 1 Enter Your Expenses		**Column A** Other Than Meals and Entertainment	**Column B** Meals and Entertainment
1 Vehicle expense from line 22 or line 29	1		
2 Parking fees, tolls, and local transportation, including train, bus, etc. . .	2	500	
3 Travel expense while away from home overnight, including lodging, airplane, car rental, etc. **Do not** include meals and entertainment . . .	3		
4 Business expenses not included on lines 1 through 3. **Do not** include meals and entertainment	4	1,100	
5 Meals and entertainment expenses. (See the separate Instructions.) . .	5		500
6 Add lines 1 through 5 and enter the **total expenses** here	6	1,600	500

Note: *If you were not reimbursed for any expenses in Step 1, skip line 7 and enter the amount from line 6 on line 8.*

STEP 2 Enter Amounts Your Employer Gave You For Expenses Listed In STEP 1

7 Enter amounts your employer gave you that were **not** reported to you in Box 10 of Form W-2. Include any amount reported under code "L" in Box 17 of your Form W-2. (See Instructions.)	7		

STEP 3 Figure Expenses To Deduct on Schedule A (Form 1040)

8 Subtract line 7 from line 6	8	1,600	500
Note: *If **both columns** of line 8 are zero, **stop here.** If column A is less than zero, report the amount as income and enter -0- on line 10, column A. See the separate Instructions for how to report.*			
9 Enter 20% (.20) of line 8, Column B	9		100
10 Subtract line 9 from line 8	10	1,600	400
11 Add the amounts on line 10 of both columns and enter the total here. **Also enter the total on Schedule A (Form 1040), line 20.** (Qualified performing artists and individuals with disabilities, see the separate Instructions for special rules on where to enter the total.) . . . . ►	11		2,000

For Paperwork Reduction Act Notice, see the separate Instructions.

Form **2106** (1990)

SCHEDULES A&B (Form 1040)

Department of the Treasury Internal Revenue Service

Schedule A—Itemized Deductions

(Schedule B is on back)

▶ Attach to Form 1040. ▶ See Instructions for Schedules A and B (Form 1040).

OMB No. 1545-0074

1990

Attachment Sequence No. 07

Name(s) shown on Form 1040: Debra Smith

Your social security number: 000 00 0000

Medical and Dental Expenses		**Caution:** *Do not include expenses reimbursed or paid by others.*			
	1	Medical and dental expenses. (See page 27 of the Instructions.)	1		
	2	Enter amount from Form 1040, line 32 [2]			
	3	Multiply the amount on line 2 by 7.5% (.075). Enter the result	3		
	4	Subtract line 3 from line 1. Enter the result. If less than zero, enter -0- ▶	4		
Taxes You Paid (See Instructions on page 27.)	5	State and local income taxes	5		
	6	Real estate taxes	6		
	7	Other taxes. (List—include personal property taxes.) ▶	7		
	8	Add the amounts on lines 5 through 7. Enter the total ▶	8		
Interest You Paid (See Instructions on page 27.)	9a	Deductible home mortgage interest paid to financial institutions and reported to you on Form 1098. Report deductible points on line 10	9a		
	b	Other deductible home mortgage interest. (If paid to an individual, show that person's name and address.) ▶	9b		
	10	Deductible points. (See Instructions for special rules.)	10		
	11	Deductible investment interest (attach Form 4952 if required). (See page 28.)	11		
	12a	Personal interest you paid. (See page 28.) [12a]			
	b	Multiply the amount on line 12a by 10% (.10). Enter the result	12b		
	13	Add the amounts on lines 9a through 11, and 12b. Enter the total ▶	13		
Gifts to Charity (See Instructions on page 29.)		**Caution:** *If you made a charitable contribution and received a benefit in return, see page 29 of the Instructions.*			
	14	Contributions by cash or check	14		
	15	Other than cash or check. (You **MUST** attach Form 8283 if over $500.)	15		
	16	Carryover from prior year	16		
	17	Add the amounts on lines 14 through 16. Enter the total ▶	17		
Casualty and Theft Losses	18	Casualty or theft loss(es) (attach Form 4684). (See page 29 of the Instructions.) ▶	18		
Moving Expenses	19	Moving expenses (attach Form 3903 or 3903F). (See page 30 of the Instructions.). ▶	19		
Job Expenses and Most Other Miscellaneous Deductions (See Instructions on page 30 for expenses to deduct here.)	20	Unreimbursed employee expenses—job travel, union dues, job education, etc. (You **MUST** attach Form 2106 if required. See Instructions.) ▶	20	2,000	
	21	Other expenses (investment, tax preparation, safe deposit box, etc.). List type and amount ▶ Tax Preparation - 200; Investment Counsel/Safety Deposit Box - 300	21	500	
	22	Add the amounts on lines 20 and 21. Enter the total	22	2,500	
	23	Enter amount from Form 1040, line 32. [23] 40,000			
	24	Multiply the amount on line 23 by 2% (.02). Enter the result.	24	800	
	25	Subtract line 24 from line 22. Enter the result. If less than zero, enter -0- ▶	25		1,700
Other Miscellaneous Deductions	26	Other (from list on page 30 of Instructions). List type and amount ▶ Gambling Losses ▶	26		200
Total Itemized Deductions	27	Add the amounts on lines 4, 8, 13, 17, 18, 19, 25, and 26. Enter the total here. Then enter on Form 1040, line 34, the **LARGER** of this total or your standard deduction from page 20 of the Instructions ▶	27		

For Paperwork Reduction Act Notice, see Form 1040 Instructions.

Schedule A (Form 1040) 1990

Charles B. WRIGHTSMAN and Jayne Wrightsman

v.

The UNITED STATES.

No. 364-66.

United States Court of Claims.

July 15, 1970.

Action to recover alleged overpayments of federal income taxes. The Court of Claims, Laramore, J., held that although meticulous bookkeeping detail was observed by taxpayers with respect to purchase, care, and maintenance of their art collection, and taxpayers devoted considerable time and effort to their collection activities, and taxpayers were wary of more traditional forms of investment, and recognized investment-aspect incident to acquisition and retention of works of art, in view of evidence showing that personal pleasure or satisfaction was taxpayers' primary purpose in acquiring and holding works of art, taxpayers were not entitled to deduct from income expenses incurred by them with respect to their art collection.

Judgment for defendant.

Collins, J., dissented and filed opinion.

1. Internal Revenue ⚷541

Art collectors, who sought to deduct from income expenses incurred in connection with art works, had to establish that their investment purpose for acquiring and holding works of art was principal, or of first importance, notwithstanding pleasure-giving quality commonly recognized as inherent in art objects. 26 U.S.C.A. (I.R.C.1954) § 212.

2. Internal Revenue ⚷541

Although meticulous bookkeeping detail was observed by taxpayers with respect to purchase, care, and maintenance of their art collection, and taxpayers devoted considerable time and effort to their collection activities, and taxpayers were wary of more traditional forms of investment, and recognized investment-aspect incident to acquisition and retention of works of art, in view of evidence showing that personal pleasure or satisfaction was taxpayers' primary purpose in acquiring and holding works of art, taxpayers were not entitled to deduct from income the expenses incurred by them with respect to their art collection. 26 U.S.C.A. (I.R.C.1954) § 212.

Hugh F. Culverhouse, Jacksonville, Fla., attorney of record, and W. A. Gartner, Jacksonville, Fla., for plaintiffs.

Joseph Kovner, Washington, D. C., with whom was Asst. Atty. Gen., Johnnie M. Walters, for defendant. Philip R. Miller and Mark Segal, Washington, D. C., of counsel.

Before COWEN, Chief Judge, and LARAMORE, DURFEE, DAVIS, COLLINS, SKELTON, and NICHOLS, Judges.

OPINION *

LARAMORE, Judge.

This is an action to recover alleged overpayments of Federal income taxes paid by plaintiffs for tax years 1960 and 1961 in the amounts of $5,911.20 and $21,199.78, respectively, plus assessed interest in the respective amounts of $1,-847.25 and $5,352.22, plus statutory interest on the amounts of recovery. The issue before us involves the deductibility under section 212 of the 1954 Internal Revenue Code [1] of certain expenses incurred by plaintiffs with respect to their art collection. Deductibility of such expenses under section 212, in turn, depends upon whether plaintiffs collected the pertinent works of art primarily as investments or, instead, primarily for their personal pleasure and enjoyment.[2] We hold that plaintiffs have failed to establish that their art collection was primarily investment-motivated and, therefore, they are not entitled to recover.

Plaintiffs, Charles B. Wrightsman and Jayne Wrightsman, were married in 1944.[3] For the tax years here involved, 1960 and 1961, the Wrightsmans filed joint Federal income tax returns. Plaintiffs have both participated in the activities incident to the acquisition and maintenance of their art collection. The Wrightsmans' acquisition of works of art commenced in 1947 when, they have conceded, their activities were in the nature of a hobby. In that initial year, plaintiffs' expenditures for art objects amounted to $3,741. By the end of 1960, their purchases totaled $5.2 million and, by the end of 1961, $300,000 more. As of March 31, 1967, plaintiffs' total purchases of works of art exceeded $8.9 million; the works of art were valued for insurance purposes in excess if $16.8 million.

Mr. Wrightsman had great skepticism with regard to conventional investments in the stock market, an attitude which stemmed from experiences during his youth in observing his father's disastrous investments in securities. One investment, however, in which Charles was able to combine knowledge and management control, two factors which he considered requisite to any investment success, was in the Standard Oil Company of Kansas. In 1918, after active service in the United States Navy, Charles moved to Fort Worth, Texas, where he engaged in the oil business as a lease broker and in several oil ventures. He accumulated sufficient funds by 1930 to purchase, and did purchase at private sale, the shares of the largest stockholder of Standard Oil Company of Kansas. He was then elected to the board of directors and, in 1932, became president of that company. He held such office through January 1951, when liquidation of that company, which had commenced in 1949, was concluded. At this time, Charles owned 93.7 percent of the outstanding stock.

Upon the liquidation, Mr. Wrightsman received a 93.7 percent interest in all of the properties, including one million dollars in cash distributed to him. With the removal of the corporate structure, his financial position changed from stock ownership to direct ownership of oil-producing properties, which he has continued to operate as an individual un-

* We are indebted to Trial Commissioner Roald A. Hogenson for his findings of fact, which have been adopted in their near entirety, and for his recommended opinion, though we have substituted our own in reaching a different result.

1. All citations to Code sections hereinafter are, unless otherwise indicated, in reference to the Internal Revenue Code of 1954.

2. Also involved in this suit is plaintiffs' claim of entitlement to deduction of $1,000 as part of a capital loss sustained on their sale in 1961 of certain works of art. Defendant has conceded that plaintiffs are entitled to recover in this regard *if* it be determined they were investors in their works of art.

3. For convenience, Mr. and Mrs. Wrightsman will hereinafter sometimes be referred to individually as Charles and Jayne, respectively.

der appropriate arrangements with the owners of the 6.3 percent interests. Thus, he commenced and has continued to receive directly a large cash flow, which had previously gone into the corporate coffers.

Aside from his investments in Standard Oil of Kansas, Mr. Wrightsman's ownership of stock, as well as that of Mrs. Wrightsman, has been quite limited. In 1959, Wrightsman Investment Company was organized, with Mr. Wrightsman as the sole stockholder, owning minor Oklahoma oil properties contributed by Charles, land on which plaintiffs' Palm Beach, Florida, home is located, and limited assets previously owned by Charles in New Mexico, Mississippi and Nebraska. Plaintiffs acquired 1,583 shares of Wrightsman Petroleum Company in 1960 and 1961, a company which had been organized by Charles' father. At the time of the trial of this case, Mrs. Wrightsman was the beneficial owner of a trust for which a bank, as trustee, had purchased stock.

Mr. Wrightsman believed that oil was one of the best possible investments, if selectively made. His trips to the Persian Gulf countries in the mid-1950's indicated to him, however, that there was a possibility of an oil glut, which caused him to conclude that he should make an effort to hedge his investments in oil with investments of other kinds. He sought advice from qualified employees. The certified public accountant in charge of his accounts recommended purchase of unimproved real estate and stock in corporations not in the oil industry. These recommendations were not followed.

By this time, Mr. Wrightsman had formed the belief that works of art were an excellent hedge against inflation and devaluation of currencies, that they represented portable international currency, since there were no restrictions on export from the United States, and that works of art were appropriate assets for investment of a substantial portion of his surplus cash being generated. These beliefs and investment intent were expressed to numerous friends and associates and the employees of his business office.

Mrs. Wrightsman's assets have been derived from income through Mr. Wrightsman under community property laws and from funds received from Charles in the form of gifts. Jayne fully shared Charles' beliefs and intent concerning investment in works of art. Their marriage has been one of constant association and travel together, with common interests and goals.

In their art collecting activities, plaintiffs have specialized in the acquisition of 18th century French works of art. Mrs. Wrightsman is not just a nominal party herein because of the filing of joint returns by the parties. She owns about three-fourths of plaintiffs' works of art, either by number or by value. Their activities in the acquisition and holding of such works of art have been conducted jointly.

Plaintiffs' mode of living from 1947 to the present time has been to reside from the latter part of November until late April at their home in Palm Beach, Florida, with occasional trips to New York City or elsewhere. Commencing about the first of May, they live for about 30 days in New York City, staying since 1956 in their Fifth Avenue apartment. From June 1 to the end of September or early October, they are in Europe, where they live exclusively in hotels.

The Wrightsmans have constantly associated with well known experts in the art world. They are art experts in their own right, as recognized by others, particularly in the testimony of Mr. Francis J. B. Watson, Surveyor of the Queen's Works of Art and Director of the Wallace Collection of London, and Mr. Joseph V. Noble, Vice Director for Administration of the Metropolitan Museum of Art.

In the acquisition by plaintiffs of works or art, each art object has been invoiced, assigned an inventory number, and noted as an approved purchase by one of the plaintiffs. The invoice is sent directly to plaintiffs' Houston, Texas, business office for payment. There the approved invoice is checked for accuracy, and a check request is prepared, following the usual business procedures employed in Mr. Wrightsman's investments in oil and gas properties. The check request, a copy of the check, and a copy of the original invoice are retained in the Houston office file. The original invoice, marked paid, with date and check reference, is returned to plaintiffs' personal files, which follow them from the Palm Beach home to their New York apartment, as the occasion warrants. Each item is reflected in the investment control account of the general ledger maintained in the Houston office. A detailed investment card record is kept with respect to each item in the works of art collection. On each card is noted the original purchase price, the date of purchase, and any items deemed to be of a capital nature requiring capitalization on the investment books of plaintiffs.

Plaintiffs have consistently catalogued their purchase of works of art. At the time of the trial herein, these catalogues consisted of 26 three-ring binder volumes, requiring a shelf space of about five feet. These catalogues are unique, represent 20 years of work by Mrs. Wrightsman, and have considerable value. Partially on the basis of this extensive cataloguing, the Metropolitan Museum has published two volumes and is in the process of completing the publication of a five-volume work on the Wrightsman Collection, authorized by Mr. Francis J. B. Watson, which will be a treatise on 18th century French works of art.

On their Federal income tax returns for the years 1960 and 1961, plaintiffs claimed deductions for certain ordinary and necessary expenses incurred in the management, conservation and maintenance of investment properties, i. e., works of art, held by them for the production of income, and incurred in the production and collection of income from those properties. These expenses, which were incurred in connection with, and are directly attributable to, plaintiffs' works or art, represent costs of insurance, maintenance, subscriptions and services, shipping, hotel, travel, entertainment and other miscellaneous expenses. Plaintiffs also claimed as deductions on their 1961 return the alleged cost of acquiring and subsequently releasing a painting due to the inability to obtain an export permit, and part of an alleged capital loss sustained on the sale of certain works of art. Disallowance by the Internal Revenue Service of the claimed deductions, and denial of plaintiffs' claims for refund of the paid deficiencies issuing therefrom, gave rise to this suit.

Plaintiffs assert that the facts and circumstances in evidence, with which they say their personal declarations of purpose and intent are in complete accord, clearly establish the deductibility of the incurred expenses as primarily investment-motivated. Defendant responds that because of the nature of the properties involved, plaintiffs are entitled to deduct the subject expenses *only* by showing a physical segregation of the works of art which precludes personal pleasure; a showing which, defendant contends, plaintiffs have failed to make. In the alternative, defendant opposes any recovery here on the ground that plaintiffs have not shown any action on their part inconsistent with the holding of their collection for pleasure, and have thereby failed to satisfy their burden of proof that the pertinent expenses were incurred primarily for an investment purpose. Although we hold that plaintiffs are not entitled to recover, neither of the alternative theories advanced by defendant constitutes, in our view, the proper application of the apposite legal standard upon which we premise our holding.

Section 212 provides, in parts pertinent to this suit:

> In the case of an individual, there shall be allowed as a deduction all the

ordinary and necessary expenses paid or incurred during the taxable year—

(1) for the production or collection of income;

(2) for the management, conservation, or maintenance of property held for the production of income; or

* * * * * *

Treasury Regulations on income tax, section 1.212–1(c) imparts, moreover, with respect to the deductible investment expense, nondeductible personal expense[4] dichotomy and the apposite standard for proper classification:

> Expenses of carrying on transactions which * * * are not carried on for the production or collection of income or for the management, conservation, or maintenance of property held for the production of income, but which are carried on *primarily* as a sport, hobby, or recreation are not allowable as nontrade or nonbusiness expenses. The question whether or not a transaction is carried on *primarily* for the production of income or for the management, conservation, or maintenance of property held for the production or collection of income, rather than *primarily* as a sport, hobby, or recreation, is *not to be determined solely from the intention of the taxpayer but rather from all the circumstances of the case.* [Emphasis supplied.]

[1] It is clear from the above that the burden of proof which plaintiffs must satisfy if they are to prevail is that as a factual matter, from an objective view of the operative circumstances in suit, they acquired and held works of art during the years here involved primarily for investment, rather than for personal use and enjoyment. Plaintiffs must establish that their investment purpose for acquiring and holding works of art was "principal," or "of first importance." *See*, Malat v. Riddell, 383 U.S. 569, 572, 86 S.Ct. 1030, 16 L.Ed.2d 102 (1966).[5] And, they must establish this notwithstanding the pleasure-giving quality commonly recognized as inherent in art objects.

The perplexing nature of the issue in suit apparently has caused defendant to seek a narrow rule possessing ease of application and certainty of result. We are unaware of any authority, however, for the interpretations which defendant places upon the applicable legal standard. Those cases cited by defendant with respect to its physical segregation-pleasure preclusion standard do not, in our view, support the interpretation urged. *See*, R. Foster Reynolds, 4 TCM 837 (1945); George F. Tyler, 6 TCM 275 (1947); Juliet P. Hamilton, 25 B.T.A. 1317 (1932). Neither do they support defendant's alternative position which turns upon whether there was action on the part of the Wrightsmans inconsistent with the holding of their art collection for pleasure. We prefer to resolve the instant controversy by the more conventional application of the legal standard involved, namely, an analysis of the particular facts and circumstances, and a determination as to plaintiffs' primary purpose therefrom. A careful review of the entire record with this conventioanl approach in mind indicates, we think, that plaintiffs have failed to sustain their burden.

Plaintiffs have carefully marshaled a broad array of evidence in support of their declared investment purpose. In this regard, we have no reason to doubt

4. Section 262 provides as follows:
"Except as otherwise expressly provided in this chapter, no deduction shall be allowed for personal, living, or family expenses."

5. The Supreme Court stated in Malat v. Riddell, *supra*, at page 572, 86 S.Ct. at page 1032:
"* * * We hold that, as used in § 1221(1), 'primarily' means 'of first importance' or 'principally'."
Although the Court was addressing itself to a capital gain provision, we are of the opinion that its definition of the term "primarily" for tax purposes is equally applicable to, and most appropriate in, the context in which the term is here encountered.

that Mr. Wrightsman was wary of the more traditional forms of investment, or that he recognized an investment-aspect incident to the acquisition and retention of works of art. Indeed, the greatly increased current value of the Wrightsman collection would seem, at least in retrospect, to confirm the financial wisdom of plaintiffs' purchases. Nor do we doubt that meticulous bookkeeping detail was observed by plaintiffs with respect to the purchase, care, and maintenance of their collection, or that the Wrightsmans devoted considerable time and effort to their collection activities. We fully appreciate, moreover, that because of plaintiffs' mode of living, much of their time was spent away from their residences wherein the majority of their works of art were maintained. It is our judgment, however, that this evidence, when viewed in proper relationship to the additional evidence below, relegates investment intent to a position of something less than primary among plaintiffs' purposes for acquiring and holding works of art.

It may fairly be said, and the record so indicates, that plaintiffs' personal lives revolve around their art collection and related collecting activities. The Wrightsmans, without any prior formal education with respect to works of art, have since the late 1940's consistently and diligently pursued a course of self-education in that field, visiting major museums and art dealer establishments in the United States and overseas, studying works of art themselves, reviewing auction catalogues and price lists, and engaging in discussions with recognized art experts, such as collectors, museum curators, dealers and others knowledgeable in the world art community. They have reviewed all of the leading art periodicals, and engaged in extensive reading in their chosen field of 18th century French art and related areas. They have acquired a substantial art library, and Jayne has engaged in extensive research, while Charles has concentrated on the restoration and conservation of art objects and the conditions of the art market. Jayne has educated herself in the use of the French language, to be qualified to engage in discussions and reading of materials in that language concerning 18th century French furniture and works of art. Whether in Palm Beach, New York, or abroad, the major portion of the Wrightsmans' day-to-day activities throughout each year is devoted to studying works of art. And, the Wrightsmans' social life in Palm Beach, New York, or abroad involves principally people knowledgeable and interested in the field of art.

As to the place and manner in which the Wrightsmans have held their collection, the record reveals that, except for occasional displays of items at other locations, plaintiffs have kept their works of art in their New York apartment, their Palm Beach home, and in the Metropolitan Museum on loan for display by that institution. As of March 31, 1967, about 77.8 percent of such objects (on an insurance evaluation basis) was in the New York apartment, about 17.7 percent in the Palm Beach home, and about 4.5 percent in the Metropolitan Museum. The works of art are on display, or in use as in the case of such items as French period furniture, in the New York apartment and the Palm Beach home, except that a small amount of furniture is stored in one room at Palm Beach.

Plaintiffs have provided air conditioning and humidity controls, considered necessary for the preservation of works of art, similar to those employed in the Metropolitan Museum. In this respect, the New York apartment is better equipped, accounting for the concentration of works of art there. Such apartment occupies the entire third floor of the building. Storage facilities for works of art have not been readily available to provide the required atmospheric controls especially needed for paintings and furniture.

The record also reveals extensive personal use by the Wrightsmans of various parts of their collection. 18th century oriental wallpaper had been installed by the previous owner on the walls of plaintiffs' Palm Beach residence which had been acquired as a completely furnished home. 18th century French parquet flooring has been installed by plaintiffs in their Palm Beach home, and in their New York apartment. Plaintiffs' paintings are never stored but, instead, a limited number are hung on the walls of their Palm Beach home, with most of them on the walls of their New York apartment. Mr. Wrightsman's bedroom in their apartment is furnished with 18th century French furniture and fixtures, and his bedroom in their Palm Beach home contains a French commode. Mrs. Wrightsman's bedroom in their apartment is furnished completely with Louis XV matching furniture and fixtures. Plaintiffs' apartment also has other rooms which contain other works of art from their collection in the form of matching furniture and furnishings.

In sum, what we wish to make clear from the foregoing is that we recognize as established *an* investment purpose for plaintiffs' collection. To be sure, many of the above-detailed facts and circumstances are entirely consistent with investment intent. On balance, however, the evidence does not establish investment as *the* most prominent purpose for plaintiffs' acquiring and holding works of art. The complete record *does* establish, to the contrary, personal pleasure or satisfaction as plaintiffs' primary purpose.

Plaintiffs place much reliance upon *George F. Tyler, supra,* wherein a loss sustained on the sale of part of a stamp collection was held deductible under section 23 of the 1939 Internal Revenue Code as having been incurred in a transaction entered into for profit. The precise factual issue before the court was whether the stamp collection was held primarily for profit or primarily as a hobby. In finding the former purpose to be primary, the Tax Court emphasized that the taxpayer from the outset undertook stamp collecting as an investment; that he consummated all purchases through a professional philatelist, who stressed the investment feature of stamps; that he purchased stamps only upon the philatelist's recommendation; that he exhibited scant interest in or knowledge of stamps; and that he participated little in those activities generally associated with stamp hobbyists. Thus it was found that although the collection and possession of stamps afforded the taxpayer some pleasure, such activities were undertaken primarily for profit.

The great disparity in facts and circumstances between *Tyler* and the instant case compels the conclusion, we think, that the *Tyler* decision in no sense advances plaintiffs' current cause. The actual importance of the *Tyler* case, for our purposes, lies in the standard there applied:

> * * * The difficulty, then reduces itself to the task of ascertaining whether petitioner has sustained his burden of proving that the desire to make a financial profit was the most important motive which led him to acquire the components of his collections. [6 TCM at 280]

The Tax Court determined, in the factual context of the *Tyler* case, that the taxpayer *had* sustained his burden of proof. We hold, in the factual context of the case before us, that the instant plaintiffs *have not.*

Also easily distinguished from the case at hand are Juliet P. Hamilton, *supra,* and R. Foster Reynolds, *supra,* to which we are referred by defendant. The *Hamilton* case involved the denial of a deduction for a loss sustained on the sale of a single painting which the taxpayer had acquired by specific bequest from her deceased father. Prior to its sale, the painting had been kept by the taxpayer in her home, except that, on several occasions, without profit to the taxpayer, the painting was placed on exhibition for inspection by art students and lovers of art. While in the taxpayer's home, the painting was sometimes made available, by special arrangement, for free inspection, 25 B.T.A. at 1317–1318. The *Reynolds* case, on the other hand, involved the allowance of a deduction for a loss sustained on the sale of certain jewelry which the taxpayer had acquired by inheritance from his deceased aunt. The jewelry, which was sold for the taxpayer by Cartier, Inc., of New York had been kept in a safe deposit box and at no time had been used by the taxpayer or any member of his family. 4 TCM at 838. We have no quarrel with the rule or reason of the *Hamilton* and *Reynolds* cases. We feel constrained to point out, however, that the rather conspicuous absence of any investment-type activity in the former or personal use in the latter serves to emphasize the appreciably more complex nature of the present controversy.

While the cases cited by the parties afford only minimal guidance for the resolution of the issue in suit, they do affirm as proper the analysis undertaken herein. That is to say, where the issue in question turns upon a taxpayer's state of mind, courts can best treat with such an issue through traditional principles of inference-drawing from an objective view of surrounding facts and circumstances, necessarily on a case-by-case basis. This, despite defendant's urging that "the issue [must] not be left to a miscellaneous assortment of factors for varying judgment in each case." Clearly, we think, by the nature of the issue it must.

[2] In accordance with such principles, and for the reasons detailed above, we hold that plaintiffs have failed to sustain their burden of proving the primacy of their investment purpose. Plaintiffs are, therefore, not entitled to recover in this action, and their petition is dismissed.[6]

COLLINS, Judge (dissenting):

I cannot agree with the court's conclusion in this case, and reluctantly I must dissent. At the outset, it should be stated that I regard this as a very difficult and a very close case. Very simply stated, my disagreement with the majority is that I feel that plaintiffs have sustained their burden of proof in showing that they acquired and held works of art *primarily* for investment rather than for personal enjoyment.

The majority have cited a number of facts and circumstances which they claim support their position that plaintiffs were engaged in the collection of art primarily for personal pleasure. As I view these same facts and circumstances, they could just as easily support a position favoring investment intent. Consequently, I feel that the factors relied upon by the court could be applied with equal weight to either side. If these facts were the only points to consider, I would have to agree with the majority since I would conclude that this would not be sufficient to satisfy plaintiffs' burden of proof.

However, there are a few other factors mentioned by the court which point directly to an investment intent. These include plaintiffs' desire to find an investment which would act as a hedge against inflation, plaintiffs' meticulous bookkeeping system, and the fact that they spent so little time at their homes where the large majority of their works of art were kept. (They spend 30 days a year in their New York apartment where 77.8 percent of their art objects are located.) These factors are the ones which, to me, tip the scales in favor of an investment intent.

I am further influenced by the fact that Commissioner Hogenson, who conducted the trial and heard the testimony of all the witnesses, found that plaintiffs had met their burden of proof and were engaged in the collection of art *primarily* for investment purposes. I feel that, in a case which is as close and as difficult as this one, some weight should definitely be attached to this advantage of the commissioner to observe demeanor and judge credibility.

I conclude, therefore, that the weight of the evidence presented is in favor of showing that plaintiffs were engaged in the collection and maintenance of art objects *primarily* for investment reasons rather than for their own personal pleasure and enjoyment. I would adopt the commissioner's findings of fact (which has been substantially done by the court) and his recommended opinion.[1]

6. At the time of oral argument on April 8, 1970, defendant made and filed a motion to reopen the record for the purpose of introducing additional evidence. Plaintiffs have timely filed a response in opposition to defendant's motion. Upon due consideration by the court, defendant's motion is denied. Judge Davis would grant the motion.

Gifford M. Mast, Jr. and Judith A. Mast, et al.[1] v. Commissioner.

Docket No. 43312-85, 43313-85, 43314-85, 43315-85, 43316-85. T.C. Memo 1989-119. Filed March 23, 1989.

David J. Duez, for the petitioners. Albert B. Kerkove, for the respondent.

Memorandum Findings of Fact and Opinion

DRENNEN, Judge: Respondent determined deficiencies in petitioners' Federal income taxes as follows:

Petitioner	*Docket Number*	*Year*	*Deficiency*	*Addition to tax under Sec. 6621(c)*[2]
Gifford M. Mast, Jr. and Judith A. Mast	43312-85	1977	$ 4,180	*
		1978	2,567	*
		1979	468	None
Terrill A. Mast and Melinda L. Mast	43313-85	1977	10,175	*
		1978	3,555	*
		1979	5,267	*
		1980	5,071	*
		1981	4,591	*
Eric W. Mast and Martha E. Mast	43314-85	1977	5,020	*
		1978	2,294	*
		1979	2,825	*
		1980	3,435	*
		1981	3,744	*
Sara B. Mast	43315-85	1977	6,805	*
		1978	1,385	*
		1979	2,007	*
		1980	1,504	*
		1981	796	None
Roderic B. Mast	43316-85	1977	5,619	*
		1978	1,150	*
		1979	2,237	*
		1980	907	None
		1981	432	None

* Applies to substantial underpayments due to tax motivated transactions.

After concessions, the issues remaining for our consideration are: (1) the fair market value of a stereoscopic photography collection donated to the University of California at Riverside ("UCR") (2) whether petitioners may allocate among themselves unequal portions of gifts of undivided interests in the donated collection and (3) whether petitioners are liable for an increased rate of interest pursuant to section 6621(c), Internal Revenue Code of 1986 (previously section 6621(d), Internal Revenue Code of 1954).

Findings of Fact

Some of the facts have been stipulated and are so found. The stipulation of facts and attached exhibits are incorporated herein by this reference.

Petitioners Gifford M. Mast, Jr. and Judith A. Mast were husband and wife with a residence at Rural Route #1, Davenport, Iowa, at the time they filed their petition in this case.

Petitioners Terrill A. Mast and Melinda L. Mast were husband and wife with a residence at 137 Lost Tree Road, Springfield Illinois, at the time they filed their petition in this case.

[1] Cases of the following petitioners are consolidated herewith: Terril A. Mast and Melinda L. Mast, docket No. 43313-85; Eric W. Mast and Martha E. Mast, docket No. 43314-85; Sara B. Mast, docket No. 43315-85; and Roderic B. Mast, docket No. 43316-85.

[2] All section references are to the Internal Revenue Code of 1954 as in effect during the years in issue. All Rule references are to the Tax Court Rules of practice and Procedure.

Petitioners Eric W. Mast and Martha E. Mast were husband and wife with a residence at 5320 Case Road, North Ridgeville, Ohio, at the time they filed their petition in this case.

Petitioner Sara B. Mast resided at 4150 East 60th Street, #702, Davenport, Iowa, at the time she filed her petition in this case.

Petitioner Roderic B. Mast resided at 4150 East 60th Street, #702, Davenport, Iowa, at the time he filed his petition in this case.

Gifford, Terrill, Eric, Sara, and Roderic Mast ("petitioners") are siblings, each of which owned an undivided 20-percent interest in a collection of antique stereoscopic negative glass plates, prints, file copies, and related material known as the Keystone-Mast collection (the Collection). In April 1977, petitioners joined in a conveyance of a 25 percent undivided interest in the Collection to UCR, which respondent has conceded to be a qualified charitable organization as described in the Code.[3] Petitioners also collectively donated a second 10 percent undivided interest in the Collection to UCR in 1981. At the time of both donations, petitioners alleged that the fair market value of the Collection was $1,427,253, which was based on an appraisal provided by Mr. Mead B. Kibbey ("Kibbey"). Petitioners each deducted varying portions of the 25 percent and 10 percent undivided interests on their Federal income tax returns as charitable contributions. The individual deductions claimed by petitioners were disproportionate and did not correspond to their prorata ownership interests in the Collection. However, their aggregate total deductions equalled 25 percent and 10 percent of the total claimed fair market value of the Collection.

On September 6, 1985, respondent simultaneously issued notices of deficiency to each of the listed petitioners which completely denied, inter alia, petitioners' charitable deductions based on a revenue agent engineer's valuation of zero for the Collection. After concessions on a number of issues, respondent continues to dispute the amounts of petitioners' charitable contribution deduction, but asserts a fair market value of $450,000 rather than zero. None of the parties contend that the fair market value of the Collection in 1981 differed significantly from the fair market value of the Collection as of the date of the gift in 1977.

Contributed Property

The central issue before us is the fair market value of the Collection at the time of the donations. The Collection consists of stereoscopic negatives, stereoscopic file prints, and miscellaneous files and ledgers. The actual size of the Collection is not completely clear. The experts presented by the parties estimate that the negative portion of the Collection consisting of negatives ranges between 105,000 to 150,000. However, an audit by UCR in 1988 revealed that there were in fact 163,135 stereographic negatives and 192,500 stereographic file prints in the Collection. The Collection is the largest archive of glass stereoscopic negatives ever assembled.

Stereoscopic image, stereograph, and stereo view are all terms which refer to a photograph viewing technique which was popular between the mid-nineteenth and mid-twentieth centuries. It involves a pair of photographs which, when viewed in a special device called a stereoscope or stereoscope viewer, produce a three-dimensional image. Stereographs are created by first taking a photograph of a desired subject with a special double lens camera. The lenses are two and a half inches apart, which approximates the distance between human eyes. A photographic image on glass or thin acetate is then produced. These were known as stereoscopic negatives or pimply negatives. Finally, a print is made from the negative. Both the negatives and the prints display two images of the same subject, each of which was slightly different due to the separation of the two corresponding lenses on the camera. It is this separation which produces a three dimensional illusion when the images are viewed through a stereoscopic viewer.

The Collection was developed under the auspices of the Keystone View Company ("Keystone"), which was founded in 1892 by Mr. B.L. Singley. Keystone was in the eye testing business. Keystone developed the Collection in an effort to control the stereograph market, and was successful in that pursuit. By the mid-1920's Keystone had the largest holdings of glass stereo negatives in the world and also had a virtual monopoly on the stereograph business. Keystone continued to add negatives throughout the 1930's, but the process of adding negatives was halted during World War II. After the war and until 1965 negatives were added to the Collection. In 1963 the Mast Development Corporation acquired Keystone and the eye testing business was moved to Davenport, Iowa. One year later petitioners' father, Gifford Mast, Sr. and Mr. John Niemeyer purchased Keystone from Mast Development Corporation. In 1965, Keystone ceased production of stereographs, continuing as a major manufacturer of eye testing equipment. Petitioners acquired the Collection after the death of Gifford Mast, Sr. The Collection was not explicitly given to petitioners, but respondent does not dispute petitioners' underlying ownership rights in the Collection.

The Collection is actually a combination of several large collections which had been developed by other major stereograph publishers including the Kilburn View Co., H.C. White Berry, Kelly and Chadwick, C.H. Graves and Keystone's main competitor —Underwood and Underwood. The stereoscopic negatives in the Collection are actually in two parts. The first part is arranged by publisher. The second part of the stereoscopic negatives in the Collection is referred to as the "unnumbered" groupings. These were those not deemed by Keystone to be important enough for regular publishing. The subjects of the stereographs include a wide range of people and places of general interest to the viewing public. Specifically, the Collection includes images ranging from portraits of Presidents and other famous individuals to landscapes and panoramas from various locations around the world.

By an Offer of Gift dated April 29, 1977, petitioners offered to donate an undivided one-fourth interest in the Collection to UCR, with a continuing obligation to donate the rest of the Collection within twenty years of the date of acceptance by UCR. Petitioners also retained the option to receive their ratable share of any royalties earned by UCR with respect to the Collection. UCR accepted the offer and possession of the Collection was taken over by UCR at Meadville, Pennsylvania. Petitioners, by a letter dated December 14, 1981, made a second contribution of a 10 percent undivided interest in the Collection in exactly the same manner as the original contribution. The Collection was later moved to UCR and placed in buildings suitable for its display.

As noted above, petitioners deducted disproportionate amounts of the donated interests as charitable contributions. The contributed amounts had no relationship to petitioners' ownership interests, which were identical. Petitioner Gifford M. Mast, Jr., testified that each individual contribution percentage was arrived at based upon a five year estimated earnings stream for each petitioner. Petitioners with higher estimated earnings deducted proportionately higher percentages of the contributed interests as charitable contributions. The aggregate total of petitioners' charitable contribution deductions equalled 25 percent and 10 percent of the fair market value estimate provided by Kibbey, which was $1,427,253. In the notice of deficiency, respondent determined that the fair market value of the Collection at the time of both donations was zero, and allowed no deductions.

Expert Valuations

Mead B. Kibbey

Petitioners' fair market value estimate, as indicated on their individual tax returns, was based on an appraisal provided by Mead B. Kibbey. Kibbey is alleged to be an expert based upon his experience as a "long time collector of photographic equipment" and his involvement with various historical societies and an art gallery. Kibbey was not a licensed appraiser, and was primarily employed in a different business. Kibbey spent 30-40 hours examining the Collection in preparation for his appraisal and concluded that it was in pristine condition.

Kibbey arrived at his opinion by applying a per unit value to the total estimated count of the various items which constitute the Collection. Kibbey originally estimated that the Collection contained 129,732 stereoscopic negatives, but later revised that number to 150,000. The bulk of the value of the Collection was attributed to the stereographic negatives and prints. Kibbey arrived at an individual value for the negatives by looking at replacement cost and arrived at an individual value for the prints based upon sales of allegedly comparable prints. With respect to the negatives, Kibbey computed a per unit replacement cost of $11, based upon current photographic costs, travel, etc. Kibbey did not assign a value for historical content. Kibbey then assigned a per negative value of 40 percent of replacement cost which was $4.25 per negative. With respect to prints, Kibbey looked to an average of allegedly comparable retail sales as listed in two catalogs. Neither catalog has been offered into evidence. The per print value based upon that catalog average was $5. Kibbey's estimate, as revised for changes in actual total unit count, was $1,427,253. In August 1987, Kibbey raised his estimate to $1,544,368 based upon the updated estimate of the total size of the Collection.

Ms. Marjorie Neikrug

Another of petitioners' experts is Ms. Marjorie Neikrug ("Neikrug"). Neikrug is a professional appraiser in that she supports herself through her appraisal activities. She has been the owner and director of a photograph gallery known as Neikrug Photographica since 1970. She is also a senior member of the American Society of Appraisers, a senior member of the Appraisers Association of America, and is also a member of a host of related organizations. Neikrug spent 35 hours personally examining the Collection for purposes of her appraisal and concluded that it was in pristine condition, which, according to Neikrug, means that Collection items can be utilized and reprinted. Neikrug recognizes a number of distinctive approaches to valuation; the income approach, the cost estimate approach, the revenue approach and the market

[3] Sec. 170(a) limits charitable deductions to contributions to organizations described in sec. 170(c).

data comparison approach. She estimates the fair market value of the Collection to be $1,592,611, based on the market data comparison approach. In arriving at that figure she estimated that the Collection contained 149,900 stereoscopic negatives.

Neikrug did not rely on either the income approach or the cost estimate approach in making her appraisal, although they were mentioned in her report.

Neikrug relied on the market comparison approach. Pursuant to that method, valuation conclusions are based on comparisons with reported sales, offers to sell by catalog, showroom or gallery pricing, and historical data. More specifically, Neikrug contacted leading galleries and received opinions as to replacement value. She also contacted auction houses and obtained estimates as to replacement value. Finally a "careful review was carried out along with other available data, background knowledge and experience as indicators of value." From this information, Neikrug developed per item values for the various pieces of the Collection. Although she makes general reference to other smaller collections which are allegedly comparable, no specific correlation is made with her assigned individual values. In fact, no direct correlation is made between her stated standards and those values. She simply states the standards and states the values.

John S. Waldsmith

Petitioners also introduced Mr. John S. Waldsmith ("Waldsmith") as an expert. Waldsmith was an independent appraiser originally retained and paid by respondent to appraise the Collection. Waldsmith has been a full-time dealer in stereo views and other photographica since 1981. He is not a licensed appraiser and had completed only one appraisal of a much smaller collection previous to his appraisal of the Collection in this case. Waldsmith is Managing Editor of Stereo World magazine, co-founder and member of the Board of Directors of the National Stereoscopic Association, and is the author of numerous articles on stereo views. Waldsmith examined the Collection extensively during visits to UCR in 1982, 1983, 1984, 1985, and 1986. His examination in this case took over 102 hours. Waldsmith agrees that the Collection is the world's largest collection of stereographic negatives ever assembled. He estimates that the fair market value of the Collection is $1,207,500. Waldsmith made his valuation determination by breaking the Collection up into component parts and then assigning average per unit values for the items in each segment. He assumed that the Collection contained 159,200 stereographic negatives and 102,100 file prints.

He asserts that the stereoscopic negatives are in two major parts. The first part is arranged in numbered order by publisher and the second part is referred to as unnumbered groupings. The unnumbered groupings were those not deemed important enough by Keystone for regular publishing. With respect to the first group, Waldsmith assigned an average per unit value of $5.00 based on sales of other similar negatives. One such sale was of a collection of 200 poor quality negatives for $1000. Waldsmith purchased some of the negatives in that collection and later sold one for $35. He also asserts that many of the negatives in the Collection would have sold for $100 in 1977, while hundreds of the negatives would have had little or no value. From this he extrapolates the average per unit value for the first major group of negatives. With respect to the second group of negatives he simply discusses their unique and historic nature and states an average value of $10 per negative. With respect to other portions of the Collection, i.e., file prints, ledgers, etc., Waldsmith generally provides a description and then sets forth a 1977 per unit sales price. Finally, he notes that the Collection may have an unascertainable value due to as yet unforeseen uses, such as television documentaries.

Penelope A. Dixon

The only expert witness presented by respondent was Ms. Penelope A. Dixon ("Dixon"). Dixon is a full-time appraiser of photography and photographic material. She has worked extensively in the photographic appraisal business. She is a senior member of the American Society of Appraisers and is a member of other related trade associations. Dixon was retained by respondent shortly before trial. Dixon's valuation estimate was primarily based upon sales of five allegedly comparable collections. Dixon's initial fair market value estimate which was rendered before she had personally examined the Collection, was $500,000. She subsequently spent two days examining the Collection for the purpose of formulating her opinion. Her final valuation, which was received by petitioners four days before trial, was $450,000.

Dixon's valuation method does not require a specific estimate of the Collection's size. However, she does dispute petitioners' various estimates of the stereoscopic negative count as excessive. At trial she disputed the UCR audit estimate of 163,135 stereoscopic negatives and insisted that the Collection contains only 105,000 stereoscopic negatives. However, she appraised the Collection based on an estimate of 135,000 stereoscopic negatives.

Dixon determined the fair market value of the Collection by estimating the price at which a comparable collection could be sold, in its entirety. Although Dixon did provide price ranges of boxed and individual stereographic prints in her report, they were apparently provided only for informational purposes. We note that those cited individual prices refer to stereographic prints, not negatives. Dixon cited five separate collections as comparable: the Philippe Halsman Archive, the Todd Webb Archive, the Darrah collection, the Underwood and Underwood collection, and the William Chase collection.

The Philippe Halsman Archive consisted of approximately 80,000 negatives and 50,000 prints from the 1940's through the 1960's. It was purchased by a Mr. George Rinhart ("Rinhart") in 1976 for $150,000. However, according to both Neikrug and Waldsmith, these negatives and prints are photographs, not stereographs. Neikrug also indicated that Evon Halsman, Philippe Halsman's wife, retained rights to the negatives for her lifetime.

The Todd Webb Archive consisted of approximately 50,000 negatives and 10,000 prints from the 1940's to the 1970's. It was purchased by Rinhart in 1978 for $60,000. According to Waldsmith these were photographs not stereographs. In addition, Neikrug testified that the Todd Webb Archive was subject to copyright restrictions.

The Darrah Collection consisted of 120,000 stereographs. It was purchased by Rinhart in 1977 for $80,000. The University of Georgia purchased 50,000 of these stereographs in 1978 for $50,000. Neikrug testified that the stereographs in this sale were prints and not negatives. Waldsmith testified that the subjects of the Darrah collection stereographs sold to Rinhart were of little interest to the general public. Moreover, Waldsmith maintains that the stereographs subsequently sold to the University of Georgia were the "dregs" of the collection.

The Underwood and Underwood Collection consists of 1.5 million photographs and stereoscopic negatives. It was purchased by Rinhart in 1978 for $117,500. This collection included approximately 100,000 stereoscopic glass negatives, 40,000 stereographs, 100,000 file prints and ledger books and over one million 5 × 7 enlargements made from the negatives. Dixon, in her report, states that Rinhart has made sales of the stereographs in groups for an average of 50 cents each. She also states that Rinhart has sold a lot of 30 stereoscopic negatives of Babe Ruth for $100. Finally, Dixon reports that Rinhart would sell between 30,000 and 50,000 of the Underwood and Underwood Collection stereoscopic negatives, which include famous pictures of Roosevelt and Mark Twain, for $100,000.

Waldsmith testified that the stereoscopic negatives in the Underwood and Underwood Collection were similar to those found in the Collection, but were of inferior quality. In addition, Waldsmith indicated that a large number of the negatives in the Underwood and Underwood Collection had been partially destroyed in that half of the image had been scratched out.

Opinion

There is no dispute in this case that an actual donation was made to a qualified charitable donee under section 170(c). The only issues before us are the fair market value of the Collection, whether petitioners may allocate among themselves unequal portions of gifts of undivided interests in property, and whether petitioners are liable for additional interest under section 6621(c) (formerly section 6621(d)) due to a substantial underpayment of tax.

Section 1.170A-1(c)(1), Income Tax Regs., provides that the amount of a charitable contribution deduction made in property other than money shall be the fair market value of the property on the date of donation. Section 1.170A-1(c)(2), Income Tax Regs., defines fair market value as "the price at which the property would change hands between a willing buyer and a willing seller, neither being under any compulsion to buy or sell and both having a reasonable knowledge of relevant facts." See *United States v. Cartwright* [73-1 USTC ¶ 12,926], 411 U.S. 546, 549 (1973); *Johnson v. Commissioner* [Dec. 42,383], 85 T.C. 469 (1985). Fair market value is a question of fact to be determined from an examination of the entire record. *Lio v. Commissioner* [Dec. 42,249], 85 T.C. 56 (1985), affd. sub nom. *Orth v. Commissioner* [87-1 USTC ¶ 9215], 813 F.2d 837 (7th Cir. 1987). The question of value is inherently factual In nature. *Kaplan v. Commissioner* [Dec. 27,230], 43 T.C. 580 (1965). The Court must consider opinion evidence presented by the parties together with all other relevant evidence in the record. *Estate of Smith v. Commissioner* [Dec. 31,262], 57 T.C. 650 (1972), affd. [75-1 USTC ¶ 13,046] 510 F.2d 479 (2d Cir. 1975). Since the parties have taken extremely divergent positions as to the fair market value of the Collection at the time of the donation to UCR, we must make that determination.

Usually, petitioners bear the burden of proving that the Commissioner's determination of the fair market value of property involved in the case is in error. Rule 142(a), *Welch v. Helvering* [3 USTC ¶ 1164], 290 U.S. 111 (1933). In the particular circumstances of this case, however, we believe the weight to be given respondent's determination of value should be modified and the burden of petitioners to show error in that determination should be mitigated to some extent. In the notice of deficiency, respondent determined the value of the collection to be zero.* At the trial respondent offered the testimony of an expert witness, who testified that the value of the collection was $450,000-$500,000. Respondent offered no additional evidence to support either his zero value determined in the notice of deficiency or the value found by his only expert witness at the trial. On the other hand, petitioners offered the testimony of several experts, one of whom had originally been retained by respondent, all of whom testified the value was much greater. Under such circumstances any presumption of correctness that might attach to respondent's determination in the notice of deficiency loses its conviction. See *Helvering v. Taylor* [35-1 USTC ¶ 9044], 293 U.S. 507 (1935); *Llorente v. Commissioner* [81-1 USTC ¶ 9446], 649 F.2d 152 (2d Cir. 1981), reversing in part [Dec. 36,955] 74 T.C. 260 (1980); *Suarez v. Commissioner* [Dec. 31,494], 58 T.C. 792 (1972). By this we do not mean that the burden of proof shifts from petitioners to respondent but only that petitioners' burden may be somewhat lightened.

In addition, as noted above, respondent offered the testimony of only one witness who was offered as an expert at the trial. We do not question the expertise of respondent's witness; she appeared to be quite well qualified. But under the rules of this Court, if a witness is to be offered as a valuation expert, a written valuation report must be served on both the Court and opposing counsel at least 15 days before the call of the trial calendar on which the case should appear (Rule 143(f)(1) Rules of Practice and Procedure, United States Tax Court). The reason for this is clearly illustrated in this case which involves a very unique type of property, consisting of many parts, which is seldom traded in the marketplace. The valuation approaches by the various experts were quite different. Respondent's valuation report was not served on either petitioners or the Court until several days before the trial. Neither petitioners nor the Court had time to fully analyze the witness report nor ask her questions about it while she was in Court. Furthermore, the parties were not left with time to knowledgeably discuss settlement, for which this case cries out.

When respondent's expert's testimony and valuation report were offered as evidence at the trial, the Court received them, over petitioners' objections, perhaps because the Court was entirely unfamiliar with the property being valued and methods used by experts in doing so, and was anxious to get as much information on the subject as was available.

All three of petitioners' experts used valuation methods which differed substantially from that employed by respondent's expert. Petitioners' experts estimated a per unit cost for the various elements of the Collection and multiplied those figures by varying total counts. Respondent's expert determined fair market value by looking at sales of allegedly comparable collections.

Petitioners' expert Kibbey examined and estimated the fair market value of the Collection at the time of petitioners' initial contribution. Although we are not overly impressed with Kibbey's qualifications as a "long time collector of photographic equipment," his methodology bears further examination.

Kibbey looked to replacement value as a basis for valuation of the negative portion of the Collection. We think, given the fact that the Collection is rather unique because of its size and content, that this is a fairly reasonable approach. His method of determining replacement value, by looking at current photographic costs, is also acceptable. However, the valuation of each negative at 40 percent of replacement cost seems somewhat arbitrary. He testified that his depreciation discount factor was conservative, but an explanation of why it was conservative was not forthcoming.

With respect to the file prints, Kibbey examined retail sales from two catalogs. Neither catalog was entered into evidence, so we must rely on Kibbey's testimony to verify the relevance of their content. He testified that the prints listed in those two catalogs were stereographs as opposed to the stereographic file prints contained in the Collection. He also testified that the file prints were stereographs kept in company files and were generally in better condition than most stereographs. Kibbey finally drew an estimate of $5 per file print from the catalog prices which ranged from $3.76 to $20.85.

We find Kibbey's estimate of the negative portion of the Collection to be relatively persuasive, but we are disturbed that a more specific mathematical computation of fair market value was not produced. We are also somewhat skeptical about accepting values for the file prints based on stereographic print prices which we have not actually seen. Again, with respect to the print portion of the Collection, averaging computations have not been supplied. In summary, we find Kibbey's opinion to be persuasive, but not convincing in and of itself. His basic methodology seems sound, but a more specific explanation of his calculations would make his opinion much more persuasive.

Petitioners' expert Neikrug used a valuation method which bears marked similarity to that employed by Kibbey. At trial she testified that she used the cost estimate approach and the market data comparison approach. She testified that the cost estimate approach was based on the cost of hiring a photographer, travelling expenses, materials, office expenses and personnel. Although she states that she used these factors, they are not delineated in her report. Neikrug's market data comparison approach relies on opinions derived from auction houses, galleries, her background and experience. Again we are left without any specific compilation of the data which she used in arriving at her estimate.

The cost estimate approach is quite similar to the method used by Kibbey. Unfortunately Neikrug does not illuminate the intricacies of her computation for us. She simply sets forth fair market values for portions of the Collection. The market data comparison approach, in theory, seems reasonable to us. However, Neikrug again provides no guidance as to its precise operation. Although Neikrug's qualifications are impressive, we have difficulty relying solely on her estimate of $1,592,611 to support petitioners' fair market value assumption.

Petitioners' expert Waldsmith made his valuation determination by breaking the Collection up into component parts and then assigning values to each segment, based on a per unit average. With respect to the negatives, those averages were derived from a few isolated sales. As for the rest of the Collection, Waldsmith simply described each component and assigned it a fair market value. We accept Waldsmith's qualifications and his stated method. However, we are left facing a gap between the stated method and Waldsmith's conclusion. Hence, his opinion cannot stand alone to support petitioners' valuation estimate.

Respondent's expert, Dixon, used a valuation method which differed substantially from that employed by petitioners' three experts. She determined fair market value based on sales of five allegedly comparable collections. To assess the viability of Dixon's valuation estimate, we must examine the comparability of those five collections; The Philippe Halsman Archive, The Todd Webb Archive, The Underwood and Underwood Collection, The Darrah Collection, and the William Chase Collection.

The Philippe Halsman Archives was not truly comparable to the Collection because it consisted of photographs, not stereoscopic cards or stereoscopic negatives. In addition, it was purchased with restrictions which Dixon did not mention in her report.

The Todd Webb Archive contained stereoscopic prints, not stereoscopic negatives. Moreover, Waldsmith testified that these prints were photographs, not stereoscopic prints. Even if the prints in the Todd Webb Archive are stereoscopic prints, evidence of their sales price only has direct relevance to the print portion of the Collection. We do not see that any immediate inference can be drawn with regard to the stereoscopic negatives, which comprise a sizable portion of the Collection. We are left then with a $60,000 figure which covers both 50,000 non-stereoscopic negatives and 10,000 prints which may not be stereoscopic. An allocation between the two groups is impossible without further information. Moreover, the Todd Webb Archive covers subjects from the 1940's to the 1970's, which is a period substantially later than that covered by the Collection.

Like the Todd Webb Archive, the Darrah Collection did not include stereoscopic negatives. Waldsmith testified that the subjects of the Darrah Collection photographs were of little interest to the general public. We see no evidence to contradict that testimony.

The size and content of the Underwood and Underwood Collection, with its 100,000 stereoscopic negatives and 100,000 stereoscopic file prints, are quite similar to the Collection. However, the negatives in that collection had been defaced. One of the two images had been defaced, destroying their stereoscopic effect. In addition, the file prints in the Underwood and Underwood Collection were only half prints. The $117,500 price which Rinhart paid for the Underwood and Underwood Collection is far less than the $1,427,453 which petitioners claim the Collection is worth. However, we are persuaded that the poor condition of the Underwood and Underwood Collection distinguishes it from the Collection.

At the outset we note that questions of fair market value are more properly resolved through settlement negotiation rather than litigation. In the absence of settlement, we are left to adjudicate the validity of conflicting experts' opinions who are convinced that both their conclusions and methods are correct. "The result is an over zealous effort, during the course of the ensuing litigation, to infuse a talismanic precision into an issue which should frankly be recognized as inherently imprecise and capable of resolution only by a Solomon-like pronouncement." *Messing v. Commissioner* [Dec. 28,532], 48 T.C. 502, 512 (1967). Unfortunately, since settlement was not forthcoming in this case, we are forced to make such a pronouncement.

While the collections chosen by Dixon as comparable are of inferential value in determining fair market value, a direct comparison is unwarranted. Dixon also included per unit price references in the Appendix of her report, but they appear to have been included solely for informa-

* By official Tax Court Order dated March 24, 1989, and signed by Judge William M. Drennen, the above sentence was added to read as indicated.

tional purposes. We also question the viability of an appraisal which was completed on such short notice and without personal inspection, although she did subsequently visit the Collection and revised her estimate down to $450,000 from $500,000. In summary, while we recognize Dixon's eminent qualifications in the photographic appraisal field, we are inclined to place little emphasis on her valuation estimate.

In assessing the persuasiveness of petitioners' expert witnesses, one of which was originally employed by respondent, we are struck by the marked similarity of their methodology. We tend to agree that a per unit method is preferable given the unique size and content of the Collection. We find Dixon's method to be unpersuasive primarily because it was based on sales prices of collections which were not actually comparable. In addition to the similarity of methods employed, we also note that the fair market values proffered by all three of petitioners' experts, ranging from $1,207,500 to $1,592,611 are fairly close. While we are concerned with the marked lack of direct computational evidence and the continuing discrepancy as to the total size of the Collection, we find that the expert testimony as presented supports, to some extent, the fair market value claimed by petitioners; but giving some weight to the testimony of respondent's expert and other evidence received, we conclude that the value of the Collection was $1,250,000.

Disproportionate Contributions

Respondent contests the disproportionate allocation of petitioners' contributions. To support this argument, respondent cites section 1.170A-7(b)(1)(i), Income Tax Regs., which provides:

> A deduction is allowed under section 170 for the value of a charitable contribution not in trust of an undivided portion of a donor's entire interest in property. An undivided portion of a donor's entire interest in property must consist of a fraction or percentage of each and every substantial interest or right owned by the donor in such property and must extend over the entire term of the donor's interest in such property and in other property into which such property is converted. * * *

We see nothing in the above cited regulation which convinces us that charitable contributions of unequal portions of undivided interests in property are prohibited. The interest donated by each petitioner does consist of "a fraction or a percentage of each and every substantial interest" owned by each petitioner. Section 1.170A-7(b)(1)(i), Income Tax Regs., does not limit or restrict the various portions of undivided interests in property which individual owners may deduct as charitable contributions. It simply requires that the fractional interest contributed consist of a fraction of the donor's entire interest.

Petitioners' evidence to support the disproportionate amounts of that portion of the total value of the Collection deducted as charitable contributions by each individual petitioner in each of the years before us consists of the written Offers of Gift given by the petitioners to UCR in all of the years, and the testimony of Gifford Mast as to how these shares were determined. The Offers of Gift specified only the percentage of the total value of the Collection that was collectively given to UCR by all five of the Masts, and did not explain how those proportions were arrived at. Gifford Mast testified how the individual portions were determined each year. As we understand it, it was based on the flow of income of each of the Masts each year, which translates into what division of the total amounts claimed each year would produce the most benefit taxwise for the group as a whole.

Nevertheless, we see no reason why petitioners should not be permitted to so determine the amounts to be claimed by each of the siblings, as long as they each knowingly and intentionally transferred their allotted portion to UCR. Respondent did not determine that they did not make the contributions claimed, nor the specific amounts they claimed, but only that they were not entitled to make deductible gifts in this manner.

We note that the contributed interests in this case are distinguishable from those in cases challenged under section 170(f)(3) which denies deductions for certain contributions of partial interests in property. *Stark v. Commissioner* [Dec. 42,896], 86 T.C. 243 (1986). Subparagraph (f)(3)(B) provides that subparagraph (A) shall not apply to: "(ii) a contribution of an undivided portion of the taxpayer's entire interest in property, and * * *." Petitioners are therefore entitled to deduct that portion of the total allowable contributions claimed on their respective tax returns.

Section 6621(c) Interest

Respondent seeks increased interest pursuant to section 6621(c). Section 6621(c) provides for an increase in the interest rate to 120 percent of the statutory rate on underpayments of tax if a substantial understatement is due to a tax motivated transaction. Section 6621(c)(3)(A)(i) includes in the term tax motivated transaction any valuation overstatement within the meaning of section 6659(c). In relevant part, section 6659(c) provides that there is a valuation overstatement if the value of any property claimed on any return is 150 percent or more of the amount determined to be the correct amount of such valuation.

Since the deductions claimed on the returns were less than 150 percent of the values we have determined, section 6659(c) does not apply, and petitioners are therefore not liable for the increased interest provided by section 6621(c).

STANDARDS OF PROFESSIONAL APPRAISAL PRACTICE

FOR PERSONAL PROPERTY APPRAISERS

A. Preamble:

It is essential that a professional personal property appraiser arrive at and communicate his or her analyses, conclusions, opinions and valuations in a manner appropriate to the function of the appraisal and of transcending clarity to the client, to any third parties involved, to the public or to any other legitimately interested entities. The intent of these standards is to guide the practicing professional personal property appraiser; to serve as establishing present appropriate standards, as well as a foundation for any further future development, in personal property appraising; and to make users of appraisal services and the public aware of these standards. Appraisers who maintain today's highest level of professional practice will observe these standards when developing and communicating an appraisal, analysis, opinion or valuation conclusion.

These standards are intended to apply to appraisers of personal property as that term is generally understood by the public, e.g., paintings, antiques, jewelry, household furnishings, collectibles, etc.

Aware that some professions may recognize personal property as including machinery, equipment, intangibles and certain business assets, we endorse action to establish uniform standards of professional appraisal practice in those disciplines by committees most closely associated with the discipline of Machinery and Equipment Appraising and the discipline of Business Valuation.

B. Competency:

Prior to agreeing to perform a personal property appraisal, the appraiser must carefully consider the knowledge, training and experience that will be required to complete the appraisal competently, and either:

1. has been tested and certified in the required field of expertise by a major recognized testing and certifying appraisal society, or

2. assumes personal responsibility in presenting alternate substantial evidence that he or she has the specialized knowledge, training, experience and resources to complete the appraisal competently, or

3. immediately discloses the lack of required knowledge, training, experience or resources

to the client, allowing the client to engage appraisal services elsewhere, or, with the client's approval, take all steps necessary and appropriate to complete the appraisal competently, such as use of necessary experts etc.

C. Definitions:

For the purpose of these standards, the following definitions apply:

Appraisal: the act or process of estimating value

Appraisal Report: any communication, written or oral, of an appraisal; the document that is transmitted to the client upon completion of an appraisal assignment.

Client: any party for whom an appraiser performs a service.

Personal Property: identifiable portable and tangible objects which are considered by the general public as being "personal", e.g., furnishings, artwork, antiques, gems and jewelry, collectibles, etc.

D. Standards:

<u>Standard I.</u>

In developing a personal property appraisal, an appraiser must be aware of, understand, and correctly employ those recognized methods and techniques that are necessary to produce a credible appraisal.

<u>Rules for Standard I</u>

Rule 1. In developing a personal property appraisal, an appraiser must:

a) be aware of, understand, and correctly employ those recognized methods and techniques that are necessary to produce a credible appraisal;

b) not commit a substantial error of omission or commission that significantly affects an appraisal;

c) not render appraisal services in a careless or negligent manner, such as improper or incomplete research or a series of minor errors that, considered individually, may not significantly affect the results of an appraisal, but which, when considered in the aggregate, would be misleading.

Rule 2. In developing a personal property appraisal, an appraiser must observe the following specific appraisal guidelines:

a) adequately identify the object(s) to be evaluated including the method of identification if other than or in addition to a personal physical inspection;

b) state and clearly define the purpose and function of the appraisal including any special limiting conditions;

c) identify the effective date of the appraisal clearly distinguishing the appraisal date from the report date when appropriate;

d) define the value to be considered consistent with the function of the appraisal, e.g., retail replacement value for most insurance appraisals; fair market value for charitable donations or estate tax valuation of property, etc.;

e) value the object by an appropriate appraisal method or technique;

f) collect, verify, analyze and reconcile such comparable sales data as are available, adequately identified and described, to indicate a value conclusion;

g) ALL PERTINENT INFORMATION MUST BE INCLUDED;

h) when applicable, consider and analyze the effect on value of:
1. any damage or imperfections relevant to the object(s);
2. the object(s)' importance as compared to other items of the same type and classification, or as it relates to an artist's total work, or as enhancing other parts of a specific collection;
3. any historical factors (provenance) which would affect the value of the object(s);
4. the market acceptability of the style and scale of the object(s);

5. the object(s)' utility, if any, in today's society as it relates to the object(s)' originally intended use;
6. any prior sales of the object(s) being appraised.

Standard II.
In a personal property appraisal report, an appraiser must communicate his or her analyses, opinions, conclusions and valuations in a manner that is clear and not misleading.

Rules for Standard II

Rule 1. Each written or oral appraisal report must:

a) clearly and accurately set forth the appraisal in a manner that will not be misleading;
b) contain sufficient information to enable the person(s) who receive or rely on the report to understand it properly;
c) clearly and accurately disclose any extraordinary assumption or limiting condition that directly affects the appraisal and indicate the impact on value of such assumptions or conditions.

Rule 2. Each written appraisal report must comply with the following specific reporting guidelines:

a) identify and describe the personal property being appraised;
b) define the purpose, function and scope of the appraisal;
c) define the value to be estimated;
d) set forth the effective date of the appraisal and the date of the report;
e) set forth all assumptions and limiting conditions that affect the analyses, opinions, conclusions and valuations;
f) where appropriate, set forth the information considered, the appraisal procedures followed, and the reasoning that supports the analyses, opinions, conclusions and valuations;
g) as the use of comparable sales is the normal valuation approach for the appraisal of personal property, explain and support the use of a different valuation approach;

h) set forth any additional information that may be appropriate to show compliance with the requirements of Standard I
i) include a signed certification in accordance with the following Rule 3.

Rule 3. Each written appraisal report must contain a certification consisting of the following elements which the appraiser certifies to the best of his or her knowledge and belief:

a) the statements of fact contained in the appraisal report are true and correct;
b) the reported analyses, opinions and conclusions are limited only by the reported assumptions and limiting conditions, and are the appraiser's personal, unbiased, professional analyses, opinions, conclusions and valuations;
c) the appraiser has no present nor contemplated future interest in the object(s) which is the subject of the report (unless specified to the contrary);
d) the appraiser has no personal interest or bias with respect to the parties involved (unless specified to the contrary);
e) the appraiser does not have a personal or business relationship with the parties involved which would lead a reasonable person to question the objectivity and validity of the report;
f) the appraiser's compensation is not contingent on an action or event resulting from the analyses, opinions, or conclusions in, or the use of, the report;
g) the appraiser's compensation is not to be dependent upon the amount of value which he or she determines at the conclusion of his or her work, neither as a fixed percentage of that value determination, nor as compensation connected to a predetermined scale relating fee to value range;
h) the appraiser has made a personal, physical inspection of the object(s) specified in the report (unless specified to the contrary);
i) the appraiser received no separate significant professional assistance (unless specified to the contrary in which case the name of the individual(s) providing such assistance must be stated and, where appropriate, should sign the report);

(j) the analyses, opinions, conclusions and valuations in the report were developed, and the report prepared, in conformity with the <u>Standards of Professional Appraisal Practice For Personal Property Appraisers.</u>

Rule 4. To the extent that it is both possible and appropriate, each oral appraisal report, including expert testimony, must address the substantive matters set forth in these Standards I and II.

E. <u>Jurisdictional Exceptions</u>:

If any part of these standards is contrary to the law of any jurisdiction or public policy clearly affirmed by competent authority in a jurisdiction, only that part shall be void and of no force or effect in that jurisdiction.

These Standards were approved by the Board of Governors of the American Society of Appraisers, Portland, Oregon, June 28, 1986, and by the Board of Directors of the Appraisers Association of American on July 7, 1986.

BIBLIOGRAPHY

Art Law, Feldman, Weil, Duke & Biederman, Little, Brown & Co., Boston, MA, 1986

Art Law, Lerner & Bresler, Practising Law Institute, New York, NY, 1989

Charitable Organizations: Special Topics, New York University 44th Annual Institute On Federal Taxation - Totaltape Publishing - Gainesville, FL 1986

Conference Report To Accompany H.R. 3838, 99th Congress, 2d Session, Report 99-841, 1986

Hearing Before A Subcommittee On Government Operations, House Of Representatives, 98th Congress, 1983

Internal Revenue Code, Maxwell Macmillan, Englewood Cliffs, NJ, 1991

Federal Tax Regulations, Maxwell Macmillan, Englewood Cliffs, NJ, 1991

Representing Artists, Collectors, and Dealers, Practising Law Institute, New York, 1985

Tax Aspects Of Charitable Giving, The Harvard Manual, Sixth Edition, Office of Planned Giving Harvard University, Cambridge, MA, 1985

INDEX

[* indicates Form, Publication or Case included in Appendix]

1994 SUPPLEMENT TO THE GUIDE TO TAX BENEFITS FOR COLLECTORS, DEALERS, AND INVESTORS

SECOND EDITION

by Robert S. Persky

PUBLISHED BY:

THE CONSULTANT PRESS, LTD.

NEW YORK, NEW YORK

• • •

But in this world nothing can be said to be certain except death and taxes."

Benjamin Franklin in a letter to Jean Baptiste Le Roy, November 13,1789

• • •

Over and over again courts have said that there is nothing sinister in so arranging one's affairs as to keep taxes as low as possible. Everybody does so, rich or poor; and all do right, for nobody owes any public duty to pay more than the law demands; taxes are enforced exactions, not voluntary contributions. To demand more in the name of morals is mere cant."

Judge Learned Hand, dissenting, Commissioner v. Newman, 159 F.2d 848, 2d Cir. 1947

• • •

ISBN 0-913069-32-9

Library of Congress Catalog Card No: 91-076614

Printed in the U.S.A

THE CONSULTANT PRESS,LTD., 163 AMSTERDAM AVE., NEW YORK, NY 10023
Telephone (212) 838-8640 Facsimile (212) 873-7065

HOW TO USE THIS SUPPLEMENT

This supplement to *The Guide To Tax Benefits For Collectors, Dealers & Investors* has been compiled for the purpose of updating the text to the *Revenue Reconciliation Act of 1993* (the "'93 Act").

It is organized in the same sequence as the main volume. Changes in the text of the main volume are indicated by chapter, page, and paragraph. This supplement contains its own index.

If you are reading the main volume for the first time it will save you time if you first mark the main volume pages which have been changed with a notation to refer to this supplement. To facilitate that process, page 11 of this supplement lists those pages of the main volume which have text changes.

If you have already read the main volume this supplement provides you with an explanation of the changes.

In the future, when using the main volume, you should also refer to the index in this supplement.

AN OVERVIEW OF THE '93 ACT

The '93 Act did not change the framework of the basic rules which govern the activities of collectors, dealers, and investors. It did change the rules in regard to the donation of tangible personal property. The major change was the permanent restoration of a benefit which had, since 1986, been periodically suspended.

The benefit is the ability to make the donation of art or other personal property, which has appreciated in value from the time of your acquisition, and to take a charitable deduction for the fair market value of the property without triggering the provisions relating to the Alternative Minimum Tax.

The '93 Act increased the graduated tax rates for individuals. Two new rates were added, 36% and 39.6%. The old maximum rate was 31%. Thus the dollar amount of the benefit received by making a charitable donation will be increased for taxpayers whose taxable income exceeds certain thresholds. The maximum rate for capital gains remains at 28%. The differential between the maximum rate for capital gains and ordinary income is again substantial and greater attention is warranted to whether you are a collector, dealer, or investor.

CHAPTER ONE

page 12 - last ¶ now should read:

Beginning in 1993, capital gains are subject to a maximum rate of 28 percent, while ordinary income may be taxed at 39.6% percent. Whether you are considered to be a collector, dealer, or investor, has again become the key fact in determining whether you can take advantage of the lower capital gain rates.

CHAPTER TWO

page 21 - last two ¶'s now should read:

A substantial differential has been reinstated by the '93 Act. Capital gains are taxed at a maximum of 28% and ordinary income at a maximum of 39.6%

It is important to remember that T.R.A. '86 did not change the character of gain as ordinary or capital, or as short-term or long-term capital gain. The statutory structure for capital gains was retained in the Code to facilitate reinstatement of a capital gains rate differential. In fact, that differential has been reinstated. Your acquisition records for the intervening years should be retained to substantiate your acquisition cost and status, i.e. collector, dealer, or investor.

CHAPTER FOUR

page 49 - last 3 ¶'s now should read:

T.R.A. '86 temporarily eliminated the difference between tax treatment by eliminating the benefit accorded on the sale of long-term capital gains property but a differential in rates has been reinstated by the '93 Act.

Capital Gains

A primary concern is whether the profit on a sale of a work of art is taxed at ordinary income rates or at the long-term capital gains rates.

The capital gains issue, in so far as the tax rate differential, has again become significant.

CHAPTER FIVE

page 53 - add a new ¶ at the bottom.

Sales and use taxes can add up. Two corporations, under common control, filed state and federal tax returns claiming wholesaler/dealer status. New York State auditors claimed that by allowing their controlling shareholder, a prominent publisher, to display all their acquired art in his residences the corporations had demonstrated that they had not acquired the art for resale. That finding was recently affirmed by a New York State tax tribunal. The corporations were assessed a total of $482,000 in sales and use taxes.

CHAPTER SIX

page 57 - numbered ¶ 3 should now read:

3. Under T.R.A. '86 unrealized appreciation in gifts of property given to a charity was treated as a preference item when computing the Alternative Minimum Tax ("A.M.T."). The result was a diminished tax benefit for some, but not all, taxpayers. The '93 Act eliminated the unrealized appreciation as a preference item. As a result there is no longer a risk of triggering the A.M.T. by making a charitable donation of appreciate personal property.

page 59 - numbered ¶ 4 is deleted.

page 78 - the first full ¶ is deleted.

page 84 - add the following new ¶ before the *QUICK REFERENCE CHART.*

A "contribution" to a charity in exchange for which the donor receives an economic benefit is deductible only to the extent that the payment exceeds the value of the benefit. If you make a $250 donation and receive two tickets to a Broadway play that sell for $50 each, you are permitted to deduct only $150. The "benefit for cash" procedure is referred to as a **quid pro quo contribution.** *Prior to the '93 Act the IRS requested charities to determine the fair market value of benefits offered for contributions (e.g. tickets, dinners, books, recordings). The charities were requested to state in the solicitation how much was deductible and how much* *was not deductible. Prior law, however, did not require the charities to comply with the request.*

The '93 Act adds a requirement that a charity receiving a **quid pro quo** *contribution in excess of $75 provide a written statement, in connection with soliciting or receiving the contribution, that (1) informs the donor that the amount of the contribution deductible for federal income tax purposes is limited to the excess of the amount of any money and/or property contributed by the donor over the value of the goods or services provided by the charity and (2) provides the donor with a good-faith estimate of the value of those goods or services (I.R.C. § 6115).*

The disclosure must be made in a manner that is reasonably likely to come to your attention. The fine print often used by charities in disclosing the value of the **quid pro quo benefits** *may be insufficient. Token benefits such as inexpensive pens and ceramic coffee mugs are not deemed to be* **quid pro quo** *items. Also excluded are payments made to an organization, organized exclusively for religious purposes, in return for which you receive a solely an intangible religious benefit that is not generally sold in commercial transactions.*

Charities failing to comply are subject to a penalty of $10 per contribution, capped at $5,000 per fund-raising event or mailing (I.R.C. § 6714). There is a defense of reasonable cause. The penalty applies if the charity fails to make a *disclosure in connection with a* ***quid pro quo*** *contribution or makes an incomplete or inaccurate disclosure.*

The new requirements may have a chilling effect on ***quid pro quo*** *gifts, particularly the popular donor print programs.*

CHAPTER SEVEN

pages 85-90 This chapter, **The Alternative Minimum Tax,** is deleted.

CHAPTER NINE

page 107 - delete reference to A.M.T. in the fourth full ¶.

page 113 - delete the second full ¶.

CHAPTER TEN

page 121 - add the following the last ¶

Advance Determination of the Value of Charitable Gifts

The House-Senate Conference Report accompanying the '93 Act states that the IRS is expected to submit a report with the year ending August 10,1994 on developing a procedure for taxpayers to seek an agreement with the IRS on the value of tangible personal property prior to donation. The report is to be made to the House Ways and Means Committee and the Senate Finance Committee.

The motive behind the procedure is to eliminate expensive and time consuming post donation disputes on valuation and to encourage charitable donations by providing a "safe harbor" valuation procedure. The agreed valuation will be binding on the I.R.S.

It is expected that the procedure, if adopted, will require (i) some minimum threshold of claimed value, (ii) the payment of a processing fee, and (iii) the submission of substantially the same documentation that is now required to be submitted with your tax return. It is our belief that the threshold claimed valuation will be a minimum of $20,000. When the program is first implemented, the threshold may be higher, so as to limit the overburdening of the program during break-in period.

Whether the I.R.S. will seek authority for the program by way of an amendment to the I.R.C. or implement it under its authority to issue regulations remains undecided.

page 130 - delete the last two sentences in the first full ¶ and substitute the following:

The '93 Act replaces the "not frivolous" standard with a "reasonable basis" standard. Thus, under the '93 Act, a taxpayer can avoid the penalties for substantial understatement and disregard of the rules and regulations by adequate discloure only if the position has a reasonable basis. Adequate disclosure means "complete, item-specific" disclosure of your position. Disclosure must be full and substantial. Disclosure isn't necessary to avoid the negligence penalty because under REG. § 1.6662-3(b)(1) a taxpayer isn't considered negligent with respect to a return position that has a reasonable basis.

page 131 - add the following to the section titled **Required Records**

The '93 Act denies a deduction for charitable contributions of $250 or more, whether cash or property, unless you substantiate the contribution by a written acknowledgment from the donee organization (I.R.C. § 170(f)(8)(A). The Senate Report states that you may not rely solely on a cancelled check to substantiate a *cash contribution of $250 or more. For contributions of less than $250, the pre-'93 Act rules continue to apply. Bona fide separate payments will not be aggregated for the purpose of the $250 threshold.*

Note that you must have the written substantiation in your possession ***prior*** *to filing your tax return.*

The acknowledgment must include the following information:

(i) the amount of cash and description (but not the value) of any property other than cash contributed;

(ii) whether the donee organization provided any goods or services in consideration, in whole or in part, for the contribution; and

(iii) a description and good-faith estimate of the value of those goods or services or, if the good or services consist entirely of intangible religious benefits, a statement to that effect. (I.R.C. 170(f)(8)(B).

No particular form is prescribed for the acknowledgment. The taxpayer must obtain the acknowledgment on or before the date on which he files his return for the tax year of the contribution. If you do not have a required acknowledgment on the last day for filing, consider filing for an extension. In the instance of large contributions you may want to save the mailing envelope or other evidence of the date of delivery.

It is expected that under regulations to be issued, charities will be able to file a return with the IRS reporting information sufficient to substantiate the amount(s) of deductible contributions. (I.R.C. § 170(f)(8)(D).

A charitable organization that knowingly provides a false written acknowledgment to a donor will be subject to the penalty for aiding and abetting an understatement of tax liability.

• • •

CHECKLIST OF CHANGED MAIN VOLUME PAGES

page 12

page 21

page 49

page 53

page 57

page 59

page 78

page 84

pages 85-90 (deleted)

page 107

page 113

page 121

page 131

INDEX

ISBN 0-913069-32-9

Supplement

$14.95